Curriculum of Global Migration and Transnationalism

Curriculum of Global Migration and Transnationalism seeks to address the question: "What is the curriculum of global/transnational migration?". The authors in this collection explore the multifaceted implications of movement for curriculum, teaching and learning, teacher education, cultural practice, as well as educational research and policy.

In this book, the authors consider the following, among other questions: Is the current experience of global/transnational mobility and/or migration really a new phenomenon, or is it an extension of existing processes and dynamics (e.g. colonialism, capitalism, imperialism)? What does global/transnational mobility imply for schools and other educational institutions and processes as spatially located entities? What approaches to curriculum are needed in the constantly shifting context of global movement? How are the "global" and "local" re-imagined through the experiences of mobility and migration?

This book was originally published as a special issue of *Curriculum Inquiry*.

Elena V. Toukan is a PhD Candidate in Curriculum, Teaching and Learning at Ontario Institute for Studies in Education (OISE)/University of Toronto, Canada. Her research examines the interplay between global education policy and local agency. Elena served as an associate editor at *Curriculum Inquiry*, and her published research appears such journals as *Education, Citizenship and Social Justice*; the *Journal of Peace Education*; *Education as Change*; and *Compare*.

Rubén Gaztambide-Fernández is a Professor in the Department of Curriculum Teaching and Learning at the Ontario Institute for Studies in Education, Canada, and the Editor in Chief of *Curriculum Inquiry*.

Sardar M. Anwaruddin received his PhD from the Ontario Institute for Studies in Education (OISE) at the University of Toronto, Canada. Currently, he is an Assistant Professor in the Department of Languages, Literatures and Linguistics at York University, Toronto, Canada.

Curriculum of Global Migration and Transnationalism

Edited by
**Elena V. Toukan, Rubén Gaztambide-Fernández
and Sardar M. Anwaruddin**

LONDON AND NEW YORK

First published 2021
by Routledge
2 Park Square, Milton Park, Abingdon, Oxon, OX14 4RN

and by Routledge
52 Vanderbilt Avenue, New York, NY 10017

Routledge is an imprint of the Taylor & Francis Group, an informa business

British Library Cataloguing-in-Publication Data
A catalogue record for this book is available from the British Library

ISBN13: 978-0-367-48217-6

Typeset in Myriad Pro
by codeMantra

Publisher's Note
The publisher accepts responsibility for any inconsistencies that may have arisen during the conversion of this book from journal articles to book chapters, namely the inclusion of journal terminology.

Disclaimer
Every effort has been made to contact copyright holders for their permission to reprint material in this book. The publishers would be grateful to hear from any copyright holder who is not here acknowledged and will undertake to rectify any errors or omissions in future editions of this book.

Printed in the United Kingdom
by Henry Ling Limited

Contents

Citation Information

The chapters in this book were originally published in the *Curriculum Inquiry*, volume 47, issue 1 (March 2017). When citing this material, please use the original page numbering for each article, as follows:

For any permission-related enquiries please visit:
http://www.tandfonline.com/page/help/permissions

Contributors

Thea Renda Abu El-Haj is a Professor and Chair of Education at Barnard College at Columbia University, New York City, USA, and is an anthropologist of education. Her research explores questions about belonging, rights, citizenship, and education raised by globalization, transnational migration, and conflict. She is currently working on two projects. In a recent publication, *Fifi the punishing cat and other civic lessons from a Lebanese public kindergarten*, in the *Journal of Education in Emergencies*, she and her colleagues write about their longitudinal collaborative ethnographic study of public kindergartens in Beirut, Lebanon, that focuses on questions of conflict and refugee policy. With the support of a Spencer Foundation grant, she is principal investigator of a US national interview study exploring the civic identities and civic practices of youth from Muslim immigrant communities. Her second book, *Unsettled Belonging: Educating Palestinian American Youth after 9/11* (University of Chicago Press, 2015), won the 2016 American Educational Studies Association Critics Choice Award.

Vanessa de Oliveira Andreotti holds a Canada Research Chair in Race, Inequalities and Global Change at the Department of Educational Studies at the University of British Columbia, Vancouver, Canada.

Monisha Bajaj is a Professor of International and Multicultural Education at the University of San Francisco, USA. She is also a Visiting Professor and Chair for Critical Studies in Higher Education Transformation at Nelson Mandela University, South Africa. Dr. Bajaj is the editor and author of six books, including, most recently, *Human Rights Education: Theory, Research, Praxis* (University of Pennsylvania Press, 2017), as well as numerous articles. She has also developed curriculum—particularly related to peace education, human rights, anti-bullying efforts, and sustainability—for non-profit organizations and intergovernmental organizations, such as UNICEF and UNESCO. In 2015, she received the Ella Baker/Septima Clark Human Rights Award (2015) from Division B of the American Educational Research Association (AERA).

Lesley Bartlett is a Professor of Education and Faculty Director of the Institute for Regional and International Studies at the University of Wisconsin-Madison, USA. She is the editor or author of a number of books, including *Rethinking Case Study Research: A Comparative Approach* and *Additive Schooling in Subtractive Times: Bilingual Education and Dominican Immigrant Youth in the Heights*. Professor Bartlett is currently the editor of *Anthropology & Education Quarterly*.

Jason Beech is an Associate Professor at the School of Education at the Universidad de San Andrés, Buenos Aires, Argentina. He is a researcher of the National Council for

Scientific and Technical Research of Argentina (CONICET), and the Director of the PhD in Education at the Universidad de San Andrés, Argentina. He has taught in several universities in the Americas, Europe, and Australia. He is interested in the globalization of knowledge and policies related to education, and in exploring the link between cosmopolitanism, citizenship, and education.

Kathy Bickmore is a Professor in Curriculum and Pedagogy and Comparative International and Development Education programs at the Ontario Institute for Studies in Education at the University of Toronto, Canada. Her interests include conflict, peace-building and democratic education, youth, and K-12 public schools, from international comparative perspectives.

Roland Sintos Coloma is a Professor and Assistant Dean of Teacher Education, and Co-Director of the Kaplan Center for Research on Urban Education at Wayne State University, Detroit, USA. A scholar of history, cultural studies, and education, his work addresses critical questions of race, gender, and sexuality from transnational and intersectional perspectives. His publications include *Asian Canadian Studies Reader* (2017), *Filipinos in Canada: Disturbing Invisibility* (2012), and *Postcolonial Challenges in Education* (2009). Roland's research has received funding from the US Department of Education, Social Sciences and Humanities Research Council, and AERA-Spencer and Connaught foundations. He served as the President of the American Educational Studies Association (2019–20), Program Co-Chair of the American Educational Research Association's Division G—Social Context of Education (2018–20), and editor of the *Educational Studies* journal (2014–17).

Sarah Dryden-Peterson is an Associate Professor at the Harvard Graduate School of Education, USA. She leads a research program that focuses on the connections between education and community development, specifically the role that education plays in building peaceful and participatory societies. Her work is situated in conflict and post-conflict settings, and is concerned with the interplay between local experiences of children, families, and teachers and the development and implementation of national and international policy. Her research reflects connections between practice, policy, and scholarship, and is strengthened through sustained collaborations with UN agencies, NGOs, and communities. Dryden-Peterson's long-term research on refugee education has played a critical role in shaping global policy on the importance of quality, conflict-informed, and future-creating education in all phases of conflict. She is recipient of the Palmer O. Johnson Award for outstanding article and a National Academy of Education Postdoctoral Fellow. Raised in Toronto, Canada, Dryden-Peterson taught primary and middle school in Madagascar, South Africa, and the United States.

Shibao Guo is a Professor in the Werklund School of Education at the University of Calgary, Canada. His research interests include citizenship and immigration, multicultural and anti-racist education, and comparative and international education. He has numerous publications, including books, journal articles, and book chapters. His latest book includes *Immigration, Racial and Ethnic Studies in 150 Years of Canada: Retrospects and Prospects* (Brill|Sense, 2018). Currently, he serves as co-editor of *Canadian Ethnic Studies*.

Awad Ibrahim is an award-winning author and a Professor at the Faculty of Education at the University of Ottawa, Canada. He is a Curriculum Theorist with special interest in applied linguistics, cultural studies, Hip-Hop, youth and Black popular culture, philosophy and sociology of education, social justice, diasporic and continental African identities, and ethnography. He has researched and published widely in these areas. He obtained his PhD from Ontario Institute for Studies in Education (OISE) at the University of Toronto, Canada, and has been with the Faculty of Education of the University of Ottawa, Canada, since 2007. Before that, he was in the United States where he taught in Bowling Green State University, USA. Internationally, he has ongoing projects in Sudan, Morocco, and the United States. His current projects include an evaluation of the Ontario (Canada) equity policy. He has more than a hundred publications and among his books, *Black Immigrants in North America: Essays on Race, Immigration, Identity, Language, Hip-Hop, Pedagogy, and the Politics of Becoming Black; In This Together: Blackness, Indigeneity, and Hip-Hop (with A. Hudson & K. Recollet); The Education of African Canadian Children: Critical Perspectives (with A. Abdi); The Rhizome of Blackness: A Critical Ethnography of Hip-Hop Culture, Language, Identity, and the Politics of Becoming; Critical Youth Studies: A Reader (with S. Steinberg); Global Linguistic Flows: Hip-Hop Cultures, Youth Identities, and the Politics of Language (with S. Alim & A. Pennycook).*

Srabani Maitra is a Lecturer in the School of Education at the University of Glasgow, UK. Her research combines interdisciplinary theories and methodologies from Sociology and Education to focus on education/learning, workplace skill training, transnational migration as well as anti-racist and anti-colonial education.

Diego Nieto is a PhD Candidate in Curriculum and Pedagogy (Comparative, International and Development Education Specialization) at the Ontario Institute for Studies in Education at the University of Toronto, Canada. His doctoral research explores the development of pedagogies of peace in the transition from war to a post-conflict scenario in Colombia, examining the experiences and conceptions youth have of diverse facets of violence and war in their lives

Leigh Patel is a Professor and Associate Dean for Equity and Justice at the University of Pittsburgh's School of Education, USA. She has published solo-authored books and dozens of refereed journals, and is a highly sought after speaker. Her work has been supported by the Spencer Foundation, American Educational Research Association (AERA), and the Nellie Mae Foundation. Prior to working in the academy, Professor Patel was a secondary school language arts teacher, journalist, and state-wide policymaker.

Fazal Rizvi is a Professor of Global Studies in Education at the University of Melbourne, Australia, as well as an Emeritus Professor at the University of Illinois at Urbana-Champaign, USA. He has written extensively on issues of identity and culture in transnational contexts, globalization and education policy, and Australia-Asia relations. A collection of his essays is published in Encountering Education in the Global: *The Selected Works of* Fazal Rizvi (Routledge, 2014). He is a Fellow of the Australian Academy of the Social Sciences.

Ellen Skilton is a Professor at Arcadia University, USA, and is an educational anthropologist and applied linguist who is interested in understanding linguistic diversity and unequal power relationships in US educational contexts. Her research has focused on immigrant and refugee education in the United States (particularly for Cambodians in Philadelphia), biliteracies, arts-based education and civic engagement, embodied learning, and most recently, interrogating whiteness and adopting antiracist practices in teacher education.

Sharon Stein is an Assistant Professor in the Department of Educational Studies at the University of British Columbia, Vancouver, Canada. Her scholarship analyzes the role of higher education in society, especially as this relates to the issues of internationalization, decolonization, economic rationalization, and climate change. Her work emphasizes the need to denaturalize and transform colonial imaginaries of justice, responsibility, sustainability, and change, particularly in the face of unprecedented global challenges. She is the founder of the Critical Internationalization Studies Network, and a member of the Gesturing Towards Decolonial Futures Collective.

Doris Warriner is a Professor in the Department of English at Arizona State University, Tempe, USA. In her scholarship and teaching, she draws on theories and approaches from applied linguistics, literacy studies, and educational anthropology to examine the educational, social, political, economic, and ideological dimensions of movement and mobility with a particular focus on the relationship between communicative practices and the lived experiences, literacy development and learning trajectories of immigrant and refugee families. A volume co-edited with Martha Bigelow *Critical Reflections on Research Methods: Power and Equity in Complex Multilingual Contexts* was published by Multilingual Matters in 2019. Recent publications have also appeared in *Curriculum Inquiry*, the *International Multilingual Research Journal*, the *Journal of Multilingual and Multicultural Development*, and *Theory into Practice*.

Shifting borders and sinking ships: What (and who) is transnationalism "good" for?

Elena V. Toukan, Rubén Gaztambide-Fernández and Sardar M. Anwaruddin

Movement is a central characteristic of the contemporary world. The movements of people across geographies were central to many of the debates that stirred political angst during the notorious year of 2016. From the Syrian refugee crisis and the thousands of migrants crossing the Mediterranean into Europe aboard sinking rafts, to Donald Trump's infamous wall rhetoric and the Brexit referendum, both the perceived threat and the fact of human movement have been at the forefront of world news. Yet it was not just the movement of people that caused a stir. In the United States, the Standing Rock protests successfully redirected the movement of oil across the land, representing one of the most significant victories for Indigenous peoples against global capital. Trade agreements were at the centre of political campaigns across the globe, and there were both excitement and dread about the prospects of corporations moving jobs to and from nation-states. The movement of images and information are also increasingly ubiquitous, as nations use the Internet to meddle in the political processes of other nations and as the phenomenon of "fake news" becomes, ironically, news itself.

The theme and structure of this special issue emerged in response to such recent events that cast migration into a public spotlight of news cycles and diplomacy, raising the question of transnationalism to pressing importance across the political–personal spectrum. But what (and whom) is transnationalism good for? It may be that the world is more interconnected by the movement of people, materials, and ideas today than it was yesterday, but what is less clear, and perhaps always changing, is what counts as movement, who benefits (and how) from such movements, and what are the conditions that, on the one hand, enable such movements, and on the other, emerge from movement itself. More to the point of this special issue, the educational possibilities that these instances of transnational movement produce are also far from decided.

Contributors in this special issue stake a position in response to the question: "What is the curriculum of global/transnational migration?" In our call, we noted that migration is experienced differently by different people. Some people cross borders willingly, pursuing the desire for opportunities and experiences, for whom distance seemingly exists "solely in order to be cancelled" (Bauman, 2000, p. 77). Some are compelled to flee situations of oppression and conflict, yet increasingly exercise agency over their own mobility through the use of global communication networks and heightened awareness of international and transnational conditions. We invited the authors to consider the following, among other questions: is the current experience of global/transnational mobility and/or migration really a new phenomenon, or is it an extension of existing processes and dynamics (i.e. colonialism, capitalism, imperialism)? What does global/transnational mobility imply for schools and other educational institutions and processes as spatially located entities? What approaches to curriculum are needed in the constantly shifting context of global movement? How are the "global" and "local" re-imagined through the experiences of mobility and migration? Noting that movement and migration are experienced by individuals, communities, and institutions in varied and complicated ways, the authors in this issue explore some of the multifaceted implications of movement for curriculum, teaching and learning, teacher education, cultural practice, and educational research and policy.

The twelve articles in this issue take up a wide range of positions, but share underlying themes. In some cases, the authors are tentative in "responding" to recent events, looking historically to suggest that perhaps we have been here before, even if the contemporary scale seems unprecedented (see, for instance, Dryden-Peterson, in this issue). What does emerge clearly from the articles is that educational projects do not only inhabit nationally bound spaces negotiated primarily under the eye of the state or between states (i.e. internationally), but are increasingly experienced transnationally. In some ways, the articles in this issue show the interplay between the national, the international, and the transnational; while the international involves interactions, treaties, travels, and exchanges of goods between national governments, the transnational denotes sustained linkages (e.g. cultural and political ties), relationships (e.g. with family members), and practices (e.g. religious activities) of non-state actors across national borders.

The articles illustrate how the collective attributes of these linkages, relationships, and practices and their wider implications are not simply the result of the sum of their parts. Rather, transnationalism represents an emerging social morphology that is increasingly shaped by vast networks that have physical and virtual dimensions, as information, capital, ideas, and people move with increasing fluidity across space and time (Vertovec, 2009). Transnational practices are not undertaken only by those who move from one place to another. The activities and identities of people who do not move are influenced by those who move. For example, when a singer goes to a foreign country to perform for a diasporic audience, the audience as a whole may connect to their or their parents' homeland (Gowricharn, 2009, cited in Kelly, 2015, see also Ibrahim in this issue). Identities, cultural practices, and social relationships are thus negotiated alongside the movements of people, ideas, and goods across national borders.

As we reflect on the content of the articles in this special issue, we return to the question of who is transnationalism good for? Is transnationalism good for people who, whether individually or collectively, make key choices that influence the course of their migratory path, but who are also impacted by effects of diplomacy, capital, and conflicts outside of their control? Is transnationalism good for nation-states, as they negotiate formalized control of movement over borders and imperial interests with varying degrees of success? And is transnationalism good for "culture" as it proliferates within movements that are felt across geographies, yet also risks suppression and appropriation by powerful global interests? Although the answers to these questions are far from clear, it is in posing the question of "goodness" that we engage with the articles in this issue to discuss what might be at stake.

Is Transnationalism Good for People?

The first set of articles examines how transnationalism serves to facilitate individuals' and groups' movement in pursuit of a range of aims: for security and peace, for opportunities to fill personal and economic potential, and for ideological freedom. These trajectories, however, are nonlinear and are fraught with unknown circumstances, hurdles, and contingencies. The four essays in this section reflect on approaches and interventions that education takes to either support or impede the aims of those who experience transnational migration.

Sarah Dryden-Peterson opens this special issue with a portrait of the experience of a teacher named Bauma, a refugee in Uganda, in her article "Refugee Education: Education for an Unknowable Future." Through the experience of Bauma and other refugee educators, Dryden-Peterson takes account of the fact that conflict and displacement are increasingly protracted over the long term. As returning home to Congo became an increasingly distant and untenable goal, Bauma adjusted to a protracted state of exile by working to raise a corps of teachers and create a school that accepts refugee children when Ugandan schools turn them away. Bauma uses the "promise" of education's possibilities to mend the disjunctures of the refugees' experience as "the light at the end of a tunnel" (p. 16). At the same time, he is compelled to consider that the aim of education cannot be clearly known when the future is uncertain. The students' mobility, access to social services, and ability to protect and exercise their rights are tied to, and restricted by, their residence in a refugee camp and their legal status as refugees, limiting their future possibilities. Dryden-Peterson suggests that it is often the task of refugee teachers and schools to take on the twofold responsibility of ensuring their students "continue building their present lives," while at the same time "preparing for their as yet unknowable futures" (p. 20). For these teachers, education that is "good" for refugee children must embrace a view of the future that is not premised on a quick exit out of the refugee experience, but that instead deals with local circumstances with a long view of what is possible.

The question of curricular approaches that address the constrained agency of newcomer refugee and immigrant students is further taken up by Monisha Bajaj and Lesley Bartlett. In their article titled "Critical Transnational Curriculum for Immigrant and Refugee Students," they ask how educators might conceptualize transnationalism and holistic understanding of youth as learners, migrants, workers, and social agents to offer recommendations for curriculum approaches that address their needs. Drawing from studies carried out in three schools in the United States, they critique "global citizenship education" as a way of conceptualizing human webs of interdependency. Rather than fostering a more equitable view of transnational relationships and dynamics, their research suggests that some forms of global citizenship education instead privilege and reinforce a Western conception of the formalized relationships between the individual and the state, and often fail to take forced migration into account.

Furthermore, Bajaj and Bartlett conclude from their studies that many United States' high schools have little support for immigrant populations, and are instead normed towards students who are characteristically white, middle-class, native English-speaking, college bound, and non-working – a reality often not in line with newcomers. Thus, the authors propose a framework of "critical transnational curriculum" that proposes four components of a culturally and socio-politically relevant pedagogy for immigrant and refugee youth. The first tenet advocates for seeing diversity as a resource for critical thinking by learning from other students' personal experiences. The second calls for engaging in translanguaging, which respects students' linguistic and cultural repertoires through such strategies as using "peer translators" in classrooms, allowing students to express themselves in their own languages for major assignments, and offering courses that are taught in multiple languages. The third tenet suggests promoting civic engagement as curriculum, sharing examples in which students learn about political processes and social issues through actions that contribute directly towards positive local changes. The fourth tenet takes on the task of cultivating multidirectional aspirations, noting, as Dryden-Peterson also does, that curriculum should aim for more than acculturation and integration as its goal because the future paths of mobility are often unpredictable and unknown. Bajaj and Bartlett's approach to critical transnational curriculum thus sees transnational experiences as an opportunity for migrant communities rather than a liability.

Taking an international comparative approach, Diego Nieto and Kathy Bickmore further critique prevalent approaches to global citizenship education, suggesting that they can impair individual agency when identity positions become reified without an equivalent analysis of structural inequalities. Their analysis shows how young people take up migration and make meaning of the circumstances that lead people to move, showing the multilayered complexity of the question, is migration "good" for people? In "Migration 'in' and 'out': Canadian and Mexican Youth Making Sense of Globalization Issues," Nieto and Bickmore present their observations of classroom experiences and focus groups with students from Canada and Mexico. They examine migration as a manifestation of globalization, looking closely at how youth endeavour to make sense of these experiences. Perhaps surprisingly, even when students had first-hand experience with territorial or transnational migration, they struggled to identify larger cultural forces propelling their movement, instead attributing their experiences with migration to isolated personal incidents. Likewise, these students critiqued anti-immigration attitudes and demonstrations of intolerance as individual level rather than structural problems.

Because the image of "global citizenship" is largely interpreted through a lens of Northern/Western domination, Nieto and Bickmore note that marginalized students can come to characterize themselves as "bad" citizens, reproducing global structural inequalities in their perceptions of localized experiences, and that "by separating localized cultural explanations of (globalized) social conflicts from their transnational structural connections, the hegemonic narratives (affirmed by citizenship curricula) mask inequitable global relations" (p. 47). The authors suggest that curricula should be transformed to better reflect the dynamics and complexities of global conflict. This is crucial if educational projects are to challenge problematic notions of what global citizenship is purported to represent for people in the context of transnationalism.

Language, for instance, is one aspect of social context in which inequalities are culturally reproduced, which is key for how transnational dynamics shape migrant experience. Many migrants speak multiple languages, yet they often need to learn a new language to access social, cultural, and economic opportunities. In her essay "Theorizing the Spatial Dimensions and Pedagogical Implications of Transnationalism," Doris Warriner delves into the linguistic dimensions of global movement and discusses how learning additional languages situates individuals in spaces and timescales, assigning them to roles and practices in processes of social identification. She argues that language learning constitutes a critical aspect of transnational migrants' lived experiences and, as such, she argues that language needs to be reconceptualized in line with the new social realities afforded by globalization and transnationalism. Such a reconceptualization, Warriner argues, would ask educators to take an intentional approach to pedagogy that attempts to connect the *inside* and *outside* of the formal classroom, thus taking into consideration the wide-ranging experiences of transnational families and their children. To that end, Warriner suggests expanding the notion of context to include linguistic and spatial dimensions of transnational mobility. She argues that pedagogical practices that are based on such an expansion will promote transnational individuals' learning, engagement, and advancement.

While focused on the experiences of people and on how individuals navigate global movement and make meaning of transnational experiences, the articles introduced in this section point to both the limits and possibilities that emerge within the context of particular nation-state. They show, directly or indirectly, that despite the crucial importance of transnationalism, nation-states continue to play a central role in shaping global mobility, whether through state policy or in the ways individuals make sense of migration. This leads us to shift the focus of our question to nation-states.

Is Transnationalism Good for Nation-States?

Transnational studies emerged partly as a response to a dominant trend in the social sciences towards methodological nationalism, which often conflates nation, state, and society as synonymous. Methodological nationalism takes for granted the specificity of national experience, assuming it as universal and ignoring particularity. By contrast, a focus on transnationalism brings attention to non-state actors, stretching analytically cross-political borders of nation-states. A large body of work in transnational studies has grown around the notion of "transnationalism from below," which points to the activities and networks at the grass-root levels and to transmigrants' agency to support and maintain such activities and networks (Vertovec, 2009).

Due to this focus on non-state actors, transnational studies have often downplayed the role of states in promoting or hindering transnational relationships, activities, and identities. Migration scholars have only recently begun to pay more attention to the roles and responsibilities of states with regards to transnationalism. Chin and Smith (2015) use the term "state transnationalism" to describe the nation-state's roles in and responsibilities for transnational activities and relationships. They write that state transnationalism "occurs when the state initiates, promotes or sustains cross-border movements and connections of people, commodities, information, capital, institutions and culture in the pursuit of its priorities and the perceived good of its citizens, expatriates or immigrants" (p. 83, emphasis original). States, then, play an active role in considering the question of transnationalism as "good" for its own explicit and implicit interests, with varying degrees of success.

The articles that we introduce in this section point, in varying ways, to the notion of state transnationalism. Collectively, these four articles shed light on the intricate relationships between the state powers that influence school curriculum and individual migrants' agency. Key to understanding this relationship, however, is the underlying processes through which state ideology regulates who is allowed to be considered a citizen in the first place. According to Lisa Patel, in her article titled "The Ink of Citizenship," the constant policing of the terms of citizenship is itself central to securing the ideological premises of a nation-state founded on settler colonialism, setting the terms for how the state manages transnational mobility. For Patel, the ways in which the conferral of citizenship and its attendant concepts of legality and belonging are negotiated illustrate the close connection between citizenship and migration through the way in which the state exercises its power to discriminate against some migrants while favouring others.

As Patel writes:

> While nations and sovereign entities have unique and important differences in their histories of conferring citizenship or membership, most share meandering histories of delineating differential terms for those who have mitigated, absolute, and blocked access to citizenship and the associative rights. (p. 63)

For Patel, citizenship operates not as a binary (either you are a citizen or you are not), but as a dialectic that shifts and turns in order to occlude more pervasive social dynamics of exclusion. Focusing on citizenship as a binary, Patel argues, misses the larger politics at stake in the complex dynamics of inclusion and exclusion that shape migration.

These dynamics of inclusion and exclusion are furthermore always eliding the fact that such conferral occurs and is dependent upon stolen Indigenous land. Focusing on the US context, Patel offers examples of the ways in which the meaning – and granting – of citizenship has always followed a dialectic relationship to conceptions of race and the politics of distribution and property rights. She describes the many ways in which the internal contradictions of citizenship manifest, with a particular focus on Indigenous and Black experience within settler society. Patel shows that the socio-political structures of settler states work "to erase Indigeneity, collapse Blackness into chattel labor, and convert land into own-able property" (p. 65).

Going beyond a binary notion of citizenship as something that individuals either have or do not have, Patel concludes that the study of transnationalism should aim to throw light on the racially stratified nature of citizenship and its relation to global migration. And it is precisely to this that authors Thea Abu El-Haj and Ellen Skilton turn their attention to in the next article, titled "Toward an awareness of the 'Colonial Present' in Education: Focusing on Interdependence and Inequity in the Context of Global Migration." In this article, the authors discuss how the "colonial present" in the United States shapes the curricular experiences of immigrant and refugee students. The authors draw on their respective ethnographic studies, one with Palestinian immigrant and the other with Cambodian refugee youth.

Drawing comparisons from their two studies, they illustrate that migrant youth face similar situations across schools in the United States. Abu El-Haj and Skilton present three key stances that the migrant youth encountered. The first stance aims to erase the colonial legacies of the United States, the second aims to "civilize" the colonized subjects, and the third aims to create an illusion of inclusion. These stances point to the various curricular strategies through which schools assimilate refugee and immigrant students in order to fit within the cultural, social, and economic logics of the nation-state. Abu El-Haj and Skilton argue that by presenting itself as a benevolent multicultural state, the United States actually attempts to obscure its "colonial present." As an alternative to hegemonic curricular practices, the authors propose a shift of focus from the nation-state to global interdependence, arguing that such a shift is necessary to nurture among students' civic identities that are stretched both within and across state borders. Such an approach might seem compelling, particularly for an audience of critical educators, such as the readers of this journal. Yet it is not so clear whether it would be "good" for the interests of nation-states like the United States.

Shifting the focus away from the United States, the next essay by Shibao Guo and Srabani Maitra discusses hegemonic practices in relationship of migration, citizenship, and curriculum in the Canadian public school curriculum. In contrast to the "melting pot" metaphor often associated with the US ideological emphasis on cohesion, Canada is often positioned in public discourses as a multicultural state that welcomes a multiplicity of national identities and expressions. Soon after being elected, for example, Prime Minister Justin Trudeau proclaimed that Canada is "the first postnational state" in the world:

> There is no core identity, no mainstream in Canada.... There are shared values — openness, respect, compassion, willingness to work hard, to be there for each other, to search for equality and justice. Those qualities are what make us the first postnational state. (quoted in Lawson, 2015, para. 44)

Contrary to such rhetoric, however, Guo and Maitra argue that the curriculum of Canadian public schools has remained fundamentally nationalist in terms of which values, behaviours, and knowledge it chooses to normalize within the authoritative curricular canon, while only superficially embracing others. "At best," they argue, "the curricula seek a tokenistic assimilation of cultural plurality while in practice insisting on a Eurocentric, singular, authentic, national culture that is generous enough to include its subordinated 'Other'" (p. 81).

As an alternative to such hegemonic curriculum, Guo and Maitra propose a transnational and transcultural framework for an ethical and inclusive curriculum. To do this, they draw on new mobilities paradigms that "desedentarize" notions of culture away from the fixed imaginaries of nationhood imposing a rigid identification assigned to place-based boundaries. A transnational optic, in contrast, reconfigures notions of culture, race, and class from being territorially unitary and static. Instead, it embraces a more nuanced conception of transnational migrant identity that is mobile and fluid. In curriculum, a transnational and transcultural framework implies moving beyond a "mere celebration of differences" towards a greater understanding of how migrants remain implicated in unequal power relations. It encourages students to build openness and empathize with others, to move across boundaries and spaces of interaction, and to foster democratic spaces in order to reflect on discrimination and injustice.

The articles mentioned so far in this section point to the interests of nation-states as promoted through school curriculum. States take advantage of existing transnational conditions and try to reap those benefits that strengthen statehood. However, not all states are equal players on the world stage. Despite historical differences due to domination and colonization, there has been a tendency among some transnational scholars:

> to treat all nation-states as if they were equal and sovereign actors within a global terrain. [However], such an approach obscures the extension of the power of some states through financial, military, and cultural means into the domain of others. (Glick Schiller, 2005, p. 443)

In his article titled "'We are here because you were there': On Curriculum, Empire, and Global Migration," Roland Sintos Coloma shows how the United States and Canada extend their imperial power to the economic, cultural, and social lives of the diasporic Filipina/o subjects. Coloma employs a postcolonial critique to discuss the making of the Filipina/o diaspora community as a racialized category with precarious economic and social conditions across North America. This observation of racialization and marginalization leads to the author's argument that "if knowledge production is indelibly central to curriculum inquiry, then a critical investigation of racialized minority and diasporic subjects in general and of Filipina/os in particular can shed light on the intersection of curriculum, empire, and global migration" (p. 92). However, Coloma finds that knowledge about the Philippines and Filipina/o transnational communities is noticeably absent in the US and Canadian school curricula. To address this imperial monoculture of knowledge, Coloma calls for working against curricular epistemicide.

All four articles introduced in this section underscore some of the ways in which states reap colonial and nationalistic benefits from the transnational movement of people, ideas, and practices. In this light, the state remains as an important actor in transnational social and political spaces. Yet, there are important differences in the exercise of power at the global level in that not all states are equally able to facilitate transnational dynamics and possibilities, as we see in the case of Canada, the United States, and the Philippines in Coloma's article. The exercise of imperialism in a global order empowers states to exercise geopolitical powers to determine how their citizens, expatriates, and immigrants experience transnational relationships, practices, and networks to differing degrees. It is, therefore, useful for studies of transnationalism and curriculum to consider both state and nonstate actors in order to gain insight into who benefits from the curriculum of global mobility.

Is Transnationalism Good for "Culture"?

The last three articles in this special issue turn our attention to cultural proliferation, cultural production, and the movement of symbols. The pull towards universalism in describing experiences that are no longer confined to national boundaries is compelling, as traditional borders dissolve not only between geopolitical entities, but also between symbolic and cultural expressions. Representations of music, language, food, and regalia are often showcased as the property of an emerging global culture that celebrates human diversity, belonging no longer to the particular historical, social, or spiritual practices from whence they came. At best, such celebrations remain superficial when limited to the outer forms of cultural expression and divorced from the land, people, and purpose that they stand for; at worst, they are a chimera to distract from the same transnational mechanisms of extraction and exploitation that undermine the heritage that they profess to celebrate. Who decides which borders are dissolved, what boundaries are crossed, and with or without whose permission?

Awad Ibrahim suggests that border crossing serves an important role in cultural production when it is localized, connecting local politics to the collective power of a boundary-less movement. In "Arab Spring, Favelas, Borders, and the Artistic Transnational Migration: Toward a Curriculum for a Global Hip-Hop Nation," Ibrahim explores the idea of the Global Hip-Hop Nation (GHHN) as an illustration of collapsing boundaries and pushing borders' limits as a semiotic, boundary-less, and arts-based nation that has its own "language" and ways of speaking. Here, the migration Ibrahim refers to is not about bodies over geopolitical borders, but about a movement of cultural production that highlights "the transnational similarities between situations of social inequality, crime, drug use, police brutality, and racism" (p. 107). He takes two examples from across the globe – a hip-hop track that helped ignite support for the Arab Spring and the work of cultural producers in the favelas in Brazil – to show what kinds of social, racial, and political movements emerge around hip-hop practices. Ibrahim suggests that despite the fact that the GHHN is global, it grounds itself deeply in the local. Hip-hoppers as cultural critics and curriculum theorists rethink literacy as "ill-literacy" by, for example, questioning the privilege of grammar over creative and semiotic production, while working across languages in politicizing their local issues through a form of transnational cultural proliferation.

Central to the ways in which symbols move across borders are the ways in which people express their feelings through symbolic work, a process that is embedded in complex affective orders; that is, the movement of culture is also the movement of emotions. Former CI editor (and co-editor of this special issue) Sardar Anwaruddin makes a compelling case for the importance of taking up the study of emotions in curricular inquiries pertaining to migration and refugee education in his article titled "Emotions in the Curriculum of Migrant and Refugee Students." Situating the flow of emotions in the context of global migration, Anwaruddin illustrates the pivotal role that emotions play in the experiences of migrants and refugees, as well as how emotions affect those in the receiving context of migration to "feel," and thus respond to, the arrival and presence of migrants. Making the argument that emotions have a categorizing function that operates in relationship to cultural processes, Anwaruddin discusses some of the ways in which a consideration of emotions might shed a different kind of light on the educational experiences of migrants and refugees, and he considers what these insights might suggest about mobile students' educational needs.

The third and final article in this section shifts the focus from cultural production and emotions to cosmopolitanism as a way to frame a global perspective and a progressive educational approach to transnationalism. Many curriculum scholars who take up the kinds of issues that occupy the articles in this special issue of CI draw from cosmopolitanism to provide a response and as a way to imagine a transnational ethic that might address the deleterious effects of power relations. Perhaps one of the most well-worn concepts for thinking about transnationalism, cosmopolitanism is not without its critics, and in their article, titled "Global mobility and the possibilities of a cosmopolitan curriculum," Jason Beech and Fazal Rizvi attempt to address these critiques. They propose a "cosmopolitan global ethic" in education and explore the possibilities of everyday cosmopolitanism for pedagogical practices that may embrace a "cosmopolitan condition." For Beech and Rizvi, all students (and teachers) in the contemporary globalized world to some extent or another (and under different conditions) live this cosmopolitan condition. In that sense, cosmopolitanism is a concept that is both descriptive and prescriptive. As such, the authors underscore that pedagogical practices should encourage students to develop interpretive frameworks (i.e. cosmopolitan outlooks) to understand the condition of cosmopolitanism in morally productive ways. Taking up a wide range of approaches to and conceptualizations about cosmopolitanism through work of various curriculum scholars, Beech and Rizvi attempt to deal critically with the universalizing trappings of cosmopolitanism. At the same time, they remain hopeful that a global approach might lead to pedagogical practices that create opportunities for a different kind of orientation towards global difference.

The production and proliferation of "culture" in curriculum of transnational migration, then, is messy, emotion-laden, and contested. Its "goodness" is in question not only from the results that are produced, but from what (and whom) is at stake along the way in the dialectic of universality and particularity that often sits in tension with one another, as much is at stake. Sustaining and engendering difference remains crucial in avoiding the repression and further marginalization of those who have less to benefit from the increasing stratification of a global cultural economy – and often, more to lose. Yet, emotion cannot always be localized, as transnational flows of information and ideas intertwine experiences and expressions inextricably, implicating pedagogy and curriculum in new ways.

Is Another Education Possible?

The articles in this special issue on global migration and transnationalism offer a glimpse into the ways in which scholars take up some of the many questions of educational experience and cultural practice. The authors offer their reflections and innovative ideas about curriculum and pedagogy with regards to movement and mobility. They remind us that displacement is never an isolated event, but rather part and parcel of a complex set of social, economic, and cultural operations. Today, most migration scholars agree that there are multiple factors that shape mobility. These factors – finding economic opportunities, seeking human security, or escaping climate disasters – are interconnected in complex ways. The multifaceted patterns of contemporary migration oppose any neat structuring of migrations based on flows and characteristics of migrants and on the countries of origin and destination.

Contemporary trends and patterns of migration are different in many ways from earlier ones. Cheaper international travel and the creation of new labour markets have transformed people's mobility experiences. Moreover, new information and communication technologies have made it easier to stay in touch with family and friends in countries of origin. Perhaps one of the most striking characteristics of contemporary migration is that migrants do not simply take their social identities from one place to another; rather, they maintain a complex web of identities and activities across national borders. Most of today's migrating individuals and families neither completely assimilate into nor remain totally segregated from the societies in their destination countries. In crossing borders, they confront complex structural forces and ideological forms, and they negotiate these in complex ways. Similarly, while some groups strengthen ties with their home cultures, others loosen them, in part depending on the discourses as well as the material resources available in the "receiving" contexts. In short, most of today's migrating individuals and communities are selectively integrated into and, at the same time, segregated from multiple social and cultural spaces.

The same kinds of selective practices are relevant to the knowledges that migrants retain and receive, learn and unlearn, engage and revise. Such knowledges influence their and their children's curricular experiences both in and outside formal schools. While this selectivity is true for all learners, it is particularly significant for migrant and refugee populations because they encounter school curricula that are shaped, to a large extent, by the interests of the receiving nation-states. Yet, migrants and refugees also extend their knowledge from "back home" and interpret the newly encountered curriculum through their own epistemic lens. As such, when it comes to the curricular experiences of globally mobile populations, a neat cartography of national borders as the dominant locus of curriculum studies no longer seems to be desirable or sustainable.

For the last century, curriculum projects have been largely a national(ist) projects, shaped and bound by local and national cultures and histories (Carson, 2009). For the last two decades, however, there has been a move towards internationalization in curriculum studies as one way to address the tensions between the local and the global. This move towards internationalization in many ways has sought to address or engage "the conditions that may be emerging for a new kind of global dialogue regarding sustainable human futures" (Smith, 2003, p. 35). Since the establishment of the IAACS and the launch of its official journal *Transnational Curriculum Inquiry*, we have seen an increasing body of work focusing on curriculum from transnational and global perspectives. A blueprint of this internationalization project has been "creating transnational 'spaces' in which local knowledge traditions in curriculum inquiry can be performed together" (Gough, 2000, p. 329).

While the project of internationalizing curriculum studies has made notable contributions to the field, its primary focus has remained bound by the political borders of nation-states. Such a focus often fails to recognize that the flow of curricular knowledge does not take a simple unilateral path between state borders. Knowledge traditions interact and collide with each other in complex and unpredictable ways, much like the movements of culture that are implicit in the kinds of flows described by Ibrahim in his article (in this issue) about the GHHN. Knowledge, like cultural practice, gets circulated, revised, and reconceptualized both within and across borders before making an impact on a school's curriculum. In response to this, some scholars have suggested that for a true internationalization of the curriculum field, scholarship needs to move beyond Western traditions of curriculum inquiry. Paraskeva (2011), for instance, has argued to the need for epistemological diversity and cognitive pluralism and recommends that we "assume consciously that (an)other knowledge is possible [and] go beyond the Western epistemological platform, paying attention to other forms of knowledge and respecting indigenous knowledge within and beyond the Western space" (p. 152).

In the afterword to this special issue titled "Provisional Pedagogies toward Imagining Global Mobilities Otherwise," Sharon Stein and Vanessa de Oliveira Andreotti take up this challenge and draw on the positions articulated across the 11 articles to suggest that a new pedagogy of global mobilities is not only possible, but it is imperative. They offer a critique of the conditions that have produced the current patterns of mobility, arguing that the "current architecture of global modernity is held up by three interdependent pillars: the nation-state, global capitalism, and humanism" (p. 136). Arguing that coloniality is at the heart of the present patterns of global mobility, they propose an anti-colonial "provisional and transitional pedagogy that would push us toward the edge of what is possible, or what appears to be possible from within our current frameworks" (p. 143). Such a pedagogy would aim, first, to unpack the historical layers of how globalization has evolved as a colonial force. Second, such a pedagogy would demand a focus on the present and a reckoning with the conditions that support ongoing colonization. The third and final "layer" of such a pedagogy involves a process of imagining a future in the present. For the authors, such a "provisional and transitional pedagogy might help us trace the desires that produce harmful knowledges, identities, imaginaries, and relationships, and face the paradoxes and contradictions of our complex collective existence" (p. 144).

In light of Stein and Andreotti's reflection, as editors we wondered what might be some of the implications of the work presented in these articles for Indigenous people, education, and sovereignty. Indeed, as we read through the articles in this issue, we were struck – although perhaps not surprised – by the absence of any sustained discussion of the implications of transnationalism and global mobility for Indigenous people, particularly for those who are engaged in struggle over sovereignty in their own lands and territories. In part, as Bauman (2000) has argued, even when populations "do not move, it is often the site that is pulled from under their feet, so it feels like being on the move anyway" (p. 87), which underscore the question, is transnationalism good for Indigenous people? In what ways might transnationalism facilitate, accelerate, and (ironically perhaps) obscure the settler project?

Patel (in this issue) points to the way in which migration is imbricated in the operations of the settler state and the ongoing colonization of Indigenous land. At the same time, transnationalism is also facilitating the strengthening of ties among Indigenous peoples and movements across the globe. In Standing Rock, for instance, transnational flows of information and connections between Indigenous groups that have existed for thousands of years facilitated the participation of Indigenous peoples from around the world, a key factor in the success of the protests. Likewise, Hip Hop has also become a key site for the production of contemporary Indigenous culture (Recollet, 2015), and Indigenous people are active participants in the GHHN that Ibrahim describes in this issue.

There are many other silences in the conversations that enliven the articles in this special issue. Yet there is no doubt that – whether through the relentless operations of empire (Coloma, this issue), through the westernized hegemony underlying many of the constructions of "global citizenship" education (Bajaj & Bartlett, this issue; Nieto & Bickmore, this issue), or the marks that such "citizenship" indelibly create (Patel, this issue) – we are all, in some way another, touched by transnational systems and processes. The question, then, is whether another education is possible that might mobilize movement itself as a key site of struggle and change. The authors in this issue seem to suggest that transnationalism might open up a space for critique and intervention within the contradictions and paradoxes that drive movement as choice for some and consequence for many more.

Disclosure statement

No potential conflict of interest was reported by the authors.

References

Bauman, Z. (2000). *Liquid modernity*. Cambridge: Polity.
Carson, T. R. (2009). Internationalizing curriculum: Globalization and the worldliness of curriculum studies. *Curriculum Inquiry, 39*(1), 145–158. doi: 10.1111/j.1467-873X.2008.01442.x
Chin, K. S., & Smith, D. (2015). A reconceptualization of state transnationalism: South Korea as an illustrative case. *Global Networks, 15*(1), 78–98. doi: 10.1111/glob.12053
Glick Schiller, N. (2005). Transnational social fields and imperialism: Bringing a theory of power to Transnational Studies. *Anthropological Theory, 5*(4), 439–461. doi: 10.1177/1463499605059231

Gough, N. (2000). Locating curriculum studies in the global village. *Journal of Curriculum Studies, 32* (2), 329–342. http://dx.doi.org/10.1080/002202700182790

Gowricharn, R. (2009). Changing forms of transnationalism. *Ethnic and Racial Studies, 32*(9), 1619–1638. http://dx.doi.org/10.1080/01419870902853232

Kelly, P. F. (2015). Transnationalism, emotion and second−generation social mobility in the Filipino-Canadian diaspora. *Singapore Journal of Tropical Geography, 36*(3), 280–299. doi: 10.1111/sjtg.12115

Lawson, G. (2015, December 8). Trudeau's Canada, again. *The New York Times*. Retrieved from http://www.nytimes.com/2015/12/13/magazine/trudeaus-canada-again.html?_r=0

Paraskeva, J. M. (2011). *Conflicts in curriculum theory: Challenging hegemonic epistemologies*. New York: Palgrave Macmillan.

Recollet, K. (2015). Glyphing decolonial love through urban flash mobbing and *Walking with our Sisters*. *Curriculum Inquiry, 45*(1), 129–145.

Smith, D. G. (2003). Curriculum and pedagogy face globalization. In W.F. Pinar (Ed.), *International handbook of curriculum research* (pp. 35–51). Mahwah: Lawrence Erlbaum.

Vertovec, S. (2009). *Transnationalism*. London: Routledge.

Refugee education: Education for an unknowable future

Sarah Dryden-Peterson

ABSTRACT

Conflict and displacement are increasingly protracted, requiring rethinking of refugee education as a long-term endeavour, connected not only to the idea of return but to the ongoing nature of exile. In this essay, I examine how refugees conceptualize education and its role in creating certainty and mending the disjunctures of their trajectories as refugees. Through a portrait of one refugee teacher, the essay explores technical, curricular, and relational dimensions of refugee education that assist refugee students in preparing for unknowable futures.

The Uncertainties of Contemporary Conflict

Abroon[1] arrived in Dadaab refugee camp in Kenya when he was nine. He and his family initially thought they would quickly return to Somalia. Yet, twenty-three years later, Abroon is still in exile, still living in Dadaab. Abroon is one of 21.3 million refugees globally who have been forcibly displaced outside of their country of origin (UNHCR, 2016). Mainstream media would have us believe that the refugee crisis generated by the contemporary conflict in Syria is unprecedented. It is true that the number of refugees globally is at its highest level since the Second World War and that, in 2015 alone, 1.8 million people were newly displaced to become refugees (UNHCR, 2016, p. 2). The most recent mass movements have resulted primarily from conflict in Syria, but also with the onset and re-ignition of conflicts in Iraq, Mali, and South Sudan, among others.

Furthermore, Abroon's experience is just one example of how the phenomena of forced migration and exile are not new. The 1.8 million newly displaced refugees in 2015 joined almost 17 million others who have remained refugees for multiple decades, from ongoing conflicts in Afghanistan, Democratic Republic of Congo (DRC), and from Abroon's country of origin, Somalia. Historically, 40 million people were displaced across Europe by the end of the Second World War. Independence movements across Africa saw more than 850,000 people become refugees in the single year of 1965. Between March and May of 1971, more than 100,000 people per day entered India from East Pakistan; by the end of 1971, there were 10 million refugees in India. One million refugees crossed from Rwanda into what was then Zaire in July 1994, 15,000 each hour on one day (UNHCR, 2000, pp. 51, 52, 59).

The degree of uncertainty that refugees face has changed since the end of the Cold War (Collier, Hoeffler, & Söderbom, 2004). Critical for refugee education is that conflict and conflict-induced displacement are increasingly protracted (Dryden-Peterson, 2015). For example, between 2005 and 2015, two-fifths of all refugees were displaced for three or more years at any one time, and, in 2014, in 33 protracted conflicts globally, the average length of exile was 25 years. The current length of displacement is nearly three times as long as it was in the early 1990s (Crawford, Cosgrave, Haysom, & Walicki, 2015; UNHCR & Global Monitoring Report, 2016).

Previously, with an understanding that conflict was short-lived and that return from exile would be imminent, refugee education was conceptualized as a return to "normalcy" through the provision of access to schooling (Nicolai & Triplehorn, 2003). As Davies and Talbot wrote, "the implication [of this thinking] is that it would almost be enough to get the children back into school and that the routines of schooling are as important as its content" (2008, p. 513). Understanding that conflict and displacement are not temporary requires a rethinking of refugee education as a long-term endeavour, connected not only to the idea of return but to the ongoing nature of exile. In this essay, I examine how refugees conceptualize education and its role in creating certainty and mending the disjunctures of their trajectories as refugees.

The Shifting Landscape of Refugee Education

When Abroon was young, his mother told him, "I want to educate these [refugee] children so that tomorrow they help themselves and they also help us." Abroon has taken on this responsibility on behalf of his mother. He now teaches in a refugee camp secondary school. "I'm making a good contribution to society," Abroon says, "because I am building their brains and their future." Teachers of refugees play a central role in helping their students to conceptualize what that future might be and how to prepare for it.

Teachers of refugees play this role within the confines of interactions among global and national structures governed by the politics of migration, funding sources, local economies, and the state of national education systems, among other factors (Dryden-Peterson, 2015). The United Nations High Commissioner for Refugees (UNHCR), the global organization mandated with the protection of refugees' rights and the provision of services, including education, poses three "durable solutions" for refugees, in effect three possible futures. They include return to the country of origin; integration in a country of first asylum (usually a low-income country); or resettlement to a third country (usually a high-income country).

Yet for Abroon, as for most refugees globally, none of these options is a realistic possibility. It has not been safe for him to return home; his country of origin, Somalia, has been engulfed in conflict for almost three decades, among the top countries of origin for refugees in every year since 1988 (UNHCR, 2016, p. 56). He has not been able to integrate into Kenya, because he does not have the right to work and xenophobia toward refugees is high (Foulds, 2016). And he cannot access resettlement, an option that is available to less than one percent of refugees globally (UNHCR, 2014). His situation is one of "radical uncertainty," where there is imperfect knowledge and the future is unpredictable (Horst & Grabska, 2015). Faced with an unknowable future, Abroon envisioned that his education might facilitate mobilities – physical and cognitive – that would help him to build a more certain future.

Like most refugees globally, however, Abroon's mobility is restricted. His access to social services and to the protection of his rights is tied to his residence in a refugee camp, limiting his freedom of movement (Lindley, 2011). And yet, it is the very concept of mobility that has shaped his educational experiences to date and that drives his future aspirations. As Abroon said:

> education is a very key tool. When war breaks out, you run away… leaving your everything. If you don't have education, then you'll become poor. But if you run away with only your shirt *and* you have the brain, you can work somewhere and earn a living…. Education is a very essential tool. Also, education is light.

Education is the "light at the end of the tunnel," Madad, fellow teacher in Dadaab and colleague to Abroon, said. Yet Abroon was thinking of a different kind of light; he meant that education is not heavy. The lack of weight meant that it was portable. Education was mobile, just as Abroon hoped that his future would be.

To examine how refugees conceptualize the role of education in creating certainty and mending the disjunctures of their trajectories as refugees, I present a portrait of Bauma Benjamin. Bauma, as a teacher, a parent, and a student, has navigated educational structures and created educational opportunities across multiple spaces: in his conflict-affected country of origin, DRC; in his country of first asylum, Uganda; in his country of resettlement, Canada; and as a transnational actor on issues of refugee education. I do not present Bauma's experiences as a journey to be reified but rather as one of many possible trajectories. His experiences of multiple contexts of conflict, exile, and migration, and the meaning he makes of each one, illuminate the roles of education in the unknowable futures inherent to refugeehood and the ways in which individuals can navigate, and shift, the structures that circumscribe them.

Portraiture is a qualitative social science methodology that intentionally seeks to pursue, understand, and convey the "authority, knowledge, and wisdom" of the perspectives and experiences of research participants (Lawrence-Lightfoot & Davis, 1997, pp. xv, 103). It involves intense engagement of the researcher and research participants in dialogue and co-construction of knowledge. This portrait draws on multiple sources of data, which derive from several discrete studies related to refugee education in Uganda (see, for example, Dryden-Peterson, 2003, 2006a, 2006b, 2011). For this essay, I draw on original data that I collected, including 12 hours of life history interviews; three one-hour semi-structured interviews in the context of Bauma's work as a teacher at a research site; seventeen interviews with Bauma's students and their families; and participant observation at Bauma's schools over six years; these research endeavours have also grown into a 14-year relationship with Bauma and his family. Most of the interviews and conversations between Bauma and myself were in French, although some were in English; I have done all of my own translations to English, yet I have included certain short fragments of text in French, with English translations that follow, in order to signal the language of the setting. Interviews with students and families were conducted in several Bantu languages, with the assistance of a long-term translator and research assistant.

I deliberately frame the portrait of Bauma with the vignette of Abroon, above, drawn from long-term research with Somali refugees in Kenya with colleague Negin Dahya (see, for example, Dryden-Peterson, Dahya, and Adelman, under review; and Dahya and Dryden-Peterson, 2016). While their experiences and meaning-making differ in multiple ways, I am compelled by the resonance across contexts of the dilemma of what education for an unknowable future consists of. I argue that the resonance of this dilemma, and the ways in which refugees navigate it, provides an important framework for understanding and re-imagining the curriculum of refugee education.

Navigating Uncertainty and Disjuncture Through Education: A Portrait

Bauma Benjamin sits on the edge of a wooden chair. It has big, thick armrests and over-stuffed blue cushions on the seat and back, and there is a bright yellow embroidered doily carefully draped across the top, behind Bauma's head. It is almost seven o'clock in the morning and, in the equatorial country of Uganda, that means the sun has just risen, no matter the time of year. The room is dark, though. There are no windows pushed through the concrete walls and the lacy, white curtain that covers the one, narrow doorway to the outside has not yet begun its fluttering dance in the as-yet calm and windless morning.

This may be the one time of day that Bauma is alone, that his guard is down, that his mind is quiet. His two children are at the back of the house, in the little laneway that separates this row of concrete homes from the next. In the rainy season, the laneway fills with a creek of dirty, sewage-like water and flocks of malarial mosquitoes. This time of year, this time of morning, it is filled with soapy and laughing children. The children splash water from brightly coloured plastic basins onto their still-warm-from-sleep skin and wriggle with the chill. The lucky ones, those for whom a day of learning stretches ahead of them, know that every inch of their bodies must be clean before putting on the perfectly washed and pressed white shirts of their school uniforms. Bauma's children are among the lucky ones.

This was not always so. When Bauma arrived in Kampala, Uganda's capital, in 2000, there were no schools that accepted refugee students (see, Dryden-Peterson, 2006a; Turney & Dryden-Peterson, 2015).

"They do not know that we are refugees," Bauma says of his children. "[My son] knows that he is Congolese, he knows that he comes from Goma. He knows that his grandmother and grandfather are in Goma. [My daughter] knows that also. They do not think they are Ugandans, but they do not think we are refugees." But not a day goes by when Bauma is not reminded that he is a refugee. The Bauma of home, the husband, the father, does not dare enter the streets of Kampala as himself.

When he kisses his wife goodbye and walks away from his immediate neighbours, he becomes a different person. Small in stature no matter the situation, in the streets of Kampala, Bauma becomes small in presence. His eyes are always focused on a destination, never a face. His body, stiff and rigid, weaves between the crowds of people shining shoes, selling tomatoes, walking to their myriad destinations. The broad smile that is always on his face when he is in the company of family and friends seems to have forever disappeared. So changed is his look and disposition that he is unrecognizable.

And that is his goal. Bauma was a human rights activist in Congo. His work began on a very personal level, protesting the persecution of his minority Bahunde ethnic group in his home districts of Walikale and Massisi. As the conflict in Congo grew and grew, he became involved with a non-governmental organization that fought, more visibly and in many districts, for the rights of civilians. Government forces and rebel militia are powerful in Eastern Congo; over five million people have been killed there since 1998 – the highest death toll in any part of the world (Council on Foreign Relations, 2015). While this massive conflict seems to escape the world's attention, the human rights activities of a small group could not escape the attention of the authorities. Bauma was imprisoned and tortured, only to escape when a fire spread through the prison and the guards fled to protect themselves. The International Committee of the Red Cross then helped him to find exile in Uganda.

Before conflict erupted, Bauma had pursued his teaching diploma in DRC, inspired by his father who was a teacher and revered as a peacemaker in their community. Bauma often describes teaching as his "calling." He has a keen responsibility to teach children, wherever he might find them. As DRC is a country of dense forests and spread-out villages, he knew that he might find himself in a situation where all he had were a group of children and the shelter of a tree. No matter the difficulty, no matter how remote, no matter how distant from a world of schools, Bauma would teach these children. When he arrived in Kampala, he found himself, he said, "as someone who is in the forest." A dense urban forest, perhaps, but one in which groups of children, especially refugee children, were not even privy to the shelter of a tree.

Without so much as a bunch of *matoke* (green bananas) to feed his own family, Bauma dedicated himself to building a school. "What prompted me [to start this school]," he said, was that "there were many refugee children who did not go to school, they passed their days in the street, just like that." Bauma's idea of "building" a school was not to construct a physical structure but rather to gather a corps of teachers who would inspire learning in Kampala's refugee children. "A school is not the building," Bauma often says; "it is the teachers." The space of the school that Bauma started in Kampala shifted constantly: a room in a church leader's home, where the children rolled up their sleeping mats and blankets each morning to make space to sit (2000–2002); the cavernous, windowless, and doorless space of a church under construction where children of all ages placed benches on the dusty floor, stacked one high for seats, two high for desks (2003–2004); a local school where they shared space with Ugandan national children (2005–2006); a brand new stand-alone classroom, built with boards and dirt, paid for with funds from the French Embassy (2007–2009); and refurbishment and extension of that classroom into a full school with concrete walls and floors and a tin roof, with funding from UNHCR and registered with the Uganda Ministry of Education and Sports (2010 to the present).

Yet, to the question of who pays his salary, Bauma had a one-word answer: *Personne* (no one). Despite the struggle this lack of compensation presented for Bauma and his family, he was unwavering in his presence, consistently demonstrated a deep care for his refugee students, and acted on his own goal of inspiring learning. In addition to his father, Bauma remembers two other important teachers in his life: an old man by the name of Leonard who answered every question his students asked; and Sidonie, a young woman from his community who also "was our neighbour." Bauma said, "she fed us, she carried me [when I could not walk through the mud]." I see these two teachers echoed repeatedly in Bauma's interactions with his students. Bauma calls every student by name; he makes sure to hear the voice of each student during every lesson. This personalized attention is rare in refugee classrooms, as in the classrooms of Bauma's DRC home and across many developing contexts (see, for example, Mendenhall et al., 2015; Schweisfurth, 2015).

Instead of writing a list of vocabulary words on the sole fragment of chalkboard he has, Bauma writes *J'apprends du vocabulaire* (I learn vocabulary), placing each student in a powerful role as active learner. At the end of each lesson, Bauma says to his students, *merci beaucoup pour aujourd'hui* (thank you for today). When I visit each of the students' homes with Bauma, he is welcomed as a friend and a frequent guest.

Through his teaching and these kinds of interactions, Bauma explains that he has two goals for his students. First, that they learn to be part of life in Uganda for now and, second, that they learn what they need to know to prepare them for their futures. But what would these futures be? This was the question with which Bauma was preoccupied, for himself and for his students. For himself, Bauma's preferred future was to return home to DRC. "In one's own village" is where one really feels at home, he says. It is a place where the future can be certain. But in the context of ongoing war and "no rule of law," where "you could be killed no matter when for no matter what reason," that future is not possible. Bauma has come to the conclusion that home, then, is what he can build for himself, his students, and his children wherever they are. When you become a refugee, Bauma says, "you must begin to *live* here [where you are], from the moment you arrive." Bauma has tried to create opportunities for his students to build a life in Uganda by enabling them to go to school and continue to learn. For himself, however, Bauma states, "I have failed at integration." It is his own inability to continue studying that led him to lose faith in the possibility of integration to Ugandan society as a possible future.

Bauma's own schooling was interrupted by conflict, repeatedly. He only just had the chance to graduate secondary school with a teaching diploma before fighting closed down the schools in his home area. "I would have preferred to do my studies in Congo," he says. "But the war interrupted all that. Then I was married, now I have ended up in Uganda with the rebels chasing me." And then, even when a research grant I held made funding available to pay for Bauma's continued education, Makerere University refused him entry in 2005. I stood with Bauma at the admissions counter as the woman explained that based on the fact that his high school diploma was in French, he could not be admitted. This restriction made it impossible for anyone educated in DRC to enter the university, effectively barring all Congolese refugees. More discouraged than I have ever seen him, Bauma lamented: "I know that I am still young. I know that my memory is good. But, I know [now] that the chances for me to study are small." The trajectory of long-term exile in Uganda that Bauma had imagined for himself, enabled by furthering his education, shrivelled up in that moment.

With education denied, Bauma began to think seriously about the need to leave Uganda. "If, last year, the university would have accepted me," he said, "I would not have thought any further about resettlement." While Bauma actively pushed his resettlement case with UNHCR, he remained committed to creating possible futures for his students, most of whom he knew did not have any prospects of mobility. He made the decision to change the language of instruction of his school from French to English, in recognition of the slim chances of their return to DRC. He registered the school with the Ugandan Ministry of Education and Sports. Even if he did not have an English-language diploma that would allow him to continue his education, he would ensure that his students did.

Eleven years after arriving in Uganda, Bauma received the news that he and his family – now four children – would begin their exile anew. That day, I received an email that read: "*J'ai finalement reçu le visa! Finalement à Ottawa!!!!!!!!* (I finally received the visa! Finally, to

Ottawa!!!!!!!!) [My wife], the children and myself have no words to say, we are filled with extreme joy!" Seven days later, they were on an airplane, for the first time, headed for a below-freezing day in Ottawa, Canada. Bauma had spent most of that intervening week making sure that his school in Kampala could continue. His four children, he knew, would be assured of an education in Canada. He also needed to ensure his students could continue building their present lives in Uganda and preparing for their as-yet unknowable futures. In fact, Bauma admitted to me not long ago that he almost did not get on that airplane, preoccupied with the tension of a future that had opened to him but remained so uncertain for his students.

Five years after arriving in Canada, Bauma's children are settled in their schools, his wife has graduated high school, and after working for three years delivering furniture, Bauma himself has finally begun his post-secondary education. Now eligible for Canadian citizenship, Bauma's future seems more certain – more knowable – than at any time since his flight from DRC. From this place of greater security, Bauma's primary commitment continues to be to inspire learning in the refugee children of Kampala in order that they might build more certain futures. Once a year since his arrival in Canada, he returns to Uganda to work with the teachers at his school, connect with the donors who support it, visit each family, and talk with the students.

Bauma's school opened access to education for refugees in Kampala, where there previously was none. His later decision to shift the language of instruction to English and to register the school with the Ugandan Ministry of Education intentionally created opportunities for his students that had not been open to him, including recognized certification of their learning and developing fluency in the language of power in their context of long-term exile. With these shifts, the school has attracted more Ugandan national students. Bauma views this coming together of refugees and nationals as a way of building community in exile, and he has actively sought to foster strong relationships between refugee and national young people. He has, for example, organized trainings for his teachers on how to have conversations about differences, stereotypes, exclusion, and empathy. He has also instituted weekly debates where all of the students at the school engage on such topics as regional political conflicts or government education policies. Bauma believes that in order to prepare his refugee students to navigate their futures, he must combine developing skills and confidence in their abilities to empathize and analyze with a deep attention to relationships, including the kind of care and respect that was modelled to him in the way his teachers Leonard and Sidonie cared for him and respected his every question.

Bauma's students remain stuck in the uncertainty of exile in a country of continued disjunctures between their aspirations and the opportunities open to them, specifically in lacking pathways to citizenship or the formal right to work (see Dryden-Peterson, 2016). Yet, the students have a kind of preparation for this uncertainty that Bauma himself did not. They have access to education and recognized certification; knowledge of the language of power in their context of exile; confidence in their ability to learn; and guided practice at building relationships with Ugandan nationals. Bauma identifies these opportunities and skills as ones his students will need as they not only inherit a future, but create it. Moreover, in the ways Bauma has created – and, through his transnational actions, continues to create – educational opportunities for refugees, he provides ongoing hope for his students of the possible fluidity of migration and the pursuit of futures that morph both in response to existing structures and in endeavours to change them.

When Bauma arrived in Kampala, Uganda, he received a letter from UNHCR stating: "This is to certify that the above-named person whose photograph appears below is a Congolese refugee known to this office. Any assistance rendered to him will be highly appreciated." On the bottom of the letter was an expiration date. The idea of an expiration date only confirmed what refugees themselves already know: assistance does expire. The mandate to protect that the global community has conferred on UNHCR is only as good as the funding and political will behind it. Funding for food and shelter dries up; nativism rises as social services in countries of asylum become over-stretched. Bauma's approach to refugee education has been that it alone has no expiration date.

Education for an Unknowable Future

The trajectories of refugees do not fit neatly into the established policy categories of return, local integration, and resettlement. Instead, they are non-linear and complex per-mutations of migration, exile, and consistently re-imagined futures. The experiences of Bauma and his students point to the need to conceptualize refugee education so that it can meet goals of cognitive mobility that accompany long-term uncertainty. Planning for refugees' extended presence in schools, however, is not politically popular. It runs counter to donors' short budgetary cycles, which are often one-year only. It can also harden national resentment, both within national contexts that are already over-stretched and struggle to meet the needs of citizens, such as in Uganda, and within contexts that are well-resourced, such as in Denmark (Tanner, 2016).

Recent shifts in refugee education policy and practice have made some headway into these political issues, toward reducing some of the uncertainty of refugee futures. Prompted in part by the experiences of students in schools such as Bauma's, UNHCR's Education Strategy now focuses on increasing access to education through integration of refugees in national schools, which have longer funding cycles and, usually, greater stabil-ity in teacher quality and certification of learning than refugee-only responses (see also, Dryden-Peterson, 2015; UNHCR, 2012). This approach, however, requires greater coordina-tion between global, national, and local actors, which can draw attention away from the core of learning and teaching. Yet, this coordination is not unimportant; for example, more refugee children had access to school and certification once UNHCR and the Ugan-dan government worked together to recognize Bauma's school (see also, Turney & Dryden-Peterson, 2015).

Beyond technical dimensions, teachers like Bauma are often open to re-envisioning, sometimes radically, the futures of their refugee students, such as the possibility of long-term exile. This future would not be possible without access to education, which Bauma recognized and acted upon, both within and outside of existing structures, to create new possibilities for his students, such as through certification, language learning, and concen-trated work toward social cohesion. Furthermore, refugee teachers often reconceptualize power relationships as they enact transformations from rote, discipline-based education to learner-centred approaches, as Bauma did. While these shifts are frequently neocolonial in their external application (Schweisfurth, 2013), in refugee settings, they are often in response to the flexibility that teachers find their students need for an unknowable future (see also, Mahshi, 2006; Soudien & Baxen, 1997). In these contexts of uncertainty, teachers are able to harness what Maber calls "creative alternative space of becoming" (Maber,

2016), in which to renegotiate the boundaries of identity and belonging as they construct school environments that are conducive to *creating* futures, rather than simply inheriting them.

The praxis of refugee education, as lived by Bauma and hundreds of other teachers of refugees whom I have observed and learned from, involves deliberation about the nature of knowledge, self-reflection about purposes and aspirations for education, and engagement with politics and power structures. Critically, the processes and outcomes of these deliberations are inherently connected to the relationships between actors – students, teachers, families, UNHCR, national governments, among others. Looking forward, Bauma's experience points also to the increasing importance of the globalization of implicated relationships, as local actors engage with Diaspora communities and others in virtual and transnational spaces, as Bauma does, bringing together resources and power as well as opening up spaces for cognitive, even if not physical, mobility.

Note

1. All names have been changed to protect the identities of research participants.

Acknowledgments

The author wishes to thank the teachers, students, agency staff, and other community members who have been involved in field-based research that informed this article. Thanks also to research collaborators, including Jacques Bwira, Kyohairwe Sylvia Bohibwa, and Negin Dayha.

Research Ethics

All research drawn upon in this essay was reviewed by the Committee on the Use of Human Subjects at Harvard University. All interview participants were aware of my role as an academic researcher and provided with an information sheet about the research, its potential risks and benefits, and their rights within the research; all gave their oral consent for participation.

Disclosure statement

The author holds no financial interest or benefit arising from the direct applications of this research.

Funding

Research that informed this article was funded by the Fulbright Commission; the Mellon Foundation; the Harvard Graduate School of Education; the Weatherhead Center for International Affairs at Harvard University; and the National Academy of Education/Spencer Foundation.

References

Collier, P., Hoeffler, A., & Söderbom, M. (2004). On the duration of civil war. *Journal of Peace Research*, *41*, 253–273.

Council on Foreign Relations (2015). *The Eastern Congo*. Washington: Author.

Crawford, N., Cosgrave, J., Haysom, S., & Walicki, N. (2015). *Protracted displacement: Uncertain paths to self-reliance in exile*. London: Overseas Development Institute.

Davies, L., & Talbot, C. (2008). Learning in conflict and postconflict contexts. *Comparative Education Review*, *52*, 509–518.

Dahya, N. & Dryden-Peterson, S. (2016). Tracing pathways to higher education for refugees: The role of virtual support networks and mobile phones for women in refugee camps. *Comparative Education*.

Dryden-Peterson, S. (2016). "Refugee Education: The Crossroads of Globalization" Educational Researcher.

Dryden-Peterson, S. (2003). *Education of refugees in Uganda: Relationships between setting and access* (Working Paper Series). Kampala: Refugee Law Project.

Dryden-Peterson, S. (2006a). 'I find myself as someone who is in the forest': Urban refugees as agents of social change in Kampala, Uganda. *Journal of Refugee Studies*, *19*, 381–395.

Dryden-Peterson, S. (2006b). The present is local, the future is global? Reconciling current and future livelihood strategies in the education of Congolese refugees in Uganda. *Refugee Survey Quarterly*, *25*, 81–92.

Dryden-Peterson, S. (2011). Refugee children aspiring toward the future: Linking education and livelihoods. In K. Mundy & S. Dryden-Peterson (Eds.), *Educating children in conflict zones: Research, policy, and practice for systemic change (A tribute to Jackie Kirk)* (pp. 85–99). New York: Teachers College Press.

Dryden-Peterson, S. (2015). Refugee education in countries of first asylum: Breaking open the black box of pre-resettlement experiences. *Theory and Research in Education*, *14*, 1–18.

Foulds, K. (2016). The Somali question: Protracted conflict, national narratives, and curricular politics in Kenya. In D. Bentrovato, K. V. Korostelina, & M. Schulze (Eds.), *History can bite: History education in divided and post-war societies*. Göttingen: Vandenhoeck & Ruprecht.

Horst, C., & Grabska, K. (2015). Introduction: Flight and exile-uncertainty in the context of conflict-induced displacement. *Social Analysis*, *59*, 1–18.

Lawrence-Lightfoot, S., & Davis, J. H. (1997). *The art and science of portraiture*. San Francisco: Jossey-Bass.

Lindley, A. (2011). Between protracted and a crisis situation: Policy responses to Somali refugees in Kenya. *Refugee Survey Quarterly*, *30*, 14–49.

Maber, E. J. T. (2016). Cross-border transitions: Navigating conflict and political change through community education practices in Myanmar and the Thai border. *Globalisation, Societies and Education*, *14*, 374–389.

Mahshi, K. (2006). An inteview with Khalil Mahshi. *Harvard Educational Review*, *76*, 64–79.

Mendenhall, M., Dryden-Peterson, S., Bartlett, L., Ndirangu, C., Imonje, R., Gakunga, D., Tangelder, M. (2015). Quality education for refugees in Kenya: Pedagogy in urban Nairobi and Kakuma refugee camp settings. *Journal on Education in Emergencies*, *1*, 92–130.

Nicolai, S., & Triplehorn, C. (2003). *The role of education in protecting children in conflict*. London: Humanitarian Practice Institute.

Schweisfurth, M. (2013). *Learner-centred education in international perspective: Whose pedagogy for whose development?* New York: Routledge.

Schweisfurth, M. (2015). Learner-centred pedagogy: Towards a post-2015 agenda for teaching and learning. *International Journal of Educational Development*, *40*, 259–266.

Soudien, C., & Baxen, J. (1997). Transformation and outcomes-based education in South Africa: Opportunities and challenges. *Journal of Negro Education, 66*, 449.

Tanner, A. (2016). *Overwhelmed by refugee flows, Scandinavia tempers its warm welcome.* Washington: Migration Policy Institute.

Turney, A., & Dryden-Peterson, S. (2015). *Should refugees live in cities? Teaching cases.* Cambridge: Harvard Education Publishing Group.

UNHCR (2000). *The state of the world's refugees 2000: Fifty years of humanitarian action.* Geneva: Author.

UNHCR (2012). *Education strategy 2012–2016.* Geneva: Author.

UNHCR (2014). *Resettlement: A new beginning in a third country.* Retrieved from http://www.unhcr. org/pages/4a16b1676.html

UNHCR (2016). *Global trends: Forced displacement in 2015.* Geneva: Author.

UNHCR, & Global Monitoring Report (2016). *No more excuses: Provide education to all forcibly displaced people.* Paris: UNESCO.

Critical transnational curriculum for immigrant and refugee students

Monisha Bajaj and Lesley Bartlett

ABSTRACT

This article explores the curricular approaches of three public high schools in the US that serve newly arrived immigrant and refugee youth, in order to define and illustrate a *critical transnational curriculum*. Drawing from qualitative research over the past 10 years at the different school sites, the authors posit four tenets of a critical transnational curriculum with examples of specific school practices: (1) using diversity as a learning opportunity; (2) engaging translanguaging; (3) promoting civic engagement as curriculum; and (4) cultivating multidirectional aspirations. A curriculum that responds to students' needs and realities as migrants, workers, and students offers not only cultural and socio-political relevance, but also recognizes the transnational lives and trajectories of immigrant and refugee youth.

Seng fled from Myanmar in 2007, narrowly escaping traffickers along a dangerous journey in which she was separated from her family for months. After working in the back of a restaurant in Malaysia as an undocumented immigrant, Seng and her family were granted asylum in the US in 2011, where she entered public schools in California, speaking no English, living in poverty, and carrying with her not only the trauma of political violence in Myanmar that forced her family to flee but also difficult memories from the migration process. Seng started at Oakland International High School, a school for newly arrived immigrant and refugee youth, soon after reaching the US. Four years later, and working almost every day after school in the back of a restaurant late into the night to help support her family, she graduated among the top of her class, securing a scholarship to attend a local four-year state college. Seng chose a major that would also allow her to work in Myanmar, given her goal to one day go back and live there.

Aasif left Afghanistan because, between the drug lords, the Taliban, and the drone strikes, he and his friends could not even play soccer without fear of violence. An 11th grader, he has learned English and is on track to graduate next year. Sitting with his best friend at Oakland International High School, a 19-year old who fled gang violence in El Salvador and travelled north to California alone, Aasif talks about how he loves eating *pupusas* at his friend's house when his aunt cooks. Aasif wants to go back and see his grandmother again, and he dreams of becoming the president of Afghanistan some day after he finishes college and when things "settle down back home."

Fleeing an abusive husband who later refused to help support the children, Carlos's mom left Carlos and his younger brother with her mother, their grandmother, in the Dominican Republic when she moved to New York in 2000 to find work. For years, Carlos attended a public school in a rural area, where he got a maximum of three hours of low-quality schooling per day. When his mother remarried and got citizenship status, she was able to request papers for her sons. Carlos had done well at his predominantly Dominican high school in New York, learning enough academic English in three years to be able to pass the demanding state English exam required for graduation. He did not plan to go on to college, but he was considering the idea of using his English and the technological skills he had picked up in an intensive after-school program to return to the Dominican Republic and work in tech support.

Seng, Aasif, and Carlos are fortunate to have landed in one of the few, but expanding, schools that tailor their services and approach to newly arrived immigrant and refugee youth. These "international" or "newcomer" high schools cater to students who have arrived within the previous four years and are English language learners (ELLs). The majority of newly arrived students, however, attend schools that have little by way of curricula, pedagogy or support services that address this population's unique realities; most US high school curricula are normed to white, middle-class, native English-speaking, college-bound, and non-working students with increasing standardization forced by high-stakes testing. Moreover, social studies curricula in the US focus on political socialization, presuming that all students are current and/or future citizens of the US They provide information about legislative processes that (1) newcomer youth may not ever have access to given many students' unauthorized status; and (b) may not be of relevance as many students may seek to return to home countries or continue on to other countries where members of their community's diaspora are living. These choices are influenced by various circumstances and larger necessities of family structures.

Global mobility – by choice or mandated by economic or political circumstances – has reached unprecedented levels. Two hundred and forty-four million people, or 3.3% of the world's population, live outside of their country of origin, with upwards of 65 million individuals classified as refugees, internally displaced persons or asylum seekers (United Nations Population Fund, 2016; United Nations High Commission for Refugees, 2016). For immigrant youth and particularly unauthorized migrants, public schools are often the sole point of engagement with the host country.

What curricular approaches have newcomer international high schools developed to address the constrained agency of newcomer youth, many of whom have fled violence and carry significant trauma from home countries only to arrive and live in poverty at the margins of urban US centres? How can we conceptualize transnationalism and a holistic understanding of youths' lives as learners, migrants, workers, and social agents to offer recommendations for curriculum approaches that address the needs and realities of newcomer immigrant and refugee youth? In this piece, drawing on fieldwork in international and newcomer high schools, we conceptualize a *critical transnational curriculum* that discusses four components of culturally and socio-politically relevant pedagogy for immigrant and refugee youth (Bajaj, Argenal, & Canlas, under review; Bartlett & Garcia, 2011; Ladson-Billings, 1995a, 1995b). The data, analyses, and conceptual insights we present in this essay have emerged from our separate research engagements over the past 10 years in three different newcomer school contexts in New York and California, namely, Gregorio Luperón High School (Bartlett & Garcia, 2011), Brooklyn International High School (Mendenhall, Bartlett, & Ghaffar Kucher, 2017), and Oakland International High School (Bajaj, Canlas, & Argenal, 2017; Canlas, Argenal, & Bajaj, 2015).

Two of these three schools (Brooklyn and Oakland International High Schools) are part of the national Internationals Network for Public Schools that coordinates approximately two dozen public (non-charter) newcomer high schools across the US. Many other high schools outside of the network, like Gregorio Luperón High School, have emerged since the 1980s, or programs within high schools, that serve newcomer immigrant and refugee ELLs. In the US, education is primarily financed and run at the state-level, though the 2001 No Child Left Behind Act, passed under then-President George W. Bush, introduced many standards-based reforms nation-wide, including high-stakes testing tied to funding and, in some cases, teacher evaluations. In 2015, the Every Student Succeeds Act turned some of that federal oversight over to states, but many of the accountability mandates linked to increased testing and budgetary cuts for non-examination based subjects continue. In the current policy climate, each of the schools, whether in or outside the Internationals Network, operates differently based on the agreements they have with their districts. These schools sometimes can raise additional funds through the Network or a partnering community-based organization for additional staff or support services. However, generally they are subject to the policies and mandates of their district. For the schools in which we have carried out research over the past decade, high-stakes exams – with some waivers and exceptions – continue to influence how teaching and learning are structured for newcomer youth. Within this larger policy context, putting our research in conversation across time and location allows us to consider how newcomer schools – through their curriculum and pedagogy – have innovated to meet the needs of immigrant and refugee youth.

Existing approaches to curriculum development frequently tout the notion of global citizenship as a way of recognizing human webs of interdependency and responsibility, beyond the local; it promotes the idea of world citizenship. However, while we support the ideas behind this effort in terms of dismantling borders, we agree with Koyama (2016) that the notion of global citizenship "suffers from the dangers inherent in the term citizenship and misconceptions of the term global," as it privileges Western normative notions about the relationship between the individual and the state (p. 1). The framework of global citizenship often fails to take into account forced migration and the limited choices the youth and families in our research have in their decisions to seek safety and survival across borders.

Instead, schools that are responsive to the needs of newcomer immigrant and refugee youth must rethink the fundamental assumption of national schooling systems – the expectation that schools should socialize students as citizens (e.g. Levinson, 2005, 2011; Stevick & Levinson, 2007). Culturally relevant and responsive schooling approaches in the US have largely focused on bridging school with the realities of families and communities, fostering academic success and cultivating a critical consciousness about unequal opportunities (Ladson-Billings, 1995a, 1995b; Suárez-Orozco, Pimentel, & Martin, 2009). Further, such culturally and socio-politically responsive approaches (Gay, 2000) to schooling for immigrants and refugees must recognize that students' identities and their sense of belonging may extend beyond or across national boundaries (Bajaj et al., under review).

Here, we identify and illustrate four key tenets in the *critical transnational curriculum* that is responsive to the needs of newcomer immigrant and refugee youth that we have seen at work in the international schools where we have done research. These include (1) *using diversity as a learning opportunity;* (2) *engaging translanguaging;* (3) *promoting civic engagement as curriculum;* and (4) *cultivating multidirectional aspirations.* The four principles of critical transnational curriculum that we discuss below offer insights for other educational contexts that are responding to the needs of diverse student bodies.

Critical Transnational Curriculum

In this section, we review key curricular principles and practices that illustrate a critical transnational curriculum for newly arrived immigrant and refugee youth. Each of the four tenets bridges the realities of students with the mandates of the educational institutions they have entered. By seeing diversity as a learning opportunity, encouraging translanguaging, utilizing civic engagement as curriculum, and cultivating multidirectional aspirations, educators, and school leaders are addressing the many educational challenges that global mobility poses for youth migrants.

Diversity as a Learning Opportunity

Schools that serve immigrant and refugee youth often frame diversity as a learning opportunity. Aware that tracking furthers social exclusion (Oakes, 1985), many schools intentionally mix students. Many newcomer schools, particularly those that form part of the Internationals Network for Public Schools, embrace the principle of heterogeneity and collaboration. Rather than track students based on academic ability, linguistic ability, race, ethnicity, grade level, age, gender, or membership in an ELL subgroup, students are heterogeneously mixed in their content classes.

Schools such as Brooklyn International High School and Oakland International High School supported heterogeneous and collaborative learning environments; classes were small, and each group worked with the same team of teachers for the first two years, during 9th and 10th grades. For example, students worked on group projects and completed different aspects of a task according to either their skill level, linguistic level or personal preference, allowing all to experience success and contribute to the project. When necessary, they engaged peer translators or even used Google Translate to communicate. Students in 9th and 10th grade stayed together, allowing for some inter-generational support and extra time to learn the pedagogical model in a small team environment. Roshan, a student who had lived in Lebanon and Turkey, stated that the international high school provided a good context for refugee students:

"Teachers know that students just got to New York. Teachers know that they don't speak that much English. Teachers know that they don't have a lot of participations. So, to get them used to it, they have to [practice]. So, the thing about 10th and 9th grade is to get ready for 11th grade. That's what the teachers try their best [to do]."

While students were grateful for their overall educational experience, particularly in terms of supportive pedagogy, it was not without its challenges. Several students remarked that they found the pedagogy, and the emphasis on inquiry-based learning, critical thinking and creativity, to be challenging because it was so different from their previous learning situations. Students noted that their previous schools had emphasized memorization above understanding. For example, Aboubakar attended private school from 1st to 8th grade in Guinea. There, he said:

> "You have to like, memorize the lessons, without knowing like what you're studying… And here, you have to like – they show you what you are studying and everything. You don't have to memorize, you just have to, like, know what you are studying."

Pedagogies are deeply cultural; they encapsulate (often implicit) ideologies about how young people learn and how an "educated person" should act and think (e.g. Schweisfurth, 2013). Students often found this pedagogical shift challenging.

Thanks to heterogeneity, students can learn from each other. Often, schools with large numbers of immigrants and refugees use the students' life stories as part of their curriculum. For example, at Gregorio Luperón High School in New York (not part of the Internationals Network, but a school tailored to newcomer Latino/a youth experiences), students were often asked to draw upon their personal experiences to write essays. In one class, students were asked to write about and then contrast their school experiences back home. Soon, it became apparent that they had had access to very different types and quality of educational experiences, depending on factors like location and income in their home countries. At Oakland International, students in the 11th grade made videos of their migration stories as part of their coursework.

Thus, avoiding tracking and homogeneous groups, schools serving international students often opt for heterogeneous grouping wherein they can use the diversity of students as an educational resource.

Translanguaging

Translanguaging, a term that originated in Wales, signals the effort to move across and beyond language boundaries (Garcia & Wei, 2014). It indicates a stance of respect for and cultivation of all of the linguistic and cultural repertoires that a student brings (Garcia & Kleyn, 2016). Schools that are responsive to the linguistic needs of immigrant and refugee students often engage in translanguaging. Schools may do this in different ways. Gregorio Luperón High School in New York is a fully bilingual high school. In their first two years, students (who are all native speakers of Spanish) learn English even as they continue to develop their Spanish academic fluency not only in a language class but also in content classes taught primarily in Spanish. They receive lots of opportunities to translate texts and learn content-specific vocabulary in English. This strategy is made possible by the availability of required state high-stakes tests in Spanish (and four other languages). In their last two years of high school, students transition to classes that are taught primarily in English, but with frequent translanguaging. For example, students might read a text in English, summarize it in Spanish, and then write responses in either language; they might make a presentation in Spanish while their peers write English definitions for key terms (Bartlett & Garcia, 2011).

In contrast, schools in the Internationals Network, such as Brooklyn and Oakland International High Schools, receive students from all parts of the world. Classes are all taught in English. However, English learning is not segregated to one classroom; rather, all teachers teach both content and English simultaneously. Further, teachers often draw on students' native languages as part of their teaching practice. For example, at Brooklyn International High School, one teacher provided students opportunities to participate in projects in which the students translated from their native language into English. Another teacher had students translate key concepts into their home language. She said: "If they don't want to explain DNA in English to me, they can explain it in French or Spanish to one of their peers who understands their language and then that peer will explain what they said." A senior official at the Internationals Network for Public Schools explained that in developing new performance assessments:

> "One of the things that we added into their graduation portfolios, which isn't required but we are having them do, is a native language project. It could take lots of different forms. It could be an original piece in their native language, it could be something that has a bilingual component to it, it could be a spoken word piece, etc."

In this way, educators demonstrated the value of the students' language resources, and encouraged them to draw across languages in their conceptual development.

Though translanguaging occurs naturally in the presence of multilingual students, teachers may benefit from learning how to cultivate and best leverage it. Recommendations include: students reading thematically in both or multiple languages from books and websites; teachers developing a listening library that contains summaries or translations of class texts in students' languages; teachers developing key vocabulary and syntax in home and classroom languages side-by-side; students doing regular turn-and-talk with partners who speak the same home language; teachers encouraging students to translate in ways that enhance students metalinguistic awareness, which is shown to improve their reading comprehension (Celic, 2009; Jiménez et al., 2015). Other sources on professional development provide not only strategies for developing translanguaging pedagogies and curricula, but also explicitly emphasize how to teach for access, equity, and social justice (Garcia, Johnson, & Seltzer, 2016).

Translanguaging is not without its challenges. It may lead some to adopt an "overly cognitive and individualistic" notion of translanguaging competence (Canagarajah, 2011, p. 2). Further, it is important to ask how teachers should address errors or interference; how to prepare students to evaluate rhetorical considerations; and whether translanguaging might pose a threat to particularly minoritized languages, such as Native American languages (Canagarajah, 2011).

Civic Engagement as Curriculum

Schools that promote a critical transnational curriculum give students direct experiences with civic engagement. Students learn how to participate knowledgably and actively by connecting their learning to social and environmental issues affecting their communities, which may be local or transnational. They acquire skills for participatory democracy by engaging directly in experiential learning. Yet living on the margins of the United States as often-unauthorized migrants or recently resettled refugees may pose a challenge for active participation. Nonetheless, a feature of critical transnational curriculum is the connection of teaching and learning processes to real-life examples of activism and civic engagement.

Gregorio Luperón High School ("Luperón") offers an example of using civic engagement as curriculum. For 12 years, the school was located in an old warehouse. There was no laboratory or gym space; the overheated classrooms had tiny windows that did not open; the school was so overcrowded that students ate lunch in shifts in the tiny cafeteria, beginning at 10:30 am. The school ran frequent fire drills, just to make sure that they could get all of the students out in time in case of an emergency. In the 2000s, the teaching staff began organizing students and their families to pressure the mayor, schools' chancellor, and other political figures for a new school. They wrote letters and planned, practiced for, and then held press conferences on the street right outside the school. They learned about the city's political processes, analysed them, and strategized how to intervene. Students learned, experientially, how to engage in the political process. Finally, after a long struggle, they achieved their goal; in 2008, a new, $41 million school was constructed.

A second example helps to demonstrate the range of such engagement and the cultivation of a collective immigrant identity and sense of solidarity among learners. In a government class in 2012, one Luperón teacher piloted a bilingual curriculum developed through a partnership between the City College of New York and the Spanish-language newspaper *El Diario* called "Social Justice & Latinos in NYC: 1913-2013." The curriculum used El Diario articles from the last century, along with other resources, to teach students about the history of Latino/as in the city. The curriculum built on students' language resources and a widely circulating newspaper, often read by parents and relatives, to encourage students to develop a social justice perspective, develop their historical and civic knowledge, and think critically about how political engagement and political representation for Puerto Ricans, Dominicans, Mexicans, and other groups had changed over time in New York.

The three schools we highlight in this article promoted a social justice orientation that helped students not only develop a critical consciousness about social inequalities in the US and beyond, but also respond to inequalities through political action. At Oakland International High School, a history teacher started a school tradition of 11th grade students organizing a May Day march as part of their study of the US civil rights movement, taking their demands for immigration reform to City Hall. The refugee students (with asylum) held signs alongside their classmates who were unaccompanied minors and other unauthorized migrants to signal collective solidarity particularly in the wake of increased deportations.

The experiential learning that fostered varied forms of civic engagement allowed students to consider contemporary stratification and inequality in local settings; ideally, a critical transnational curriculum would also include global settings reflecting the transnationalism of students' lives, though these examples were harder to identify in our data. Creating a deliberate space that fostered such forms of critical education socialized students into active participation in their communities, which was particularly important for students and families whose civic participation led to political repression and forced them to flee (this was true for many of the youth from Myanmar in Bajaj et al.'s research in California).

As the existing literature suggests, civic engagement curricula must be carefully designed. Such curricula when linked with community action and participation may generate an unequal relationship between the community and educational institutions if parents and communities are not consulted or involved. While authentic civic engagement as curriculum is challenging to develop especially in schools with tremendous diversity of national background and citizenship status and can often be secondary to the mandates of state exams, that the three schools we discuss were trying to foster pan-immigrant solidarity and active forms of civic participation among students in preparation for their future was laudable.

Multidirectional Aspirations

There is a widespread assumption in educational scholarship that acculturation, assimilation, and political socialization are key tasks for public schools. It is worth questioning how successful schools have been at "integrating" immigrant students who live in poverty. Further, it is important to note that schools making this assumption are excluding transnational students who may have multiple current national identifications and different plans for the future. As Hamann and Zuniga (2011) articulate, "the regular practice of schools can be a source of routine rupture for transnationally mobile children" (p. 141). Here, we argue that schools working with immigrant and refugee students need to rethink those assumptions, and should instead be preparing students for transnational possibilities.

All of the students in the opening vignettes – Seng, Aasif, and Carlos – had hopes and dreams that transcended an entire career in the United States. Immigrant students may return to home countries for stretches and come back to the US for a variety of reasons related to family structures, economic opportunity, family's fears of negative peer influence in the US, authorization status, etc. (see, e.g. Bartlett & Garcia, 2011). Thus, a critical transnational curriculum, contrary to current US social studies and citizenship education approaches, requires preparing youth for multiple post-secondary options that include work and post-secondary studies in different countries. Few schools have excelled in this area.

The schools featured here foster multidirectional aspirations in several ways. First, the mere fact of cultivating native languages is one key factor in preparing youth for multiple possible futures. By maintaining and even, as in the case of Luperón, further developing their mother tongue, students sustain the possibility of securing professional work back home. Second, teachers in these schools intentionally expanded the curriculum well beyond a focus on the US. Even in classes on government or US history, teachers incorporated parallels from students' home countries. For example, in a Luperón social studies class, after discussing the civil rights movement in the US, students were asked to critically discuss the treatment of people of Haitian descent in their hometowns in the Dominican Republic, which led to comparing the contrasting experiences of those at the border to those in resort areas and those in bigger cities. Teachers were careful not to assume that a students' lack of knowledge of US history meant the students did not know history. Instead, they encouraged students to draw upon and compare what they had learned in their previous educational experiences, and they incorporated specific students' life stories when discussing contemporary events. Further, teachers de-centred US-centred perspectives and sources by contrasting accounts of events, for example, by contrasting an Al Jazeera and a New York Times report of an international conflict. Third, counsellors at these schools were aware of diverse possibilities for the future, and worked with youth to help them elaborate possible plans. For example, students were encouraged to investigate post-secondary opportunities and costs in various locations, including back home.

It is clear that more could be done on this front. It is essential to develop students' language resources and global ties in order to facilitate their transnational imaginaries. Students' realities and futures (by choice or by circumstance) are not always limited to life in the United States. When possible, teachers should approach subjects in a way that allows students to bring their own interests and experiences. While some subjects – e.g. US history – may be mandatory, they can (and should) be taught in ways that decentre white middle class masculine narratives and diversify the topics and actors under consideration. This area of multidirectional aspirations needs further development in order for deepening the critical transnational curricular approach we have outlined in this article.

Discussion and Conclusion

In elaborating a critical transnational approach, we build upon scholarship that advocates for relevant and sustaining pedagogy that allows students' realities to be reflected in the curriculum. We highlight four dimensions of how specific newcomer schools engage in culturally responsive curriculum and pedagogy tailored to students' interests and needs. This approach is valuable not only because it addresses a growing population in the US, but also because it can interrupt the dogma of a homogeneous national identity. One indicator of curricular relevance is persistence in school. The Internationals Network for Public Schools boasts an 82% high school graduation rate (within six years) amongst its 22 schools (including Brooklyn International and Oakland International discussed in this article), compared with much lower rates both for peers (56% in six years) and amongst ELLs who, for example, have a 60% high school completion rate in California and 46% in New York (Deeper Learning Network, n.d.; Scott, 2012).

Outdated curricula that centre the experiences of middle-class people of European descent in the US force a large number of students into the margins. For example, on the days he is not at Oakland International High School, Juan, an unaccompanied teenager from Guatemala, works as a day labourer to pay rent and buy food. Worker, unauthorized migrant, breadwinner, *and* student (with interrupted formal education): these realities are complex and require transnational understandings of students' past experiences, present realities, and future trajectories. A curriculum that fails to recognize the realities and needs of migrant students and families is a lost opportunity. Conversely, responsive and tailored approaches, such as the critical transnational curriculum we have illustrated in this article, can offer newcomer students important preparation for life, post-secondary transitions, and the development of a critical understanding of social inequalities and civic participation.

Obviously, the ability to tailor curriculum and make schooling relevant is often constrained by policy reforms such as high-stakes exams, English-only legislation in some states, and limited funding for curricular innovation. Despite these odds, many newcomer high schools are securing external funding and leveraging community partnerships in order to critically engage with students as transnational global agents. Examining models of innovative praxis for newly arrived immigrant and refugee youth can suggest important directions to scholars, students, and practitioners who seek to deepen and expand culturally responsive approaches for this increasing population in schools across the world. A critical transnational curriculum can offer students important resources and tools for gaining knowledge and engaging in social analysis and action.

Acknowledgments

The projects described in this article were funded by a variety of sources. Monisha Bajaj's research in California was funded by the University of San Francisco's Jesuit Foundation Research Grant and a Spencer Foundation Small Grant (201600033). Lesley Bartlett's research in New York was supported by a Ruth Landes Memorial Grant from the Reed Foundation.

Disclosure statement

No potential conflict of interest was reported by the authors.

Funding

University of San Francisco's Jesuit Foundation Research; Spencer Foundation Small [grant number 201600033]; Ruth Landes Memorial Grant from the Reed Foundation.

References

Bajaj, M., Argenal, A., & Canlas, M. (under review). Socio-politically relevant pedagogy for immigrant and refugee youth.

Bajaj, M., Canlas, M., & Argenal, A. (2017). Between rights and realities: Human rights education for immigrant and refugee youth in an urban public high school. *Anthropology and Education Quarterly, 48*(2).

Bartlett, L., & Garcia, O. (2011). *Additive schooling in subtractive times: Bilingual education and Dominican immigrant youth in the heights*. Nashville: Vanderbilt University Press.

Canagarajah, S. (2011). Translanguaging in the classroom: Emerging issues for research and pedagogy. *Applied Linguistics Review, 2*, 1–28

Canlas, M., Argenal, A., & Bajaj, M. (2015). Teaching human rights from below: Towards solidarity, resistance and social justice. *Radical Teacher, 103*, 38–46.

Celic, C. (2009). *English language learners day by day*. Portsmouth: Heinemann.

Deeper Learning Network. (n.d.). Deeper learning network spotlight. *Internationals Network for Public Schools*. Retrieved from http://deeperlearning4all.org/network/international-network-for-public-schools

Garcia, O., Johnson, S.I., & Seltzer, K. (2016) *The translanguaging classroom: Leveraging student bilingualism for learning*. Philadelphia: Caslon.

Garcia, O., & Kleyn, T. (2016). *Translanguaging with multilingual students: Learning from classroom moments*. New York: Routledge.

Garcia, O., & Wei, Li. (2014). *Translanguaging: Language, bilingualism and education*. New York: Palgrave.

Gay, G. (2000). *Culturally responsive reaching: Theory, research, and practice*. New York: Teachers College Press.

Hamann, E., & Zúñiga, V. (2011). Schooling and the everyday ruptures: Transnational children encounter in the United States and Mexico. In C. Coe, R.R. Reynolds, D.A. Boehm, J.M. Hess & H. Rae-Espinoza (Eds.), *Everyday ruptures: Children, youth, and migration in global perspective* (pp. 141–160). Nashville: Vanderbilt University Press.

Jiménez, R.T., David, S., Fagan, K., Risko, V., Pacheco, M., Pray, L., & Gonzales, M. (2015). Using translation to drive conceptual development for students becoming literate in English as an additional language. *Research in the Teaching of English, 49*(3), 248–271.

Koyama, J. (2016). *The elusive and exclusive global citizen*. (Working Paper No. 2015-02). Mahatma Gandhi Institute of Education for Peace and Sustainable Development/UNESCO Retrieved from http://mgiep.unesco.org/resources/

Ladson-Billings, G. (1995a). Toward a theory of culturally relevant pedagogy. *American Educational Research Journal, 32*(3), 465–491.

Ladson-Billings, G. (1995b). But that's just good teaching! The case for culturally relevant pedagogy. *Theory Into Practice, 34*(3), 159–165.

Levinson, B. (2005). Citizenship, identity, democracy: Engaging the political in the anthropology of education. *Anthropology and Education Quarterly, 36*(4), 329–340.

Levinson, B. (2011). Toward an anthropology of (democratic) citizenship education. In B. Levinson & M. Pollock (Eds.), *Blackwell companion to the anthropology of education* (pp. 279–298). Malden: Wiley Blackwell.

Mendenhall, M., Bartlett, L., & Ghaffar-Kucher, A. (2017). "If you need help, they are always there for us": Education for Refugees in an International High School in New York City. *Urban Review, 49*, 1.

Oakes, J. (1985). *Keeping track: How schools structure inequality*. New Haven: Yale University Press.

Schweisfurth, M. (2013). *Learner-centred education in international perspective: Whose pedagogy for whose development?* London: Routledge.

Scott, D. (2012). Graduation data shows states struggle with English learners. Retrieved from http://www.governing.com/blogs/view/gov-graduation-data-shows-states-struggle-with-English-learners.html

Stevick, E.D., & Levinson, B.A.U. (Eds.). (2007). *Reimagining civic education: How diverse societies form democratic citizens*. Lanham: Rowman and Littlefield.

Suárez-Orozco, C., Pimentel, A., & Martin, M. (2009). The significance of relationships: Academic engagement and achievement among newcomer immigrant youth. *Teachers College Record, 111* (3), 712–749.

United Nations Population Fund. (2016). Migration overview. Retrieved from http://www.unfpa.org/migration

United Nations High Commission for Refugees. (2016). Figures at a glance. Retrieved from http://www.unhcr.org/uk/

Immigration and emigration: Canadian and Mexican youth making sense of a globalized conflict

Diego Nieto (iD) and Kathy Bickmore

ABSTRACT
This paper discusses findings from focus groups with youth located in underprivileged surroundings in one large multicultural city in Canada and in a moderately large city in Mexico, examining their understandings and lived experiences of migration-related conflicts. Canadian participants framed these conflicts as a problem of racist attitudes towards immigrants in an otherwise welcoming city. Mexican youth understood emigration as a questionable individual dream to overcome precarious economic conditions, bringing about violence to those travelling and family fractures for those who stay. We identify tensions between these dominant narratives about mobility and conflict – usually also present in intended curriculum – and students' first-hand, every day experiences with migration in each setting. We point out to youths' contrasting imaginaries of citizenship – sense of agency and identity positions – with regards to migration in each setting, showing the limited opportunities they have to make sense of their lived (globalized) conflicts beyond their own localized cultural explanations. We argue that connecting the recognition of cultural differences in the world with the power imbalances, unequal positions, and historically structured global inequities revealed by issues such as migration, must become a crucial effort in citizenship education on global issues.

Migration is a window into the concrete realities of globalization – including conflicts between those who move and those who stay, competition for employment, movement of capital in search of cheap labour, and struggles over citizenship. Dominant discourses of mobility and education are epitomized by demands for global knowledge economy capabilities and by de-politicized notions of humanitarian ethics. However, young people's actual political, economic, and socio-cultural concerns and experiences of transnational mobility vary from place to place, revealing tensions with how the usual intended school curriculum seeks to explain this globalized world.

In this paper, we explore how understandings of global mobility take different shape for youth in underprivileged spaces in urban Canada (global North, receiving immigrants) and Mexico (global South, sending emigrants). Comparing the ways these youth locate themselves in relation to their actual experiences with migration – a shared global event, linked with important social conflicts in both contexts, we argue – reveals something of how they imagine their own and others' citizenship in the face of transnational phenomena. This allows us to localize the experience of globalization in relation to specific spaces of citizenship and thereby to challenge typical curriculum notions of globalization driven by hegemonic economic or cosmopolitan goals.

Localizing Social Conflicts and Citizenship Curriculum Through Migration

Citizenship reflects the relationship of individuals and groups, often mediated by the state, to ideals as well as actual processes for collective decision-making, justice, and inclusion/ belonging to a political community (Gordon, Long, & Fellin, 2015). These citizenship practices and ideals, relations and institutions may open or impede opportunities to deal with social conflicts through democratic processes that help to build sustainable peace. When disputes related to pressing migratory issues emerge (e.g. around labour exploitation, refugee status, anti-immigrant expressions, etc.), democratic peace-building questions repressive measures of population control, and seeks instead opportunities to redress the structural and cultural roots of these social conflicts (Bickmore, 2015; Galtung, 1996).

While dominant liberal democratic theory assumes that justice and therefore sustainable peace can be achieved by ignoring social differences and individualizing disputes, our research is based on the understanding that justice, and therefore peace, requires recognizing and responding to unequal structural positioning, attached to the cultural and epistemological marginalization of specific social groups across borders (Young, 2007). In short, we share Santos's (2001) assertion that globalization processes entail *localization*, where power relations give some entities privileged positions in structures of transnational processes, sustained by means of their capacity to designate – culturally and epistemologically – a rival social condition or entity as local.

From this starting point, any analysis of citizenship curriculum with regard to globalization processes such as migration must address the ways in which school curriculum contributes to these processes of localization: the ways in which different actors are placed and take up different positions in transnational structures of power. Accordingly, our research examines globalization through particular educational processes of localized youth in relation to migration as a relevant local/globalized social conflict, in contexts differently positioned in the structures of the global system.

Consequently, we turn away from most approaches to peace/conflict/citizenship education, which prescribe solutions that assume the superiority of Northern expert knowledge disconnected from the lived concerns and understandings embedded in any community (Lederach, 2003). Similarly, this approach contests Western neoliberal ideas about citizenship and peace/conflict which, despite enormous differences in social realities, have spread globally through the curriculum, overlooking the varied local–global scales and historical roots of social conflicts and migration processes (Meyer, Bromley, & Ramirez, 2010; Salomon & Nevo, 2002).

This project focuses on student's relations to the school curriculum on citizenship education and social conflicts, including intended content and pedagogy, and the implicit (modeled and practiced) social relationships and ideological perspectives embedded in what is and is not taught (Apple, 1979). In that respect, research shows that school curricula on citizenship in Canada and Mexico has not successfully addressed widespread political disengagement and social conflicts or violence (Cox, Bascopé, Castillo, Miranda, & Bonhomme, 2014; Hughes, Print, & Sears, 2010). In Mexican schools, institutional pressure to transmit large amounts of information often "prevents inclusion of the students' experience and imposes contexts" of affluent classes to marginalized youth (Tibbitts & Torney-Purta, 1999, p. 17). Implemented citizenship curricula in Canada often emphasize formal civic structures or de-politicized individual behaviour such as environmental care or charitable aid (Chareka & Sears, 2005; Llewellyn & Westheimer, 2009); marginalized youth may also juxtapose a contradictory sense that people like themselves may be at fault, seeing themselves as "bad" citizens (Kennelly & Dillabough, 2008; Tupper & Cappello, 2012). Thus, there is an apparent mismatch between the citizenship usually taught in schools and that actually lived by many young people.

Underprivileged Spaces and Migration Dynamics

The Peace-Building Citizenship Learning project, from which this paper stems, focuses on the mismatch outlined above as it is expressed in urban underprivileged spaces. Participant schools' neighbourhoods in both contexts suffer from economic marginalization when compared to their surroundings, which comes along with class, race and cultural-related stigmatization due to crime rates and incidents involving gang and other types of violence. It is important to recognize, in this regard, that lived citizenship experiences are radically different for youth inhabiting marginalized areas of urban contexts, in contrast, for instance, to those who live in wealthy areas.

Taking these factors into consideration, the project explores the actual expressions of the lived citizenship experiences of youth (age 10–15, grades 5–9) in such contexts, by discussing with them – and their teachers – various social conflicts they identify as relevant in their lives. The research aims to open up opportunities to learn about potential peace-building citizenship actions in their schools: three elementary and intermediate public schools in a large multicultural city in Ontario, Canada, and four in a moderately large city in Guanajuato, Mexico.

During focus groups, participants in this study identified a variety of social conflicts affecting their lives. In Ontario schools, for instance, students showed concern with sexual and racial discrimination (particularly islamophobia), bullying and cyber-bullying, and poverty and homelessness. In Guanajuato, issues such as domestic and gender-based violence, drug-related trafficking and violence, pollution, bullying, and authorities' abuse of power (police violence and state corruption) were of particular concern for students. Significantly, in both contexts, it was common for participants to discuss migration issues at some length, showing how relevant it is for youth in these underprivileged areas.

This comparative finding drew our attention to the importance of connecting local expressions of conflicts with transnational dynamics, as well as connecting citizenship practices and ideals with people's movement across borders. In fact, migration has played a central role in the history of each of these spaces. In participating Canadian schools, students represented a great variety of racial and ethnic backgrounds – Caucasian, Black (usually West Indian or North African), Tamil, Middle Eastern, South Asian, Caribbean and Latino, Roma-Hungarian – expressive of urban Canada's historical and contemporary waves of immigration. In Guanajuato, while the experience of transnational immigration was hardly present in these schools – rendering classrooms ethnically and racially homogenous for the most part – their neighbourhoods, too, had been shaped by historical processes of population mobility. These include domestic rural–urban migrations, working class settlements growing around industrial factories, and rural borders progressively being co-opted by urban expansion. More recently, a prominent issue has been the constant flow of people towards the "North" in search of opportunities.

In what follows, we present and compare the exchanges in each location that focused specifically on migration-related conflicts. It draws from data collected through focus groups lasting 60–70 minutes with roughly five students each, including eleven focus groups in Ontario and sixteen in Guanajuato. The focus groups were animated by visual prompts representing diverse instances of social conflict relevant to each context, thus aiming to root our research in their first-hand, every day, local–globalized citizenship learning experiences.

Making Sense of Migration as a (Lived) Social Conflict

In this section, we discuss youths' understandings of the causes, actors, and social conflict processes involved in migration, and some relevant experiences they narrate, in order to contrast the characteristic ways in which transnational migration was lived in each setting. For Ontario youth, anti-immigration attitudes connote patterns of a culture of racism, whereas for Mexican kids (e)migration is a consequence of dreams to achieve a better life up North.

Ontario: Anti-immigrant Expressions as Racism

The student participants in Ontario, a receiving context for migrants, consistently framed migration as a cultural conflict in which the arrival of migrants awakens racist rejection from some Canadians. The following are responses from students to an image of a "Go Back to Where You Came From" sign:

Group 1A[1]
S5Mg7 [Black West Indian]: Deportation, maybe.
S2Mg7 [Middle Eastern]: Racism.
S1Mg7 [White]: Like, people aren't getting the respect that they deserve, when they are not native to Canada; they are immigrants from countries that don't have the same rights.
Group 2A
S1M [South Asian]: It is basically racism – against Islam and Muslims [peers agree].
S2M [South Asian]: And immigrants.

The students easily identified specific populations who suffered bias after arrival in Canada. They added that these newcomers were sometimes bullied in school, based on their ostensible limited competence in English or in Canadian cultural norms.

Group 3D

S2Fg6 [North African]: people new to this country do not know much English or do not know how to behave.

S5Mg5 [Black West Indian]: People from other countries don't know how to behave, so they might get bullied.

S2Fg6 [North African]: … once [a student from Syria] got here: she got bullied.

For these students, the causes of migration – apparently as they were taught in school – are disease, discrimination, dictatorship and war in other places, which make people seek refuge in Canada.

Group 1D

S3Fg6 [Black West Indian]: We were just working [in class] on why people come to Canada: because there are different diseases, or maybe because there's Taliban. There are problems why people are running away from their own countries.

Group 2B

S4F5g6[Brunette]: Canada is a pretty safe place.

S3F5g6 [White]: Unless the terrorists come here.

Group 3D

S4Mg6 [Latino]: [We recently had a whole unit] about refugees. We found out the many countries they went through – Turkey, Hungary, Iraq – and people didn't want to let them through.

These students embraced the dominant image of their country and city as a secure place where multiculturalism is lived and defended, where discrimination against migrants is limited. Almost simultaneously but in contrast, some students spoke of relatives suffering unfair treatment.

Group 2A

S5F [South Asian]: Everyone isn't treated equally, cuz if you look at our community it's [a] very stereotyped multicultural community… We have people from all over the world in one place.

S2M [South Asian]: I've seen, like, my aunt came two years ago and was not always treated well.

Group 3B

S4M [Central Asian]: Some of the people in my family have been criticized because of skin color and where they are from.

Above, students share experiences of racism that migrants in Ontario suffer, while reiterating the prevailing narrative that this should be condemned. At the same time, one of the schools had a significant population of Hungarian Roma youth (among many global migrants), singled out in the school as particularly troublesome. Some students there recognized that stereotypes emerged due to past experiences of cultural dissonance between newcomer and other populations. Others blamed patterns of victimization on these migrants' (perceived) bad behaviour.

Group 3D

S1Mg6 [South Asian]: In our school, …almost every Hungarian we see, they would cause a fight. So, every time a Hungarian came, people were biased against them. … [However] Once I met a Hungarian. I thought, he is going to be mean … When I started to talk to him I realized, he is so nice … taking away all [my] stereotypes against Hungarians.

Group 3E

Facilitator: Does anti-immigration racism happen in your life?

S3F5g6 [East Asian]: Some people.

S1M5g6 [Black]: Yeah

S2M5g6 [White]: A little bit.

S3F5g6 [East Asian]: Like Syrians.

S1M5g6 [Black]: Like Hungarians. People say to them, "go back to your country."

S5F5g6 [East Asian]: Because most of the Hungarian are trouble makers.

S3F5g6 [East Asian]: They say bad words to you. … They do not keep their money… They just … waste all their money.

S1M5g6 [Black]: Exactly …

S2M5g6 [White]: It is not completely their fault that …they cannot afford good food. They can only afford sugar food or junk food. So they are always hyper.

S4M5g6 [South Asian]: Some people, they just do not like them when they first see them. So they just start to bother Hungarians that were mean to them. I know a kid got bullied who was Hungarian, but he did not do anything wrong…. .

S5F5g6 [East Asian]: Because they … do not speak English yet. They just think they can do whatever they want, because they do not understand Canada … Since they do whatever they want, other people say, "you're just driving people crazy, just get back home."

Thus, while many students were quick to condemn the racist character of anti-immigrant expressions in abstract terms, reiterating a dominant multicultural narrative, they rarely connected migration with structural inequities in their surroundings or the global system.

Many Ontario students also struggled to make sense of a cartoon depicting global economic inequality (pits excavated from southern continents, piled on northern continents). A few mentioned, in other instances, that immigrants might face poverty or difficulties finding employment, but such statements were scarce compared to their condemnation of racist attitudes. The prevalent understanding was that migration-related conflicts were rooted in people's (mistaken) beliefs and biases, not linked to structural processes and inequities.

In sum, participating Ontario students' understandings of migration were based on cultural explanations – (un)acceptable attitudes by a "We" toward "Others." They also tended to root the causes of migration at a distance, not viewing themselves or the places they inhabit as participants in the reproduction of unequal structural patterns of migration. This reinforces idealized views of Canada as welcoming and safe, even when contradicting some of the students' own experiences of transnationality.

Guanajuato: Emigrating in Search of Individual Dreams

In apparent contrast to Ontario youth's cultural understandings of immigration, in Guanajuato (Mexico), student participants connected migration with economic problems: the
search for work opportunities and improved living conditions. Most had experienced this
conflict directly; in almost all focus groups, multiple students mentioned close relatives
and parents who had migrated North in search of adequately paid work or to reach the
dream of a better future.

Group 1F[2]

**Facilitator [Showing a cartoon of a Mexican confronting a wall with McDonalds
window and US flag]:** What is this conflict about?

E3Fg7: You can see Mexicans trying to cross the border for a good job. Better paid. To
send [money] to their families.

Group 2A

Facilitator: Do you know people who have gone to the North?

E5Mg4: My dad left with my uncle.

E4Fg6: My uncles and aunts.

E1Mg5: My siblings.

E5Mg4: My brother wants to leave but my dad does not want to let him go...

E2Fg5: Yes, a boy said his uncle had gone because he had no money and was sending
money to his mother.

The lived reality of these students, as of many others in the global South, is that it is
almost normal that people leave the country; these fractures are a common part of their
lives. Guanajuato students identified two ways emigration patterns represented violence.
First, it left them abandoned by parents or close relatives; the bad material conditions and
underemployment their parents endured in Guanajuato obliged them to travel. Second,
students said that they had learned that the promise of a better future via migration
quickly turned into a nightmare, because of the risks involved in illegally entering or as
exploited workers in another country.

Group 1D

Facilitator: Why is [migration] a problem?

E5Fg7: That they abandon us ... It's a family problem...

Group 1F

Facilitator: Do you know many people who have gone North?

E5Fg7: Many people, and even more from here, but we know that they don't make it:
they are exploited, the *migra* [immigration police] catches them, also the *mara*
[criminal gangs], women get raped and mistreated, and men get everything they
have taken away and get killed.... A friend, he left about a year ago because of
lacking money, but he tells me they are treated very ugly...

E1Fg7: My uncle says he's doing very badly: they don't let them out and pay little.

[Peers tell similar stories]

Group 3C

E1Mg5: Many choose to go for a better quality of life and a better economy. People prefer to go to the US to find jobs, but what usually happens is that they end up working as waiters or farmers, so [people in the US] don't have to do that work. They work hard but the minimum wage is low.

Students reported that emigration had been mentioned in Geography, Spanish, or Civics/Ethics classes, and that teachers warned them of the dangers involved for those who dared to take this path, arguing that it was better to stay in school in Guanajuato.

Group 1E
E1Fg8: We learned about migration of Mexicans to the US to seek a better economy for their family, and there was discrimination because they were called Indians, or they were kicked out, or sometimes, when they were crossing the border, they died from hunger and cold.

Group 2B
E1Mg4: Migration is talked about in the History book.
E2Fg6: The teacher told us that when they go somewhere else it's because they cannot get any job, and when they are on their way to the other country they can get killed … In the Civics and Ethics book we learned that Mexico is considered a country that expels migrants. Many leave for lack of employment, or to study another language.

Significantly, when considering the causes of migration conflicts, Guanajuato participants pointed to economic patterns such as low salaries and unemployment. However, when they identified potential mitigating actions, they emphasized (like Ontario participants) cultural patterns of behaviour. They viewed the problem as rooted in individuals' attitudes towards money, success, and schooling, more than in the economic imbalances suffered within their own context and in the global economy.

(Dis)Empowered Subjects' Imaginaries of Citizenship

Students' understandings of social conflicts reveal ways in which globalization is experienced in their own lives, given the specific positions they occupy in these processes. Youth's views of social conflicts also reveal their ethical–political judgements (what they consider fair or good), and their own sense of responsibility and agency with regard to such issues. As we have seen, although most students recognized structural patterns of inequity and harm, they often replicated dominant narratives of what we could call "cultural blame" regarding migration, even contradicting some of their own lived experiences. These narratives place the burden of conflicts and inequities in the culture of specific individuals or populations, while disconnecting them from structural and transnational processes. In what follows, we trace these narratives to reveal connections and tensions between how they imagine citizenship and identity and their sense of agency and belonging in a (globalized) political community.

Ontario: The Welcoming Multicultural Imaginary

As Ontario students condemned racist anti-immigrant attitudes in their multicultural urban setting, they expressed their own ideals about good citizens. For them, "We" – Canadians – have a duty to welcome those who arrive, regardless of their race or national origin.

> *Group 1C*
> **S3Fg6 [South Asian]:** [This city] is like, there's tons of different people, and you can never just assume that there's a person and they are just one thing. ... And, you know, you have all types of different stuff in your blood. So ... there's a whole bunch of different types of religions and stuff in Canada. It's not fair that you just deny a few people and let the other ones come.
>
> *Group 3A*
> **S3Fg5 [East Asian]:** Canada is a country of different cultures. ... I'm sure half of Canada welcomes other countries. There are millions of refugees coming to Canada ... They should be welcome to come to Canada.

In addition, these young Ontarians exhibited a sense of agency to do something about anti-immigrant attitudes. They said people should speak up against racism, or organize campaigns to help newcomer refugees accommodate into Canadian society. Similarly, some said "positive encounters" with unfamiliar others could be a great opportunity that they would enjoy, to unlearn biases.

> *Group 3A*
> **S5Fg6 [White]:** [I heard on the radio about]... a small town where Syrians [refugees] came and [a woman] asked everyone in the town to come and meet them. She is just a regular person [mom] with two children that can help Syrians feel welcome.
> **S3Fg5 [East Asian]:** Most of this [conflict] is happening because of miscommunication, and what we could do is have people from different religions and stereotypes have discussions about those issues or rights and [develop] mutual understanding or respect.
> **S5Fg6 [White]:** I think it would be nice to meet [recent immigrants] and learn about their families too...
>
> *Group 3D*
> **S4Mg6 [Latino]:** You do not know what [Hungarian students] have gone through; their parents treat them bad... [So] make friends and ask them if something bothers them.

Ontario youth were critical of those who "do not understand that everybody is equal and should be welcomed." Thus, they reproduced the imaginary of Canada as a welcoming multicultural nation and advocate a humanitarian cosmopolitan duty to help those in need, without necessarily analyzing the power relations, structural positions and historical roots of the conflicts involved. Decisions to help were framed as free choices based on a private belief, but separated from political obligations stemming from shared history, systemic global relationships, or their own participation in perpetuation of those problems.

Ontario students' identification as Canadians in the North of the global world positions them as the locus of acceptance and tolerance of the "Other" – embracing the privileged (White) Western cosmopolitan imaginary even when contradicting their own racialized local positions and life experiences.

This tension was expressed as they critiqued related contradictions in their experienced curriculum. They questioned the way they study war and conflict, slavery and other world issues always at a distance and in the past – if they are addressed at all, without having opportunities to discuss and understand how conflicts happen and are handled locally and in the present, such that they would feel they could do something about them.

Group 3A

S5Fg6 [White]: We have actually talked about [immigration] a lot ... especially during the election with Justin Trudeau... But I kind of wish we would still talk about it a little bit more... it's an ongoing topic.

S3Fg5 [East Asian]: Right now [in class] we are doing a project about conflict. People are thinking about war... [We] talked about Syrian refugees, we also talked about bullying, but I wish we kind of talked about conflicts. Because when [the teacher] talked about conflicts, they weren't small conflicts in the world; they do matter.

S2Mg6 [White]: No one really focuses on conflicts that happen in the community, which is definitely important.

Group 1D

S2Fg6 [Black]: I wish in school we could sometimes talk about ... stuff that happens, even stuff like racism and homophobia, even in our own families, like, discriminations that happened in our families.

S3Fg6 [Black]: I think it's kind of unfair, cuz these are actual problems that unfortunately are still happening. Like, racism: we talked about the older days, but unfortunately it's still happening today! ...What I wanna know is, what's happening, so, what I could change? ...we should be learning about... things that are going on, so the whole world could be helping out!

Guanajuato: Prepare Yourself So You Can Work (and Stay)

There is a stark contrast between the sense of agency and ethical–political identification expressed by the Ontario youth and the Guanajuato youths' ways of dealing with migration conflicts in their lives. While Ontario students had strong moral judgements against anti-immigrant attitudes, Guanajuato students apparently accepted emigration as a given, something that individual people had to do to overcome their difficult situations. They hardly ever framed emigration as an unfair consequence of unequal global relations. A couple of them denounced the treatment received by Mexicans in the USA, thereby judging the conflicts embedded in migration – similarly to students in Ontario – mainly through the cultural experience of discrimination, but downplaying the economic and political relations that reproduce marginalization and suffering.

Group 2C

E4Fg5: I think it is an injustice because Americans do not let Mexicans to go to their country, whereas they can come in and out of Mexico. Surely they despise them because they are Mexicans.

Group 3C

E5Mg5: They migrate to live better elsewhere. Sometimes they don't get that opportunity because of overpopulation and because [Americans] think they are drug traffickers, or Mexicans...

E4Mg6: Sometimes they discriminate because of the ethnicity. If we go there they would discriminate against us.... The idea the US has of us is that we are lazy.

These young people found it difficult to imagine what they could do about the constant pressure their family members endured to leave the country. Often, this question was followed by silence until some student stated, hesitantly, that maybe citizens or the government could remind people of the importance of continuing in school in order to obtain a good quality of life. Some students even suggested that they might obtain a salary comparable to what is available in the United States or Canada. Students generally replicated their teachers' narratives of hard work and study as their only option in face of the migration-related realities they were suffering.

Group 1B

E4Mg8: We can tell them that here too, by studying, they can get the same money they make there, but putting an effort in studying and pursuing a career.

Group 3C

E4Mg5: Sometimes we do not prosper because we do what we have to and that's it. Instead, the US and Canada are at the top because they work hard and together.

E3Fg5: We need to study more to be able to work easily and receive better wages.

E4Mg5: They need to instill in them the joy of studying and teach them the consequences of not studying. Sometimes they migrate because they are not informed.

Despite some classroom lessons, these students had not had opportunities to make sense of the structure and politics of migration-related conflicts, beyond the decisions of individuals either to emigrate or to stay in school. Without the analytical tools to recognize connections among migration, economic inequality, and discrimination, young people are pushed towards accepting a political identity as the subordinate in these globalized relationships. While the Ontario students embraced the idea of being tolerant citizens of the world, the Guanajuato youth took on their status as second-class citizens – not only within their own country, but also in the world system.

Discussion: Localizing the Curriculum of Migration

Although all the participants in this study lived in marginalized communities, the migration-related experiences of student participants in Guanajuato, Mexico and Ontario, Canada reflect their different identity positions in the global system. Guanajuato youth framed transnational emigration as a close personal problem, but did not identify actors, actions, or relations capable of confronting or explaining the economic inequalities or cultural violence embedded in migration dynamics (nor what to do about them). Ontario youth recognized themselves and their neighbours as transnational immigrants, but identified only the bad (racist) attitudes of others as causes of conflict. Dominant narratives reiterated by students in both contexts emphasized localized cultural beliefs and attitudes as explanations of migration conflicts – not unequal identity positions in the global system – at times contradicting their own experiences. This curriculum of migration transcending from dominant narratives tells us that we need to learn about "other's cultures" and develop a sort of cosmopolitan cultural competence. In practice, this becomes a simple reification of *Other*'s backgrounds and cultural markers that do not help to understand the connections between their suffering and circumstances, and the relations we have to each other in global structures of injustices and power.

When hegemonic narratives about social justice conflicts overemphasize a politics of cultural difference, they obscure unequal opportunities structured by the division of labour, decision-making hierarchies, and institutional and cultural norms and standards existing in the world (Young, 2007). We argue that by separating localized cultural explanations of (globalized) social conflicts from their transnational structural connections, the hegemonic narratives of migration affirmed by citizenship curricula mask inequitable global relations. They end up both limiting students' sense of agency to individual, non-structural actions and reifying their identity positions in the global system.

In this way, they reproduce *a curriculum of blame*, as it detaches individual actions from large-scale social processes. If migrants are uneducated, unhealthy, unemployed, or have suffered violence, it is because of their life choices or their cultural background, and not because of these transnational structures and social processes. If people are racist or have anti-immigrant biases, it is a problem of *their* particular (lack of) culture and not of the (dis)positions of people and countries in the map of transnational relations of power: the way it sustains feelings of superiority/inferiority and privilege/subordination in the global world.

As seen in the contrasting sense of agency between Ontario and Guanajuato participants, simplified individual-cultural narratives of social conflicts encourage political subjects to embrace – or to be (un)able to reject – unequally positioned (superior or subordinate) identifications within the world system. Challenging the common view that globalization has made the world smaller and people more able to understand *the place of the Other*, we find that distances and imbalances are widened when young people understand the causes and actions shaping migration conflicts as mere belief, cultural and attitude differences, *as opposed to* part and parcel of a historically structured unjust transnational system.

Transforming curricula about local expressions of globalized conflicts such as migration could present a significant opportunity to challenge this gap between individualized experiences of social conflicts and their political, structural, and transnational character. The curriculum of globalized migration could get beyond discussing the values, principles, and stereotypes that govern interpersonal and cultural interactions (a typical depoliticized multicultural curriculum of migration). Instead, such a curriculum might make visible the connections between personal acts and systemic consequences – thereby opening democratic space to critically question the traditions and identities that sustain systemic hierarchies in the world.

We close this essay by making a call for a localized curriculum of migration, one that traces globalization consequences to concrete localities, to the places where the consequences of globalization *externalities* are concretely felt. That is, a curriculum that attends to places and spaces from where we can trace concrete consequences of transnational patterns of power such as free trade agreements, border controls, and imperial and (neo) colonial wars. Localizing the curriculum of migration means that emerging conflicts related to the movement of people are learned and understood as a human-made process, neither natural nor the responsibility of *deviant* individuals or *different* cultures, but as a social process where responsibilities and capacities for agency could emerge.

Notes

1. In codes, letters refer to focus groups (A, B, C, D...) within numbered school sites (1, 2, 3...). Students are S (Canada) or E (México)#, female or male, and grade#. When relevant and possible, we have also included racial or ethnic background and school grade, based on field notes (students did not necessarily self-identify, and in Mexican schools, there were essentially no evident ethnic/ racial differences).
2. All focus groups in Mexico were conducted in Spanish and translations made by the authors or other Spanish speakers from the research team.

Disclosure statement

No potential conflict of interest was reported by the authors.

Funding

This work was supported by the Social Sciences and Humanities Research Council of Canada (SSHRC) insight [grant number 494798].

ORCID

Diego Nieto 🆔 http://orcid.org/0000-0002-6163-1573

References

Apple, M. W. (1979). *Ideology and curriculum*. Boston: Routledge & K. Paul.

Bickmore, K. (2015). Incorporating peace-building citizenship dialogue in classroom curricula: Contrasting cases of Canadian teacher development. In R. Malet & S. Majhanovich (Eds.), *Building democracy in education on diversity*. Rotterdam: Sense.

Chareka, O., & Sears, A. (2005). Discounting the political: Understanding civic participation as private practice. *Canadian and International Education, 34*(1), 50–58.

Cox, C., Bascopé, M., Castillo, J. C., Miranda, D., & Bonhomme, M. (2014). Educación ciudadana en América Latina: Prioridades de los currículos escolares [Citizenship education in Latin America: Priorities of school curricula]. *IBE Working Papers on Curriculum Issues*, (14). Retrieved from http://www.ibe.unesco.org/en/document/citizenship-education-latin-america-priorities-school-curricula-ibe-working-papers

Galtung, J. (1996). *Peace by peaceful means: Peace and conflict, development, and civilization*. London: Sage.

Gordon, D., Long, J., & Fellin, M. (2015). Education for national belonging: Imposing borders and boundaries on citizenship. *Journal of Social Science Education, 14*(3), 2–8.

Hughes, A., Print, M., & Sears, A. (2010). Curriculum capacity and citizenship education: A comparative analysis of four democracies. *Compare: A Journal of Comparative and International Education, 40*(3), 293–309.

Kennelly, J., & Dillabough, J. (2008). Young people mobilizing the language of citizenship: Struggles for classification and new meaning in an uncertain world. *British Journal of Sociology of Education, 29*(5), 493–508.

Lederach, J. P. (2003). *The little book of conflict transformation*. Intercourse: Good Books.

Llewellyn, K., & Westheimer, J. (2009). Beyond facts and acts: The implications of 'ordinary politics' for youth political engagement. *Citizenship Teaching and Learning, 5*(2), 50–61.

Meyer, J. W., Bromley, P., & Ramirez, F. (2010). Human rights in social science textbooks: Cross-national analysis, 1970–2008. *Sociology of Education, 83*(4), 111–134.

Salomon, G., & Nevo, B. (Eds.). (2002). *Peace education: The concept, principles, and practices around the world*. Mahwah: Lawrence Erlbaum.

Santos, B. d. S. (2001). Nuestra America. *Theory, Culture & Society, 18*(2–3), 185–217.

Tibbitts, F., & Torney-Purta, J. (1999). *Citizenship education in Latin America: Preparing for the future*. Washington: Human Rights Education Associates.

Tupper, J., & Cappello, M. (2012). (Re)creating citizenship: Saskatchewan high school students' understandings of the 'good' citizen. *Journal of Curriculum Studies, 44*(1), 37–59.

Young, I. M. (2007). Structural injustice and the politics of difference. In A. Laden & D. Owen (Eds.), *Multiculturalism and political theory* (pp. 60–88). Cambridge: Cambridge University Press.

Theorizing the spatial dimensions and pedagogical implications of transnationalism

Doris Warriner

ABSTRACT

The construct of transnationalism has been used to describe and examine how people maintain connections with their homeland while learning about and participating in the practices of the receiving context. This notion has influenced a great deal of research that seeks to capture how transnational connections are created and sustained – and also how participation in an adopted society's practices might coexist with continued engagement with the people and practices in another space. In recent years, social scientists across disciplines are bringing increasingly nuanced perspectives to the study of transnationalism and globalization – for instance by distinguishing the society from the nation-state (Glick Schiller, 2005) and culture from territory (Appadurai, 1996/2003), and by taking into account the dangers of what has been named "methodological nationalism" (Wimmer & Glick Schiller, 2002). Yet, widely circulating discourses of how movement and mobility influence teaching and learning often lack such nuance, complexity and texture, with consequences for educational policy and practice. Here, I describe the key tenets of transnationalism, interrogate what we mean by the "social contexts" of teaching and learning, and argue for rethinking the spatial dimensions of teaching and learning in a time of transnationalism and globalization.

Since 2015, we have witnessed large numbers of unaccompanied children from Central America move across the southern border of the USA in search of safe haven. Even larger numbers of asylum seekers are fleeing Syria and other politically unstable situations in the Middle East to try to obtain refuge in northern Europe (also known as "the refugee crisis"). Attacks in Paris, Brussels, San Bernardino and Orlando have increased suspicion of those considered outsiders, immigrants and refugees. Primary voters in the USA rally around a call to "make America great again" (in part by excluding immigrants from Mexico), and voters in Britain decide to leave the EU in what came to be understood by the public and the media as "a referendum on migration and migration policy" (also known as the "Brexit") (Papademetriou & Banulescu-Bogdan, 2016, p. 2). Anti-immigrant sentiments are spreading as those on the move are increasingly viewed with suspicion, fear and anxiety. Public anxiety about terrorism, crime and even cultural difference influences everyday, commonplace, public discussions and understandings of globalization and immigration.

As the Transatlantic Council of the Migration Policy Institute has observed, the public's anxieties and fears about immigration and difference are both intangible and robust:

"One of the principal fears associated with immigration—and one that is particularly difficult to address effectively—is that it erodes the norms and values that bind societies together. *This fear is exacerbated when newcomers are perceived as not adapting to the host-country language, culture, and identity—or worse, as bringing and retaining cultural norms and practices that are seen as fundamentally in conflict with the cultural ethos of the majority.* Communities that are seen as living apart from the mainstream—whether religiously, ethnically, or linguistically segregated—reinforce these fears and make publics wary of systematic difference." (Papademetriou & Banulescu-Bogdan, 2016, 8; emphasis mine)

As educational researchers and policy-makers, it is increasingly important that we understand how such anxieties and fears are shaping the experiences of our students or influencing their educational trajectories. We also need to consider what analytic perspectives, tools of inquiry and pedagogical approaches might be used to understand the complicated dynamics at hand.

Social scientists from various disciplines bring increasingly nuanced perspectives to the study of transnationalism and globalization – for instance by distinguishing the society from the nation-state (Glick Schiller, 2005) and culture from territory (Appadurai, 1996/2003), and by taking into account the dangers of what has been named "methodological nationalism" (Wimmer & Glick Schiller, 2002). However, while educational researchers, sociolinguists and applied linguists have been making rapid and steady progress on how we theorize and investigate such topics (e.g. Blommaert, 2010; Duff, 2015; Lam & Warriner, 2012; Vertovec, 2004, 2009; Warriner, 2007a; Warriner & Wyman, 2013; Wei & Hua, 2013), advances in our theoretical, methodological and pedagogical understandings have not necessarily influenced public discourse in a substantive way. Our interests in connecting questions about migration, transnationalism and educational opportunity to questions about how migrant families and individuals are able and willing to learn new ways of communicating (even while maintaining meaningful connections to people, practices and institutions elsewhere) seem to exert little influence over public conversations and debates that need more nuanced insights and advanced methodological approaches.

In this article, I briefly synthesize key insights from scholarship theorizing the spatial dimensions of transnationalism and the advantages of this way of conceptualizing and analysing transnational processes and experiences before considering the economic, political and social dimensions of transnationalism and the increasingly interconnected nature of our economies, societies and technologies. I also describe and analyse the ways in which language and literacy constitute critical aspects of the transnational experience. The vast majority of transnational migrants speak multiple languages or need to acquire a new language in order to access educational, social and economic opportunities. With a focus on the lived experiences of immigrant and refugee families, I make a case for rethinking the spatial and linguistic dimensions of teaching and learning in a time of transnationalism and globalization. With a view of social context as more than just place (or setting), social relations, economic trends and ideological influences, I emphasize the value of viewing language and literacy as key dimensions of context. Although linguistic anthropologists have long discussed how language is a quintessential part of context, educational researchers and practicing teachers do not always think of context as including language. Taking into account the linguistic dimensions of context adds nuance to our understanding of teaching and learning processes in a time of transnationalism and globalization. One pedagogical implication of this shift would be to approach language education policies, processes and programmes in more intentional and systematic ways.

With such considerations in mind, I ask two focal questions: (1) what approaches to curriculum are needed in the constantly shifting context of global movement? and (2) how might the "global" and "local" be re-imagined through the experiences of mobility and migration? I show that, although it is important to focus on questions of formal curriculum and instruction in relation to learners' lived experiences, we must also look *outside the classroom* (and other formal learning environments) if we are to truly understand the social contexts of learning for immigrant and refugee families and children – and create innovative pedagogical practices that promote learning and advancement in those spaces. I demonstrate the value of paying increased attention to the linguistic dimensions of the social contexts of learning and how such dimensions influence experiences of transnationalism and processes of globalization.

Attending to the linguistic dimensions of the social contexts of teaching and learning outside formal educational environments involves expanding our notion of context to include not just setting and situation but audience, purpose and the communicative channels that are used, valued or legitimated. For instance, it is important to take into consideration how intercultural communication, risk-taking and learner autonomy collectively provide migrants, immigrants and refugees greater access to social, educational and economic opportunities. First, I provide a review of key insights from the literature on transnationalism.

Transnationalism, Language Practices and Pedagogy

Transnationalism, as a manifestation of globalization, has been described as the "sustained linkages and ongoing exchanges among non-state actors based across national borders—businesses, non-government-organizations, and individuals sharing the same interests" (Vertovec, 2009, p. 3). The modifier "transnational" has been attached not only to migrants and their movement but also to practices used to create or sustain connections between individuals living in different locales – or when individuals or communities "incorporate daily activities, routines and institutions located both in a destination country and transnationally" (Levitt & Glick Schiller, 2008, p. 284). Faist (2010) views transnational social formations as "pluri-local transactions" that do not conflate society, state and territory but rather separate the "inner logic of social action…[from] the spatial dimension of social life" (p. 74). As Faist (2010) observes, migrants' complex ties, interactions and relationships across borders shape not only public policy but also local practices in the country of origin *and* in the country of settlement.

Gupta and Appadurai have also influenced how we understand and theorize processes of transnationalism and pointed out the problems with conceiving of social or cultural belonging only in terms of national affiliation. Gupta (1992/2003), for instance, drew attention to the role of "imagined communities" (see also Anderson, 1983) in fostering allegiances and affiliations, and this has challenged conventional notions of belonging (which are based on a more territorial notion of identity). Appadurai (1991/2008), too, argued that identities might not be clearly tied to a single territory or place but instead might be influenced by flows that transcend territorial, cultural or national boundaries. Indeed, even though many theories of learning encourage us to view social context in terms of place, the notion of transnationalism pushes us to move beyond this and think more broadly of the social contexts for learning as networks, relationships and communicative practices. Drawing on spatial theory, I am interested in how space might also be conceptualized as "networks of social relations and understandings" (p. 28), how such networks are socially produced and the role of language in that process. By reconceptualizing context to include not just setting and location but also a space that has been socially constructed (Bartlett & Vavrus, 2017), we are able to identify and analyse the processes by which contexts emerge. Following Basch, Glick Schiller, and Szanton Blanc (1994), Ong (1999), Bartlett and Vavrus (2017) and others, I show that, if we theorize belonging and movement only in terms of nation-state boundaries, decisions about not only *what* is investigated but *how* it is investigated are limited in consequential ways.

These are a few of the scholarly contributions that show the value in rethinking how transnational movement and transnational connections are conceptualized and operationalized. By replacing dichotomies (e.g. here vs. there; homeland vs. host country; assimilation vs. segregation; us vs. them) with notions of fluidity and flow, researchers are able to provide a more nuanced account of transnational processes and identities, while also giving attention to the situated and complex ways in which people on the move might establish and/or maintain transnational connections. By focusing on the different social practices migrants might use to intentionally and actively maintain connections to their homeland while also making connections in their new context, a growing body of ethnographic work illuminates some of the ways that refugees and immigrants have used a range of resources and practices to actively build, sustain and nurture transnational connections. Such work shows in rich detail how the transnational movement of material goods, people and practices influences not only the conditions and local experiences of the transnational migrant but also processes of teaching and learning (Abu El-Haj, 2009; Burns & Roberts, 2010; Duff, 2015; Jacquemet, 2005; Lam & Warriner, 2012; Leander, Jiménez, Eley, & Smith, 2015; Li & Zhu, 2013; Warriner & Wyman, 2013).

One reason that transnationalism should be of particular interest to teachers, teacher educators and educational researchers is that local manifestations of global processes require multiple modifications in instructional practice, curricular goals, learning processes and questions of assessment and accountability. It is important to examine much more than the local; we must also investigate and theorize the relationship between local practices and global influences. One way to understand how people "incorporate daily activities, routines and institutions located both in a destination country and transnationally" (Levitt & Glick Schiller, 2008, p. 284) is to systematically examine their practices. For instance, a close look at language and literacy practices among transnational migrants illuminates the need not only for multiple modifications in instructional practice (e.g. to build on and expand existing repertoires) but also for new understandings of learning processes in relation to questions of social identity. With a focus on language and literacy practices in relation to identity and processes of transnationalism, for instance, Duff (2015) observes that language education efforts and materials "instill transnational sensibilities and desires together with the languages, cultures and topics being discussed" and that research on the sociolinguistics of globalization "offers possibilities for curricular and pedagogical innovation" (p. 76). In Warriner (2007b), I examine the kinds of sensibilities, identities and trajectories that are encouraged or facilitated by particular kinds of testing regimes, and I argue that we often find that "the policies and testing practices often utilized in adult ESL education stand in stark contrast to the different kinds of knowledge, literacies, and identities that help individuals access economic, social and cultural capital outside the classroom context" (p. 322). Han (2013), King (2013) and Noguerón-Liu (2013) employ theories of transnationalism to understand how individuals use existing and emerging linguistic resources in a range of different ways to develop and sustain connections with people, practices and events elsewhere. Also, Prinsen et al. (2015) use social network theory to examine online practices of Dutch-Moroccan migrant youth in relation to their emerging identities and opportunities with a focus on "individuals successful at managing identity movements across social worlds" and find that "there are multiple ways in which youth seek and find resilience" (p. 34). Collectively, this scholarship sheds light on the various ways that studies of transnationalism might inform the policies and practices of teachers working with transnational migrants by influencing their understanding of the relationship between identity, learning and transnationalism.

Pedagogical Implications

By examining the experiences, practices, and everyday negotiations of contemporary language learners, researchers have provided accounts of transnationalism that shed light on how meanings might "emerge dialogically, recursively, and relationally in language curriculum, language teaching, and language use" (Warriner & Wyman, 2013, p. 11; see also Kramsch & Whiteside, 2008). These accounts demonstrate the influence of transnational connections on meaning making and show that "contemporary language learners are simultaneously situated in and influenced by multiple spaces and timescales" (Warriner & Wyman, 2013, p. 12). Han (2013), for instance, examines the emergent informal nature of multilingual repertoires among African and Chinese traders and the role of those linguistic resources in fostering and supporting transnational connections. Examining data from a longitudinal case study of one bilingual, Ecuadorian family, King (2013) shows that locally relevant ideologies of language and language learning influenced how family members saw their roles, their languages and their practices – with consequences for language learning and processes of social identification. Noguerón-Liu (2013) examined how adult learners of English used digital technologies to access and maintain transnational social networks and to establish or strengthen connections with people from their nation of origin. The analysis shows that the use of such resources in turn fostered digital literacy socialization (see also Noguerón-Liu & Warriner, 2014).

Other researchers focus on how ideological forces influence situated social practices in ways that shape the experiences of transnational migrants. In a special issue of *Applied Linguistics* on "Transnational Identities," De Fina and Perrino (2013) critically reflect on the relationship between situated local practices and processes of social identification among transnational migrants. With attention to questions of scale, they show that practices are varied and that ideologies (e.g. of language and of learning) are multiple and contested. At the same time, while investigating the "processes of globalization that permeate all aspects of human life and culture" (p. 509), they argue that it is important to realize that globalization does not always create economic opportunity (even though this is often assumed). Indeed, globalization often has undesirable consequences for migrants and language learners/users (Kramsch & Vinall, 2015; Park, 2015; Shin & Park, 2015; Warriner, 2015). Park (2015), for instance, points out that when learners and their teachers view the

English language as a "commodity" (and assume that an "endless investment in language learning" will ensure opportunity), they fail to understand the actual social contexts of learning, the ways that language learning and use are embedded in social relations of power and how other factors influence the kinds of opportunities available to those who can read, write and speak English.

So, given these considerations and insights, what might the curriculum of global/transnational mobility and migration look like? For starters, it might involve greater critical language awareness and an explicit discussion/debate with students about the influence that ideologies of language have on language use and other social practices, particularly in relation to questions of domain, situation or purpose. In addition, some argue that we should view the classroom as "a globalized social space" (Burns & Roberts, 2010, p. 411) where the boundary between the classroom and larger worlds is more permeable than fixed; where questions of identity and agency cannot be separated analytically from questions about instruction and participation and where globalization and transnationalism (and their consequences) require a re-envisioning and re-structuring of English language teaching. For instance, teachers, researchers and policy-makers might revalue bilingualism, other linguistic resources and the aspirations of the learners (some of which may require bilingualism). Ideally, teachers and curriculum designers attend to such considerations while developing and delivering instruction. Burns and Roberts (2010), for instance, argue that teachers, researchers and policy-makers need a more systematic investigation of "the realities of adult migrant learning experiences" and "the creation and implementation of curricula that speak to these realities, rather than close them off or drive them into narrowly focused channels" (p. 416).

One way to achieve this is through practices that take into account "the wider structuring processes of globalization" (Burns & Roberts, 2010, p. 410). For instance, by discussing lived experiences and challenges they have encountered, learners might begin to identify and/or debate different ways of responding to or engaging with such challenges – and how certain language and literacy practices might be mobilized. Another is through modifying how participation in the classroom is organized and how the local classroom community is imagined (Auerbach, 1992; de Costa, 2010). Routinely, teachers are asked to make such modifications and accommodations in the classroom context. However, given that "the central tenet of a participatory approach is that curricula must emerge from and be responsive to the particular context of each group of participants" (Auerbach, 1992, p. 10), then the curricula must also go where learners encounter challenges and opportunities to use language—outside the classroom. It may also work well to allow a curriculum to emerge when learners are actually in the process of experiencing "the material conditions of [their] lives" (Cooke, Winstanley, & Bryers, 2015). In spaces outside of the classroom (e.g. in real-world settings), where learners spend most of their time and confront significant challenges on a routine basis, researchers could work with learners to evaluate the situation(s) at hand, develop priorities, modify goals, "set their own agendas" and "devise their own learning materials" (Cooke et al., 2015, p. 215).

While evaluating the situation at hand, developing priorities for instructional goals or creating learning materials to use in the out-of-school environment, it is important for researchers and practitioners to understand and value transnationalism (and its accompanying practices) and to be aware of the many different ways that transmigrants maintain connections with people and practices elsewhere (Levitt & Glick Schiller, 2008). The particular activities and practices that get taken up and promoted in spaces outside the conventional classroom context could/should be guided by questions such as what kinds of competencies count in what environments? and what are the consequences of not having them?

As an example, consider how difficult it can be to identify a health care provider, set up an appointment, get to the doctor's office (or clinic) and interact with health care professionals. Add to this the communicative challenges involved in understanding a diagnosis, picking up a prescription and following the instructions on the label of the medication. Even for those who share (or are familiar with) the language and cultural background of the provider, it can take time to understand the system and navigate it. For those moving into new (political and cultural and linguistic) spaces of transnationalism with a limited understanding of English and/or little knowledge of the health care system and how it works, the level of complexity increases and there is an increased chance for miscommunication between health care professionals and transnational migrants, immigrants and refugees. This is true whether or not the migrant ends up in the USA, the UK or a context where English is not the dominant language. Many such challenges have been described as problems of "health literacy." While some define health literacy as "the knowledge and competences of persons to meet the complex demands of health in modern society" (Sorensen et al., 2012), others define it as "the degree to which individuals have the capacity to obtain, process, and understand basic health information and services needed to make appropriate health decisions" (Institute of Medicine, 2004, p. 4). However we define it, it is clear that health literacy represents an example of something critical missing from the experiences of migrants and refugees crossing transnational boundaries or experiencing transnationalism.

So what kind of curriculum is needed to address the language, literacy and communication challenges involved when transnationalism influences how people navigate the health care system and/or negotiate meaning when communicating with health care professionals? It is certainly possible to deliver the instruction in a classroom environment but with participatory approaches and by including topics such as health and health care as the content of the curriculum. The learner and their priorities or concerns might influence the content of the curriculum as well as the pedagogical approaches used. As Cooke et al. (2015) note, participatory approaches "critically explore the shared concerns and resources that learners bring to the classroom" and "involve reflection on the material conditions of learners' lives and experiences and, where appropriate, involve students in action to effect change" (p. 214). Learners "set their own agendas" and "devise their own learning materials" while teachers help learners "take action" on issues they deem important and in ways they deem appropriate (p. 215; see also Mehmedbegovic, 2012; Shepherd, 2012).

Another way to bridge learners' lives with the goals of a classroom is through principled eclecticism (Cushing-Leubner & Bigelow, 2014) – an approach that encourages "the integration of eclecticism into classrooms and other language learning environments coupled with intentional decision-making, rooted in theoretical understandings of language acquisition, concepts of cognitive and social-emotional development, and understanding of motivating factors for learner investment and engagement" (p. 248–249). In such spaces, risk-taking is valued, errors are embraced and the goals of instruction are student-driven:

"When students take responsibility for their own learning, seek clarification and negotiate meaning and deeper understandings independently, and experience decreased inhibition to use the language, this is called *learner autonomy*." (p. 250–251)

The learner is increasingly viewed as having agency, even when that agency might be limited and constrained by social and historical context, and teachers view "learners as complex individuals whose language use, meaning-making and actions are mediated by their social and cultural worlds" (Vitanova, Miller, Gao, & Deters, 2015, p. 5).

While theorizing the ways that teachers might draw on learners' existing resources (e.g. orality) to foster learning, Bigelow & Vinogradov (2011) have argued that "adults need contextualized, meaningful instruction that is age and level appropriate, and this instruction needs to be explicit and systematic" (p. 123) – where the language forms that are being taught are "located within a memorable, interesting, meaningful context" (p. 123). By listening and attending to learners' concerns (e.g. about transnationalism) and interests (e.g. in experiences of migration or resettlement), teachers can help guide students as they work to communicate about real-life issues (p. 124).

Such approaches make sense for improving teaching and learning in formal educational environments. But there is another promising approach. Rather than "bring the outside in" to the classroom, what if we brought the teaching and learning to contexts and situations outside of the classroom – for instance, to contexts of transnationalism and intercultural communication as experienced in a health care setting? As researchers and teachers, we might start by identifying the communicative challenges and opportunities encountered in that setting, and then work to understand them before developing materials that could be used in the setting to teach and learn ways of reading, writing, listening and speaking that were needed in that situation for a particular communicative purpose. Drawing on notions of transformative participation (Pittaway & Bartolomei, 2013; Block, Gibbs, & Haslam, 2013; Refstie & Brun, 2011) – or "power sharing between researchers and participants in identification and development of local knowledge" (Pittaway & Bartolomei, p. 166) – researchers are well-positioned to devise a curriculum of transnational mobility and migration in partnership with those on the front lines of transnationalism and transnational processes. With the idea that "knowledge and meanings are constructed and co-constructed through the interaction of the researcher and the research participants" (Pittaway & Bartolomei, p. 166), knowledge would be created in and through interaction, collaboratively, in a "real-world" setting. Drawing on the notion of "reciprocal research" or "community consultation" (Pittaway & Bartolomei, 2013), researchers and practitioners could develop processes that increase participants' involvement and participation. Focusing on learners' lived experiences and priorities requires implementing pedagogical practices that foster engaged learning and educational advancement in an era of transnationalism.

In this scenario, the curriculum evolves in response to and engaged with specific experiences of mobility and migration, collaboratively negotiated in dialogue with "the material conditions of learners' lives and experiences" (Cooke et al., 2015, p. 215). Such responsive engagement attends simultaneously to the "global" and the "local" (and the dynamic relationship between them). Influenced by and tailored to the learner, the context, the situation and the purpose of the interaction, the pedagogical response is never one-size-fits-all. Whether and how the user needs to learn how to read instructions on prescribed medication depends on not only their level of English language proficiency but also whether they have just received a prescription, what it is for and what risks are involved with not being able to doing so.

This is one example of a real-world space of transnationalism that poses challenges to educational policies and practices that are less directly connected (or responsive) to the everyday experiences of the target audience. To improve experiences of mobility and migration for users of different languages from a variety of contexts, we must revisit and rethink the value of terms such as "global," "local" and "transnational" and how to provide "a globalized social space" (Burns & Roberts, 2010) of teaching and learning in different real-world contexts.

Conclusion

In sum, transnationalism and mobility require a range of responses from schools and other social institutions: raising students' critical language awareness; bringing participatory approaches into the classroom; allowing the curriculum to be student-driven and the ped-agogy to be learner-centred; re-envisioning the social contexts of learning to include non-school environments. I have also explored how notions of the "global" and the "local" might be re-imagined and how this re-imagining might improve experiences of mobility and migration. I have shown that in contexts shaped by globalization and transnational-ism, it is important to focus on questions of curriculum and instruction, particularly in rela-tion to learners' lived experiences, and that it is important to re-envision pedagogical practices in ways that promote learning, engagement and advancement.

In an era of increasing globalization coupled with the spread of anti-immigration rheto-ric and practices, many teachers, teacher educators, educational researchers and applied linguists are eager to use research-based understandings and tools of inquiry to question and resist fears and anxieties about cultural, linguistic and religious difference; to show that those differences are not in and of themselves a threat to existing norms, values, pri-orities and practices; and to question assumptions regarding what defines or constitutes a community, a society or a nation. Ongoing and future work in this domain requires a seri-ous reconsideration of the social contexts of teaching and learning in order to envision and create spaces in which learners might learn new ways of interacting with specific sit-uations, other users of their new language and everyday challenges. A more intentional approach to managing the dynamics and challenges that accompany transnationalism might be productively combined with a proactive stance towards intercultural communi-cation and multilingualism as well as a deeper understanding of the many different spatial dimensions of transnationalism.

Acknowledgments

I wish to thank Bryan Brayboy, Lesley Bartlett and the editors of this special issue. Their input and feedback have greatly strengthened the clarity of my focus.

Disclosure statement

No potential conflict of interest was reported by the author.

References

Abu El-Haj, T.R. (2009). Becoming citizens in an era of globalization and transnational migration: Re-imagining citizenship as critical practice. *Theory into Practice, 48*(4), 274–282.

Anderson, B. (1983). *Imagined communities: Reflections on the origin and spread of nationalism.* New York: Verso.

Appadurai, A. (1996/2003). Sovereignty without territoriality: Notes for a postnational geography. In S. M. Low & D. Lawrence-Zuniga (Eds.), *The anthropology of space and place: Locating culture* (pp. 337–349). Malden: Blackwell.

Appadurai, A. (1991/2008). Global ethnoscapes: Notes and queries for a transnational anthropology. In S. Khagram & P. Levitt (Eds.), *The transnational studies reader: Intersections & innovations* (pp. 50–63). New York: Routledge.

Auerbach, E.R. (1992). *Making meaning, making change. Participatory curriculum development for adult ESL literacy. Language in education: Theory & practice 78.* Washington: Center for Applied Linguistics.

Bartlett, L., & Vavrus, F. (2017). *Rethinking case study research: A comparative approach.* New York: Routledge.

Basch, L., Glick Schiller, N., & Szanton Blanc, C. (1994). *Nations unbound: Transnational projects, post-colonial predicaments and de-territorialized nation-states.* New York: Routledge.

Bigelow, M., & Vinogradov, P. (2011). Teaching adult second language learners who are emergent readers. *Annual Review of Applied Linguistics, 31*, 120–136.

Block, K., Gibbs, L., & Haslam, N. (2013). Ethics in research with refugees and asylum seekers: Processes, power and politics. In K. Block, E. Riggs, & N. Haslam (Eds.), *Values and vulnerabilities: The ethics of research with refugees and asylum seekers.* Toowong: Australian Academic Press.

Blommaert, J. (2010). *The sociolinguistics of globalization.* New York: Cambridge University Press.

Burns, A., & Roberts, C. (2010). Migration and adult language learning: Global flows and local transpositions. *TESOL Quarterly, 44*(3), 409–419.

Cooke, M., Winstanley, B., & Bryers, D. (2015). Whose integration?: A participatory ESOL project in the UK. In J. Simpson & A. Whiteside (Eds.), *Adult language education and migration: Challenging agendas in policy and practice* (pp. 215–224). London: Routledge.

Cushing-Leubner, J., & Bigelow, M. (2014). Principled eclecticism and the holistic approach to language teaching and learning. In S. Çelik (Ed.), *Approaches and principles in English as a foreign language education* (pp. 245–263). Ankara: Eğiten Kitap.

de Costa, P. (2010). From refugee to transformer: A Bourdieusian take on a Hmong learner's trajectory. *TESOL Quarterly, 44*(3), 517–541.

De Fina, A., & Perrino, S. (Eds.). (2013). Transnational identities. [Special issue]. *Applied Linguistics, 34* (5), 1–8.

Duff, P. (2015). Transnationalism, multilingualism, and identity. *Annual Review of Applied Linguistics, 35*, 57–80.

Faist, T. (2010). Transnationalization and development: Toward an alternative agenda. In N. G. Schiller & T. Faist (Eds.), *Migration, development and transnationalization: A critical stance* (pp. 63–99). New York: Berghahn.

Glick Schiller, N. (2005). Transnational social fields and imperialism: Bringing a theory of power to transnational studies. *Anthropological Theory, 5*(4), 439–461.

Gupta, A. (1992/2003). The song of the nonaligned world: Transnational identities and the reinscription of space in late capitalism. In S.M. Low, & D. Lawrence-Zuniga (Eds.), *The anthropology of space and place: Locating culture* (pp. 321–336). Malden: Blackwell.

Han, H. (2013). Individual grassroots multilingualism in Africa Town in Guangzhou: The role of states in globalization. *International Multilingual Research Journal, 7*(1), 83–97.

Institute of Medicine. (2004). *Health literacy: A prescription to end confusion.* Washington: The National Academies.

Jacquemet, M. (2005). Transidiomatic practices: Language and power in the age of globalization. *Language & Communication, 25*(3), 257–277.

King, K. A. (2013). A tale of three sisters: Language ideologies, identities, and negotiations in a bilingual, transnational family. *International Multilingual Research Journal, 7*(1), 49–65.

Kramsch, C., & Vinall, K. (2015). The cultural politics of language textbooks in the era of globalization. In X. L. Curdt-Christiansen & C. Weninger (Eds.), *Language, ideologies and education: The politics of textbooks in language education* (pp. 11–28). New York: Routledge.

Kramsch, C., & Whiteside, A. (2008). Language ecology in multilingual settings: Towards a theory of symbolic competence. *Applied Linguistics, 29*(4), 645–671.

Lam, W. S. E., & Warriner, D. S. (2012). Transnationalism and literacy: Investigating the mobility of people, languages, texts, and practices in contexts of migration. *Reading Research Quarterly, 47* (2), 191–215.

Leander, K., Jiménez, R. T., Eley, C., & Smith, P. H. (2015). Transnational immigrant youth literacies: A selective review of the literature. In P. Smith & A. Kumi-Yeboah (Eds.), *Handbook of research on cross-cultural approaches to language and literacy development* (pp. 322–344). Hershey: IGI Global.

Levitt, P., & Glick Schiller, N. (2008). Conceptualizing simultaneity: A transnational social field perspective on society. In S. Khagram & P. Levitt (Eds.), *The transnational studies reader: Intersections & innovations* (pp. 284–294). New York: Routledge.

Li, W., & Zhu, H. (2013). Translanguaging identities and ideologies: Creating transnational space through dynamic multilingual practices amongst Chinese university students in the UK. *Applied Linguistics, 34*(5): 516–535.

Mehmedbegovic, D. (2012). In search of high-level learner engagement: Autobiographical approaches with children and adults. In D. Mallows (Ed.), *Innovations in English language teaching for migrants and refugees* (pp. 67–77). London: British Council.

Noguerón-Liu, S. (2013). Access to technology in transnational social fields: Simultaneity and digital literacy socialization of adult immigrants. *International Multilingual Research Journal, 7*(1), 33–48.

Noguerón-Liu, S., & Warriner, D. S. (2014). Heteroglossic practices in the online publishing process: Complexities in digital and geographical borderlands. In A. Blackledge & A. Creese (Eds.), *Heteroglossia as practice and pedagogy* (pp. 179–197). New York: Springer.

Ong, A. (1999). *Flexible citizenship: The cultural logics of transnationality.* Durham: Duke University Press.

Papademetriou, D. G., & Banulescu-Bogdan, N. (2016). *Understanding and addressing public anxiety about immigration.* Washington: Migration Policy Institute.

Park, J. S. Y. (2015). Language as pure potential. *Journal of Multilingual and Multicultural Development.* doi: 10.1080/01434632.2015.1071824.

Pittaway, E., & Bartolomei, L. (2013). Doing ethical research: 'Whose problem is it anyway?' In K. Block, E. Riggs, & N. Haslam (Eds.), *Values and vulnerabilities: The ethics of research with refugees and asylum seekers* (pp. 151–170). Toowong: Australian Academic Press.

Prinsen, F., de Haan, M., & Leander, K. M. (2015). Networked identity: How immigrant youth employ online identity resources. *Young, 23*(1), 19–38.

Refstie, H., & Brun, C. (2011). Towards transformative participation: Collaborative research with 'Urban IDPs' in Uganda. *Journal of Refugee Studies, 25*(2), 239–256.

Shepherd, S. (2012). Responsive teaching and learner centredness. In D. Mallows (Ed.), *Innovations in English language teaching for migrants and refugees* (pp. 167–175). London: British Council.

Shin, H., & Park, J. S. Y. (2015). Researching language and neoliberalism. *Journal of Multilingual and Multicultural Development.* doi: 10.1080/01434632.2015.1071823

Sorensen, K., Van den Brouke, S., Fullam, J., Doyle, G., Pelikan, J., Slonska, Z., & Brand, H. (2012). Health literacy and public health: A systematic review and integration of definitions and models. *BMC Public Health, 12*, 80–93.

Vertovec, S. (2004). Migrant transnationalism and modes of transformation. *International Migration Review, 38*(3), 970–1001.

Vertovec, S. (2009). *Transnationalism*. New York: Routledge.

Vitanova, G., Miller, E. R., Gao, X., & Deters, P. (2015). Introduction. In P. Deters, X. Gao, E. R. Miller, & G. Vitanova (Eds.), *Theorizing and analyzing agency in second language learning: Interdisciplinary approaches* (pp. 1–16). Buffalo: Multilingual Matters.

Warriner, D. (2007a). Transnational literacies: Immigration, language learning, and identity. [Introduction to Special issue]. *Linguistics and Education, 18*(3–4), 201–214.

Warriner, D. (2007b). "It's just the nature of the beast": Re-imagining the literacies of schooling in adult ESL education. *Linguistics and Education, 18*, 305–324.

Warriner, D. S. (2015). "Here, without English, you are dead": Ideologies of language and discourses of neoliberalism in adult English language learning. *Journal of Multilingual and Multicultural Development*. doi: 10.1080/01434632.2015.1071827

Warriner, D., & Wyman, L. (2013). Experiences of simultaneity in complex linguistic ecologies: Implications for theory, method, and practice. *International Multilingual Research Journal, 7*(1), 1–14.

Wei, L., & Hua, Z. (2013). Diaspora: Multilingual and intercultural communication across time and space. *AILA Review, 26*, 42–56.

Wimmer, A., & Glick Schiller, N. (2002). Methodological nationalism and beyond: Nation-state building, migration and the social sciences. *Global Networks, 2*(4), 301–334.

The ink of citizenship

Leigh Patel

ABSTRACT
Nations actively write themselves onto human bodies. They etch and scratch their borders onto human flesh with figurative, often contradictory, ink that delivers stark material impact. The impacts hold their greatest force in metering the hinged consequences of contingent citizenship for some and unfettered citizenship for a few others. In this essay, I consider the often overlooked logics of these national scriptings and the curricular potential we lose when we perpetuate the faulty idea that migration is only about movement across countries.

Migration is all but synonymous with the trajectory of a person or a people's movement from location to location. The study of and teaching about migration pivots around the process of moving from place to place. Because migration is tantamount to movement, there are resultant outcroppings of foci in research, praxis, and curriculum. What are the motivations that have caused people to move? Under what conditions? What do they experience during migration? What do they experience in the "receiving" country versus the "host" country? Migration scholarship in particular documents undocumented status and the lived impact of not having legal authorization. In educational research and policy, the default of movement across nations has been papered over by an intense focus on dominant language acquisition, and more recently, racism-blind curricula of diversity and cultural competency (Ahmed, 2012; Patel Stevens, 2009). Social studies textbooks discuss the push and pull factors that move people across borders and land masses. All of this misses a vital feature of migration.

Migration surely is about movement, catalysed by and catalysing consequences between geographic locations. But nations are not static entities in global migration. People are not mere moveable and moving entities on a stable Risk[1]-like plateau of a planet (Smith, personal communication, 2016). Nations actively write themselves onto human bodies. Ferreira da Silva (2015) wrote that the following 110 years after Du Bois' 1903 declaration that the problem of the twentieth century would be the colour line, race and nation would be the primary descriptors through which European particularity mapped itself onto global space. Nations etch and scratch their borders onto human flesh with figurative, often contradictory, ink that delivers stark material impact. The impacts hold their greatest force in metering the hinged consequences of contingent citizenship for some and unfettered citizenship for a few others. In this essay, I consider the often overlooked logics of these national scriptings and what we lose when we operate under a faulty, pervasive premise that migration is only about movement across countries.

Citizenship as Dialectic

With migration largely corresponded to movement, migration studies are understandably organized around the impact of not having legal authorization. They place particular attention to the conditions that shape and the consequences that ensue when migrants do not have legal authorization to be in a nation/state (e.g. Gonzales, 2015; Yoshikawa & Kalil, 2011). Studies document and explain how and why unauthorized migration occurs, and how undocumented migrants navigate risks along migration journeys and in new countries. For example, migration scholarship focused on education sheds light on the ways that undocumented youth navigate the interactions with state entities that confer drivers' licenses, mediate federal financial aid for college, and allow and/or deny access to health care.

It is easy to read migration scholarship and understand the conferring and denial of citizenship as the single most impactful societal designation for migrants, either opening up legitimacy or sequestering life into limbo status. Citizenship, though, simultaneously contains within it and obscures complex histories and logics of race and property. It is a concept that was and continues to be sourced in the idea of piecemeal gifting to offset absolute status. Because of these histories and uses, it is more aptly understood as dialectic than binary. As such, the questions in migration studies should not be whether one has citizenship, but rather how its conferral furthers relative profit and debt.

While nations and sovereign entities have unique and important differences in their histories of conferring citizenship or membership, most share meandering histories of delineating differential terms for those who have mitigated, absolute, and blocked access to citizenship and the associative rights. In the United States, the founding documents of the government first addressed the form of governance and then quickly, within four years, began explicitly codifying whiteness and pre-existing "free" status as prerequisites for naturalization processes.

Later iterations of amendments and pivotal court rulings would include detailed phenotypical descriptions to racially stratify who was eligible for citizenship and who was relegated to the permanent class of foreigner (Harris, 1993; Lopez, 2006). The designations were neither consistent nor logical, but cumulatively they worked to re-inscribe whiteness as a protected status of property ownership. For example, in 1922, Takao Ozawa was denied his appeal for citizenship because he was not Caucasian, and therefore not white. The following year, Bhagat Singh Thind's appeal for citizenship was denied because he was determined to be Caucasian but not white (Lopez, 2006; Takaki, 2012). Racially coded logics of ownership prevailed through contradiction, with the conjoined collective impact of whiteness as the ability to own and land relegated to property. Despite this historical and ongoing vacillation of the codified, protected rights for some and diminished rights for others, citizenship is presented in a much simplistic fashion in the United States curriculum.

Curriculum that introduces the concept of citizenship is most commonly overtly taught in history and social studies courses. The primary publishers in the United States, including

Pearson, McGraw Hill and Glencoe, and Houghton Mifflin introduce and address the concept of citizenship in similar ways. For example, in McGraw Hill's 2014 textbook, *Discovering Our Past: A History of the United States*, the book states that "A citizen is a person who owed loyalty to a nation and is entitled to its protection. For the most part, anyone born on U.S. soil is automatically a U. S. citizen." It gestures to the limitations on citizenship by stating, "Our rights and freedoms have some limits. For example, government can limit our freedom of speech or our right to hold a protest if it threatens public health or safety…Limits on rights and freedoms must be equally applied to all people" (p. 215). Across the five most popular textbooks used in the United States, there is a consistency in the introduction of citizenship as the arbiter of equal rights and limited, also equally, when safety is threatened. This presents an ironically disjointed echo of the also disjointed nature of the wider rhetoric about citizenship as inherent and its actuality as contingent and withheld differentially. Thus, the understanding of citizenship as binary, as something one either has or does not have, is an insufficient and dysfunctional framing.

Understood as a dialectic, citizenship embodies irrationality. It is not a singular feature of a person or population's existence, nor is it statically defined by a nation. Nations, however, rely on conveying it as a static status, in part, to reify their own status as an entity. Yet, citizenship is not the source of rights. It is a tool of codification for metering relative status under a governing order. In stratified societies, it is contradictory by its very purpose in those societies. It is where less is dispersed to many in order to sequester more for a select few. The United States, as with all nations animated by logics of stratification, was codified on the premise that all beings cannot be granted equal and equitable rights and responsibilities. The constitution's preliminary words of equal creation of men are, in code and in practice, verily erased by the underlying and long-lasting codes and lived realities of liminality, exclusion, and revocability. Freedom and democracy proclaim themselves most loudly through politicians and school textbooks but are, in fact, untranslatable within the realities of contingent citizenship and property rights for a few.

When migration studies defer to citizenship as the arbiter of rights, they further the erroneous and overly neat tropes of lawfulness. They unwittingly contribute to blurring the societal structure that operates on hinged projects of well-being and suffering. The projects have been, necessarily under projects of layered well-being, always raced and gendered. The optic referent for manifest destiny in most United States textbooks is an 1872 painting by John Gast, that features a floating white woman, named Columbia, looking westward and symbolizing the vision and self-anointed duty of the US government to civilize and modernize evidently savage lands and peoples. Underneath Columbia are white male settlers who are carrying out this settler work. This image predominates as the image of manifest destiny and this iconic status speaks to the overall project of whiteness as property that included top-ranked yet still distinct dreams of white male and white female settlers.

Black Americans and Native Americans encounter, more than any other populations, simultaneous conferral and denial of US citizenship. Native Americans, living on homeland that predates US nationhood, were not granted birthright citizenship in the United States until 1966. But their rights as sovereign subjects on Turtle Island were not upheld by the US government preceding or following birthright citizenship. The United States' Voting Rights Act of 1964 guaranteed the right to vote for all Black Americans, but it is renewable every 25 years, meaning also that it is fundamentally temporary. Unsurprisingly, it has also been those with liminal status who have most eloquently indicted racialized citizenship that is promised and withheld (Du Bois & Edwards, 2008).

In her 2014 book, *Citizen: An American Lyric*, Claudia Rankine weds poetry and criticism to illuminate the incessant revocations of citizenship from Black Americans based on the construct of race. She uses the second person singular voice in the book to bring the reader into the experience of being made to bear witness to one's own revoked and permanently revocable status.

> In line at the drugstore it's finally your turn, and then it's not as he walks in front of you and puts his things on the counter. The cashier says, Sir, she was next. When he turns to you he is truly surprised.
>
> Oh my God, I didn't see you.
> You must be in a hurry, you offer.
> No, no, no. I really didn't see you.
> (Rankine, 2015, p. 77).

Rankine's short poem lifts up the underside scratching of hypervisibility and invisibility in a racially coded nation. In addition to social commentary, social activism has been a location where people have demanded for citizenship to make good on its surface promises.

In 1909, journalist and activist Ida B. Wells spoke about racial violence. In a speech entitled, "This Awful Slaughter," Wells spoke excoriatingly to the first convening of the National Association for the Advancement of Colored People about the ways that Black women, men, and children were being terrorized by a national campaign of lynching. Without uttering the terms racial injustice or racial justice, she laid out a clear appraisal of the problem of this coordinated lynching campaign as well as a solution. Wells noted that what would "resolve" this violence on Black people was neither education nor agitation, but the nation coming good on its promise of rights to its citizens. Wells called the nation on its hypocrisy and made explicit the dialectics in conferring citizenship in order to deny it. When migration studies focus on citizenship without contending with the contingent racialized coding of citizenship, they contribute to this chasm between word and deed. Wells' indictment and demands remains as relevant as when she delivered the speech well over 100 years ago.

A Multivariate Contradiction

Disrupting the idea of citizenship as a binary, as a condition that one either has or does not, also allows for recognizing the differential contingencies made possible under citizenship's rule. The idea of citizenship has been a key to formulating not just contingent relationships, but has bundled together sets of contingencies at the same time. In the United States and many other nations, inscriptions of legal citizenship are, in reality, more of a palimpsest of whiteness as property, the logics barely legible when superficial rhetoric is deconstructed. This palimpsest makes generous use of equivocations to etch on top of distinct yet connected locations of contingent citizenship.

In a settler society, such as the United States, Canada, Australia, and Israel, the societal architecture works to erase Indigeneity, collapse Blackness into chattel labour, and convert land into own-able property. It is not an event, but an ongoing structure that relies on distinct yet connected locations relative to the pursuit of land ownership by a few

(Wolfe, 2006). Because this structure is so reprehensible, it desperately needs narratives that tell a more palatable version of how society operates and where it comes from. The fictions become a malignant counterpart to the societal structure, denying its existence to ensure its existence.

In the United States, narratives of meritocracy and equality are crucial for blurring in order to perpetuate the racially stratified reality. The conceptual tissue that connects the narratives of meritocracy, equality, and linear progression is equivocation. Equivocations (e.g. we all put our pants on one leg at a time, All Lives Matter, etc.) are necessarily for what Chinua Achebe (1989) called a malignant fiction in stratified societies, as they render illegible the underlying scripts that explicitly locate populations differentially. Equivocations lop off the tops of the most protected status and submerge the most vulnerable realities into a forced dysconsciousness of equal. The settler's needs for own-able land, working and own-able chattel, and disappearing Indigenous who can righteously demand rematriation are not speak-able, read-able, or write-able in these equivocations. This illegibility protects settlers' interests.

Purportedly, the settler himself has no elevated status in equivocations of everyone having equal rights. The gendered male settler hero has both his race and gender privilege blurred through the unilateral writings of equality. Equivocations erase societal domination and subjugation through their inked assertion of equality. They are the sound of everyone having an equal opportunity to succeed in a meritocracy, everyone having equal rights under the law, and all of society benefitting from linear progression. While none of these premises are borne out in a single statistical reality of well-being, they are all but unshakeable as rhetoric that is asserted on a daily, if not hourly basis in the United States. The citizen stamp uses bold, red ink stamp, "ALL" on top of societal disparities.

Citizenship is a binary in nationalist imaginaries, belying the quixotic and impermanent nature of nation/states themselves. Although the question, "where are you from," is ubiquitous and almost unerring in its assertion, citizenship itself, from-ness, is piecemeal. Put another way, there is no "there" in the question of "where you are from?" The question is a way to assert who can be questioned (the outsider), as well as who can question (the insider) (Patel, 2015; Selasi, 2015). Author Taiye Selasi asserts that this question is an encoded version of the question, "Why are you here?" It is the everyday custom agent not needing a uniform.

Collateral Losses from Citizenship and Migration as Movement

What do we lose with this consistent oversight of the ways that nations actively write and rewrite their borders onto human bodies, parsing them into their desirability for a larger structure? We lose a potentially liberatory perspective on the fact that global migration and the pressures that create, contain, and discipline movement, are in fact creations. This is not to say that moving is unnatural and that populations were meant to stay geographically static. It is, however, wholly ignorant and illogical to equate the global capitalist and imperialist push and pull of populations that have been made vulnerable across nations' borders with individualistic, romanticized ideas of wanderlust. Defaults to movement, and binary positions of being pro and again migration as movement, detract from the ways that citizenship is promulgated as a disciplining status onto some. That citizenship status designations are creations means that they can be interrupted, but to best interrupt them, we need to better understand them.

To destabilize, to unsettle, the prevailing irrationality of how citizenship writes itself unevenly onto raced and gendered bodies, there must first be a more honest reckoning with the mixed histories and realities of citizenship. Curriculum that perpetuates national-ist fantasies of havens for migrants but is silent on Indigenous erasure should fall to the wayside for accurate histories and ongoing projects to be taught. Ample curriculum exists to interrupt the dominant narratives of citizenship taught in the most dominant text-books. The public pedagogies of movements including the Dream Defenders and Black Lives Matter are providing a re-imagining of citizenship that is not codified through nationalist impulses. Taking a note from these radical imaginaries of citizenry and with due attention to settler structures, the frequently race- and gender-silent analyses of citi-zenship in migration studies must speak into its own void. While extant migration studies name specific ethnicities and races, naming a studied race is nt the same as mapping the material work of racialization.

Perhaps most daunting, though, the binary logic of citizenship itself should be appre-hended. Social critic and poet Fred Moten expounded on the binaries even found in free-dom narratives that do a disservice to the foundational and founding logics of piecemeal apportioning:

> Often, historical books on American slavery attempt to show all the different ways in which the enslaved people are both radically interdicted from enjoying any kind of normative per-sonhood. Then the opposite side of it is, people often try to show how they managed to achieve that kind of subjectivity against all those odds and against the grain of that interdic-tion. The first few chapters of [*The Half Has Never Been Told*] show that the fundamental prob-lem with slavery in the United States in the 19th century wasn't that it interdicted individual personhood on the part of the enslaved, but that it imposed individual personhood as a kind of regulative, parseable condition. (Moten as quoted in Duplan, 2016, para 5)

In a settler society, humans and land are fundamentally parseable, all pursuant to their potential contribution to the land ownership project of the settler status. Black popula-tions are parseable into both chattel and labour. Indigenous populations are parseable into history and a savage threat to be dominated. Migrant populations can be parseable into both anti-black model minority symbols and coolie labour. These projects of parcelled out personhood depict more accurately the contingent racialized realities of social loca-tions than does the binary logic of citizenship. Citizenship written by these inks cannot begin to explain the illegible yet overtly erased place of the Native American in US history. That inked citizenship cannot speak of the bequeathed and constantly questioned status of Black Americans. Nonetheless, settler markings of citizenship unendingly seek authori-tative writing, leveraging binaries of legality and illegality to distort the more sophisticated desire for parsed peoples.

Global migration is constrained by default binary analyses of citizenship and citizenries because of the relative silence on racialized codifications of citizenship. Migration is about the writing of nations onto bodies. This writing is defined at a global level by race and racial logics (da Silva, 2015; Du Bois, 1899). The logic of racialized and gendered parsing of piecemeal personhood permeates migration, much more than movement. Its mother tongue, its first ink, is citizenship.

Note

1. Risk is a board game popular in the Westernized world that is composed acquiring armies and conquering as many other countries as possible. It was first created in 1958 by Parker Brothers Corporation.

Disclosure statement

No potential conflict of interest was reported by the author.

References

Achebe, C. (1989). The truth of fiction. *Hopes and impediments: Selected essays*.

Ahmed, S. (2012). *On being included: Racism and diversity in institutional life*. Durham: Duke University Press.

da Silva, D.F. (2015). Globality. *Critical Ethnic Studies, 1*(1), 33–38.

Du Bois, W.E.B., & Eaton, I. (1899). *The Philadelphia Negro: A social study* (No. 14). Boston: Published for the University.

Du Bois, W.E.B., & Edwards, B.H. (2008). *The souls of black folk*. London: Oxford University Press.

Duplan, A. (2016, July 13). A body that is ultra-body: A conversation with Fred Moten and Elysia Crampton. *Ploughshares at Emerson College.*Retrieved from http://blog.pshares.org/index.php/a-body-that-is-ultra-body-in-conversation-with-fred-moten-and-elysia-crampton/

Gonzales, R.G. (2015). *Lives in limbo: Undocumented and coming of age in America*. Oakland: University of California Press.

Harris, C.I. (1993). Whiteness as property. *Harvard Law Review, 106*, 1707–1791.

Lopez, I.F. (2006). *White by law: The legal construction of race*. New York: University Press.

Patel, L. (2015). *Decolonizing educational research: From ownership to accountability*. New York and London: Routledge.

Patel Stevens, L. (2009). Maps to interrupt a pathology: Immigrant populations and education. *Critical Inquiry in Language Studies, 6*(1–2), 1–14.

Rankine, C. (2015). *Citizen: An American Lyric*. London: Penguin.

Selasi, T. (2015). *Don't ask me where I'm from; Ask me where I'm local* [Video file]. Retrieved from: https://www.ted.com/talks/taiye_selasi_don_t_ask_where_i_m_from_ask_where_i_m_a_local?language=fr

Takaki, R. (2012). *Strangers from a different shore: A history of Asian Americans*. Boston: Little, Brown.

Wolfe, P. (2006). Settler colonialism and the elimination of the native. *Journal of Genocide Research, 8*(4), 387–409.

Yoshikawa, H., & Kalil, A. (2011). The effects of parental undocumented status on the developmental contexts of young children in immigrant families. *Child Development Perspectives, 5*(4), 291–297.

Toward an awareness of the "colonial present" in education: Focusing on interdependence and inequity in the context of global migration

Thea Renda Abu El-Haj and Ellen Skilton

ABSTRACT

Across the world, the number of displaced people has risen to unprecedented levels. In the United States, rightwing politicians call for closing borders to Muslims, refugees, and immigrants. These conditions lead the authors to ask *how to educate with and for immigrant students who are positioned as enemy aliens – "impossible subjects" – within their new nation?* We take a comparative approach, looking across our studies with Palestinian immigrant and Cambodian refugee youth in the US to think about how their experiences in US schools can inform an education for justice. In looking across two ethnographies, done more than a decade apart from each other, we illustrate the remarkable similarities between discourses about these different groups of students. In this article, we focus on three stances toward immigrant incorporation that the young people in our research studies encountered – stances through which they learn about the meanings of and expectations for citizenship and belonging. Our argument is that despite the differences between these stances, all three erase the "colonial present" that shapes the lives of immigrant youth and their families. We call for an education that decentres the nation, and focuses attention on the co-dependent inequities at the centre of our global interdependence.

On 11 September 2001, as news about the events in the US was just breaking, a teacher walked into the principal's office in the school in which I (Abu El-Haj) – a Palestinian American scholar – would later conduct critical activist ethnographic research. According to the principal, this teacher demanded that he "round up all the Palestinian kids." Over the past decade and a half, I have told this story often because it so well illustrates the position in which many youth from Muslim im/migrant[1] communities (as well as communities presumed to be Muslim) have been placed, not only in public spaces and communities, but also *inside their schools*. From taunts of "terrorist," to girls having their *hijabs* torn of their heads, to beatings, and unjust disciplinary sanctions, youth from Muslim im/migrant communities have faced the burden of proving that they are "loyal" subjects of the US – a condition they can never sufficiently meet. Many of the people who are being framed as enemy-aliens, have, in fact, been displaced by either direct US military action, or US economic and military support for violent regimes from which they are fleeing (as was the case with the Palestinian youth).

Nearly a decade before 9/11, in the midst of a class-action suit filed on behalf of Cambodian plaintiffs, I (Skilton) – an Anglo-American scholar and ESL tutor in a three-year ethnographic study in homes, schools, and communities in Philadelphia – found that students, school district officials, and organizations struggling to meet the needs of their own minoritized communities, questioned the legitimacy of Cambodian students as full members of the United States. Although Asian Americans have often been framed as either "forever foreigners" or "honorary whites" (Tuan, 1999), the experiences of Cambodians point to yet a third space – "the other Asians who have often faced challenges in schooling and high poverty rates" (Reyes, 2007). In addition to the ways in which Cambodians may not have fit the stereotype of successful Asian Americans, many have also experienced not just the traumatic upheaval of the genocidal Pol Pot regime, but also the "liminality" of the refugee camp (Long, 1993), and later, the realities of living in poverty in the US. Even more relevant to our argument are the ways in which the US has simultaneously "welcomed" Cambodians while also playing a major (yet often hidden) role in the conflict that has framed their lives.

The latest round of US-led wars and military actions across many nations began soon after 9/11, and continues to this day. Across the world, the number of displaced people has risen to unprecedented levels (UNHCR, 2016). In the US, and many other "Western" states, rightwing politicians call for closing borders to Muslims, to refugees, and to immigration. These conditions lead us to ask *how to educate with and for im/migrant students who are positioned as enemy aliens, "impossible subjects" (Ngai, 2004), within their new nation.* Although as ethnographers we are wary of generalizing across national contexts, many of the themes about immigration that we encounter in the US resonate with research undertaken in other countries (Jaffe-Walter, 2016; Rios-Rojos, 2014) As we reflect on this question, we take a comparative approach, looking across our studies with Arab im/migrant and Cambodian refugee youth to think about what we can learn from their experiences in US schools. In looking at the experiences of Cambodians and Palestinians, it is easy to focus on the significant differences of language, geography, history, and geopolitics between these groups. Quickly, however, it is possible to notice uncanny parallels in their experiences in schools. In reading through transcripts of interviews with, and observations of, teachers and students done more than a decade apart from each other, the discourses about these students contain remarkable similarities. In what follows, we focus on three stances toward immigrant incorporation that the young people in our research studies encountered: (1) Erasing colonial legacies, (2) civilizing the colonial subject, and (3) producing the illusion of inclusion. Through each of these stances, young people were learning about the meanings of and expectations for citizenship and belonging. Our argument is that despite the differences between these stances, all three embed what Derek Gregory (2004) calls "the colonial present," and are built on narratives that erase this very present. Gregory (2004) writes of the "colonial-rather than the imperial" in order to signal "the active sense of the verb to 'colonize': the constellations of power, knowledge, and geography that … continue to colonize lives all over the world" (p. xv). These narratives depend, as Gregory argues, on both colonial amnesia that denies the past and present workings of colonial power, and colonial nostalgia, in which the powerful fantasize about the loss of "Other" cultures, but also long for the prior relationships between the ruler and the ruled. Thus, in listening for colonial narratives, we hear multiple silences around the United States' colonial past and present. As we hear these silences locally, we acknowledge echoes of longstanding colonial power relations in many parts of the world which, although distinctive to particular contexts, tend to depend on both amnesia and nostalgia for maintaining the status quo. We then address the limits of cultural citizenship and critical cosmopolitanism, in order to consider a more radical critique for educating beyond the nation-state for peace and global justice.

Stance 1: Erasing Colonial Legacies

Given the virulent anti-immigrant discourses that pervade much contemporary political talk in the US, it is no surprise that im/migrant youth experience explicitly hostile encounters not only with their peers, but also with some of their educators. This thread runs through the data from both our studies. For Skilton, there were examples of administrators asking why we needed bilingual Asians, teachers who posited that Cambodian students would have known nothing about real Cambodian culture without teachers' input, and adult ESL teachers who were telling strangers in public spaces to stop speaking their native language because they "lived in America now." Although the following examples come from the lives of Palestinian youth, the commonalities across our studies are strikingly similar.

Some educators expressed a nostalgia for an imagined immigration of the past with a smooth transition to national assimilation. For example, Tom Blackburn,[2] a teacher in Abu El-Haj's research who described himself as being of German ancestry, spoke of the differences between the Arab Muslim (and other new immigrant) communities, and historic waves of white European immigrants.

> [I]f you talk about our parents, grandparents, and great grandparents' immigration from Western and Eastern Europe … what I see is the difference where they came … here wanting to start a new life and buy into the program here and want to create a better society. *What I see with the immigration that's coming in now, it's more or less I'm going to come in and get everything I can possibly get for me, or get what I can get and then go back to my other country* … I don't see them buying into the American dream (emphasis added).

We hear, in Mr Blackburn's yearning, what Gregory (2004) calls colonial nostalgia – one that longs for a colonial historical imaginary. It reflects a white fantasy that denies both the reality that assimilation was neither a seamless process for those immigrants who became white, and the racialized exclusions that were fortified through the expansion of white supremacy (Ignatiev, 1995; Ngai, 2004). However, Mr Blackburn's narrative also reflects an erasure of the Unites States' "colonial present" (Gregory) that contributes to creating the conditions that lead people to migrate to the US. Rather than understanding the dire conditions from which many migrants are fleeing, immigrants are described as greedy people who are taking "our" good life in order to benefit their families elsewhere, or to return home.

This stance toward immigration also denies the contours of contemporary migration patterns. Academics debate the extent to which today's globalization reflects a new phenomenon; nevertheless, it is clear that today's technologies make it possible for people to stay connected to families and communities through direct and immediate means. These technologies also create opportunities for people to be engaged much more directly in politics beyond their immediate surroundings. Thus, many young people develop and maintain a transnational sense of belonging to multiple places, peoples, and politics.

For the young people with whom we worked, the demands to "buy into the program" did not line up with the identifications and understandings they had developed through their migration experiences. Cambodians in Skilton's study were often positioned as "other Asians" living in poverty and attending largely African-American schools – positioned by others and themselves as always Cambodian and never quite American. All of the youth in Abu El-Haj's research viewed themselves as Palestinian – members of a political imaginary seeking an independent state, even as they also carved out a sense of themselves as belonging to the US – a sense that was always partial. Cambodians and Palestinians could see the contradictions between the colonial fantasies with which they were being asked to line up, and the local and global injustices they knew so well. Thus, these young people – who were framed as enemy aliens in the US, and who remembered the conditions of violent conflict and occupation they and/or their families had experienced – demanded a lifting of the veil of the US colonial present. They required an education that confronted unjust conditions both in the US and in other countries, particularly those directly affected by US economic, political, and military policies.

Stance 2: Civilizing the Colonial Subject

Nowhere are the parallels between the discourses about Palestinian and Cambodian youth clearer than in the forces that position female passivity and rule-following as a desired quality for school success. Both Cambodian and Palestinian women and girls were framed in terms of needing to be saved, protected, and freed from the oppression assumed to be foundational to their respective communities' cultural values and practices.

Early on in Skilton's research (1997, 2009; Skilton-Sylvester & Chea, 2010), she was shocked to find an inquisitive, thoughtful, engaging third grader transformed in her regular education classroom to a mere shadow of herself. The teacher, a middle-aged white man, explained without hesitation that she was on the "barefoot, pregnant, obedience track" and had a "scary dad" at home. This same student, in high school, was asked if she was planning to get pregnant and leave school early. As she reported:

> I have this counselor that was working at my school… and I can tell he's like "you guys come to this country and aren't even happy to come to this country, you guys don't even try to learn, you know." And he'd look at everybody as just one category which really upset me a lot. … So one day my boyfriend dropped me off at school and he's like, "Are you gonna drop out and just have kids?"

The vision of this student as on the path to early pregnancy, meek and uncritical (and not caring about her education) was not only false, it also ignored the ways that US schools and society rewarded behaviours and created contexts in which silence and obedience flourished. Although these are connected to the same forces that position female passivity and rule-following as a desired quality for school success for many, the ways that this played out for Cambodian and Palestinian young women and girls were particularly fraught with assumptions that they were doomed to a life of oppression and passivity because of their "cultures."

Consider the Palestinian young woman, Haneen Haddad, who in the face of a female teacher "going on" about her *hijab*, decided to remove her headscarf so that the teacher could see her hair. Upon removing her scarf, Haneen recalled that the teacher told her, "you look more [like a] girl now." In deciding to respond positively to the teacher's request, this student was not only acquiescing, she was also being positioned as an object to be saved by western society, freed to be a "girl" – a *visible* subject. The principal of the school at which Abu El-Haj worked commented repeatedly about his hope that an Arab American after school club would "give girls voice."

Others have written eloquently of the "Western" desire for Muslim women to be saved (Abu-Lughod, 2013), but what we want to highlight here are the ways that the story of Cambodian and Palestinian emancipation by a liberal and benevolent "West" is built on a fairy tale of epic proportions. This "civilizing" mission obscures a social and geopolitical reality in which the United States (and not just Pol Pot or the Israeli government) has used its military might to create instability, and further its own interests while writing the fiction that it is the beacon for democracy worldwide. In fact, an emphasis on personal trauma, a psychological understanding of events and outcomes fundamentally erases history, inequality and the responsibility of the US in creating and/or supporting the trauma and conflict in the first place.

Stance 3: Producing the Illusion of Inclusion

Although colonial erasure and "civilizing" discourses remain steadfast educational stances that im/migrant youth face, the image of the US as a multicultural salad bowl has become a national trope – one that gets taken up in schools as the primary discourse for managing "diversity." Although manifesting as a more benign discourse, multiculturalism does its own work obscuring the "colonial present" – projecting a reformed US that has left behind its racist past, and reformed itself into a harmonious pluralist polity (Brown, 2006; Melamed, 2006; Moallem & Boal, 1999). Multiculturalism paints a picture of a nation in which each person can maintain and share a rich diversity of cultural beliefs and practices. Where multiculturalism is celebrated in schools, it professes to create and celebrate a harmonious, diverse citizenship inclusive of all.

Bill Andrews, a teacher in Abu El-Haj's study who identified as African-American, described this imagined nation:

> See, the beauty of America is not that it's a melting pot like they used to say. It's not. It's a salad bowl. But when you have a salad bowl, when you put the lettuce in, it retains its own identity … but it's so good together. And that's what America is. It's not a melting pot. Everybody's not going to blend. Everybody's going to be who they are. But we're all in that salad bowl called America.

It is critical to pay attention to the version of culture that is imagined to be in this salad bowl – one in which there are no conflicts between these distinct flavors. This is an uncontested culture; in a sense, it is lightly worn.

Moreover, there is a disciplinary aspect to this salad bowl image of US multiculturalism. It promotes an image of the US as a world peacemaker – and a US education as its diplomatic service. For example, the principal of the school in Abu El-Haj's study told her that he noticed when Arab Muslim students initially arrived, they were "aggressive" toward the US. He argued, over time, this aggression was ameliorated *through an education* that assimilated them into a multicultural community.

> I have come to understand that maybe if they [Muslim im/migrants] viewed Americans as the enemy … if this is what was basically professed where they were before … then coming here and having lived here for x number of years, I've definitely seen an assimilation. [For example] Amir Khalid was an angry, angry man when he came here. You know, he drew pictures of planes and bombs and guns and all kinds of stuff. I worked closely with him and his father … I saw, little by little, he was venturing out from his group and he was involved in the Asian club. It was Asian break-dancers. It looked like break-dancing and they were Asian kids plus Amir.

The trope of US respect for cultural diversity plays a critical role in constructing a harmonious national imaginary. Without the rich diversity of this multicultural landscape upon which he could fashion himself anew, Amir might have remained locked into his anger and aggression.

What gets obscured in all the pretense that the US is a multicultural haven – a fantasy United Nations – are deeper political conflicts that structure relations of power across the world. Unfortunately, for the im/migrant youth in our research, the only acceptable performances of difference were cultural ones that subsumed any political conflicts to benign displays of food, clothing, or music. For example, while Palestinian American youth in Abu El-Haj's study were often invited to participate in the school's annual multicultural fair, they were forbidden from displaying the Palestinian flag, or from wearing the black-and-white checkered scarves (kefiyyas) that have come to be a symbol of the Palestinian struggle for independence. Moreover, critical discussion about US support for Israel, and the US "war on terror" were virtually silenced in their schools.

Beyond Multiculturalism

Critical educational scholars have long acknowledged that multiculturalism is an inadequate framework for addressing deeper structural inequalities that shape our society (see for examples, Abu El-Haj, 2006; Castagna, 2014; Motha, 2014). Cultural recognition and cultural citizenship have been proposed as frameworks for addressing inequalities in democratic states (Flores and Benmajor, 1997; Kymicka, 1995; Ong, 1996; Rosaldo, 1994; Taylor, 1992). These frameworks argue that institutional structures and norms must recognize and draw on group affiliations and cultural resources in order for marginalized groups to be full participants in diverse democratic societies. And yet, these discussions and debates still centre around forging new pathways for inclusion into the nation-state. In fact, in Skilton's 2009 article on democratic citizenship education, she describes the need for recognition of Cambodian (and other Asian) experiences in the curriculum. Participants in her study often discussed the emphasis on Rosa Parks and Martin Luther King during Black History Month, but had a powerful sense that their heritage was not part of the fabric of the school curriculum. One of the participants in Skilton's study, Nhor, a Cambodian woman in her 20s who had just read about the Cambodian genocide for the first time, said:

Some people don't know about the Khmer Rouge. People in America don't know that slavery is in every country. There's a lack of teaching.… When I was growing up, my parents would say, "You guys are bad children. You don't know how good you have it." And we were like, "Oh yeah, Khmer Rouge, whatever." Now I really know.

In this moment of recognition, she saw, for the first time, the atrocities of her parents' experiences in Cambodia, her own life in new terms, and the connections between human exploitation in the United States and abroad. She also used this moment to critique her education, not merely in terms of a request for recognition (although it initially may be read that way), but as a call for making visible the underlying structures that are anti-human and that exist in a variety of forms (all with similar roots) around the world. Years later, rereading this description (highlighted in Skilton-Sylvester, 2009), Skilton recognized her own growing awakening. Deeply embedded in the narrative of Pol Pot is a story of a vicious, ideologically-based, quest for power and control, associated with the Khmer Rouge. What is not hinted at in any of the stories of Cambodians in the US, are the ways that the US government also helped create the context for the genocide in direct and powerful ways. How many US citizens do not know that history?

Recognition, it turns out, is not enough. Even when it is done well (e.g. utilizing Moll and González's (2004) funds of knowledge approach), recognizing what families and neighbourhoods bring to schools still leaves nationalism intact (even if inadvertently). As Dunbar-Ortiz states in her 2015 book, *An Indigenous Peoples' History of the United States*:

> The main challenge for scholars in revising US history in the context of colonialism is not lack of information, nor is it one of methodology… Rather, the source of the problems has been the refusal or inability of US historians to comprehend the nature of their own history, US history. The fundamental problem is the absence of the colonial framework.

As long as unequal colonial power relations are invisible in our analysis, we are unable to even see the ways that the nation is obscuring our understanding.

One of the most dramatic stories from working with Cambodian students came from a high school student, at a predominantly African American school, who was asked (along with her African American classmates) to write about what it feels like to be black. At first glance, this may seem like an example of Cambodian culture needing to be recognized – a call for an expanded cultural citizenship. We might imagine that we want the teacher to ask students to write about what it feels like to be part of a minoritized group – to specify the ways that the US recognizes and does not recognize who they are. What we are arguing here, however, is that an expanded view of citizenship that continues to frame identity in terms of the nation state, on the one hand, and in terms of salad bowl multiculturalism, on the other hand, completely misses the point and leaves any possibility for emancipatory transformation buried deep below the surface.

One might wonder if what we are suggesting is a kind of *critical cosmopolitanism* (Hawkins, 2014), *cosmopolitanism from the ground* (Hansen, 2010), or *cosmopolitanism from below* (Hall, 2006). According to Hawkins (2014), this orientation does acknowledge the ways that historical and current contexts and conditions "mediate what happens, and who people [can] be and become, within them" (p. 107). However, in spite of their attention to those who may be less powerful or those who have not voluntarily chosen to move across national boundaries (e.g. refugees and immigrants), these less elitist forms of a cosmopolitan orientation are still limited in scope. They pay scant attention to the ways that the world we educate students to understand, question, and critique is a colonial, parasitic one in which those who have power and resources survive and thrive on the backs of those who do not. We are calling for a stance that attends to interdependence and inequity, within and across nation-states, focusing squarely on the relations of power that shape the colonial present.

Our argument about the shared limitation of the three stances toward immigration, described above, is that they all rely on an obscuring of the colonial present. In his 2005 novel, *Never Let Me Go*, Kazuo Ishiguro creates a nightmarish world in which human clones are bred and raised in order to harvest their organs so that other humans can live long lives, disease free. Told from the perspective of the narrator Kathy H, the reader slowly comes to the realization that she, and her friends, have been bred only to die young, sacrificing their organs one by one so that humans may live. Described as occurring in "England, late 1990s," Ishiguro does not bother to set his tale in a dystopic imagined future; rather, he appears to be commenting on the world that already exists – one in which the good lives of the few are parasitic on the lives of the many "Others."

Toward a Wide Awake Curriculum that Decentres the Nation

The kind of curriculum we are proposing rejects the facile, decontextualized comfort of multiculturalism. It also builds upon but pushes beyond a model of cultural citizenship. Cultural citizenship expands democratic politics to consider group rights; however, it still centres on the nation-state. We also expand critical cosmopolitanism's concern about global inequities, by centering attention on fundamental and asymmetrical power relationships that structure our interdependent and deeply unjust world. This wide awake curriculum requires not only denaturalizing the US (or any nation-state) as the primary locus for attention and concern, but also challenging the narrative of the US's "radical innocence" (Pease, 2009) both at home and abroad. Education that supports young people to understand inequality and oppression in relation to both the past and present, and to work for justice and equity, must expand the scale for such work to include global contexts of injustice and a wide awake look at the historical foundation of the present and who the colonial narratives render visible and invisible, reasonable and unreasonable. As we decentre the nation in our analysis, we call for an education that puts power at the centre of inquiry, and particularly the untrustworthy power of colonial narratives to shape "truth," create fictional heroes and villains, and limit what is imagined to be possible. Uncritical perspectives on the nation-state leave intact a willful blindness to the role the United States and other colonial powers continue to play in contributing to devastating economic and political conditions in too many countries – conditions that are often intimately interwoven with the reasons that people migrated in the first place.

Elsewhere, Abu El-Haj (2015) has made the case for an education that creates opportunities for substantive inclusion for transnational youth. For Abu El-Haj, this means that young people need opportunities to learn about and understand structural inequalities and oppressions that traverse local and global contexts. It also requires educating young people to develop civic identities and practices that support them to take action for justice within and across the borders of nations. Here, we want to conclude with a call for an education that disrupts the colonial present at every turn and teaches students (and the teachers who teach them) how to actively call into question these fictions in their lives in and out of school. For example, we have been particularly encouraged by the ways that the #blacklivesmatter movement has actively and persistently pushed back at the colonial present in the US and around the world. As teacher educators, we find that in spite of its significant limitations, multiculturalism remains the only visible frame that educators typically turn to in the context of their awakening to the personal and structural realities of their im/migrant students' daily lives. Even when educators engage with the realities of structural racism, a focus on the nation often remains intact. Without a persistent focus on decentering the nation, we limit the possibilities for getting and staying "woke," learning with and from im/migrant youth, and building a more just and equitable world.

Notes

1. Arzubiaga, Nogeuron, and Sullivan (2009) suggest using im/migrant to denote the variety of people included in the category of immigrant (for example, immigrant, transnational migrant, and refugee).
2. All names are pseudonyms.

Disclosure statement

No potential conflict of interest was reported by the authors.

References

Abu El-Haj, T. R. (2015). *Unsettled belonging: Educating Palestinian American youth after 9/11*. Chicago: University of Chicago Press.

Abu El-Haj, T. R. (2006). *Elusive justice: Wrestling with difference and educational equity in everyday practice*. New York: Routledge.

Abu-Lughod, L. (2013). *Do Muslim women need saving?* Cambridge: Harvard University Press.

Arzubiaga, A. E., Nogeuron, S. C., & Sullivan, A. L. (2009). Education of children in im/migrant families. *Review of Research in Education, 33*, 246–271.

Brown, W. (2006). *Regulating aversion: Tolerance in the age of identity and empire.* Princeton: Princeton University Press.

Castagna, A. (2014). *Educated in whiteness: Good intentions and diversity in schools.* Minneapolis: University of Minnesota Press.

Dunbar-Ortiz, R. (2015). *An indigenous peoples' history of the United States.* Boston: Beacon.

Flores, W. V., & Benmajor, R. (1997). *Latino cultural citizenship: Claiming identity, space and rights.* Boston: Beacon.

Gregory, D. (2004). *The colonial present.* Malden: Blackwell.

Hall, S. (2006). *Interview of Stuart Hall.* Retrieved from http://www.youtube.com/watch?v=fBfPtRaGZPM

Hansen, D. T. (2010). Cosmopolitanism and education: A view from the ground. *Teachers College Record, 112*, 1–30.

Hawkins, M. R. (2014). Ontologies of place, creative meaning-making and critical cosmopolitan education. *Curriculum Inquiry, 44*, 90–112.

Ignatiev, N. (1995). *How the Irish became white.* New York: Routledge.

Ishiguro, K. (2005). *Never let me go.* New York: Vintage.

Jaffe-Walter, R. (2016). *Coercive concern: Nationalism, liberalism, and the schooling of Muslim youth.* Stanford: Stanford University Press.

Kymicka, W. (1995). *Multicultural citizenship: A liberal theory of minority rights.* New York: Oxford University Press.

Long, L. (1993). *Ban Vinai: The refugee camp.* New York: Columbia University Press.

Melamed, J. (2006). The spirit of neoliberalism: From racial liberalism to neoliberal multiculturalism. *Social Text, 24*(4), 1–24.

Moallem, M., & Boal, I. A. (1999). Multicultural nationalism and the poetics of inauguration. In C. Kaplan, N. Alarcon, & M. Moallem (Eds.), *Between woman and nation: Nationalisms, transnational feminism, and the state* (pp. 243–263). Durham: Duke University Press.

Moll, L. C., & González, N. (2004). Engaging life: A funds-of-knowledge approach to multicultural education. In J. A. Banks & C. A. McGee Banks, *Handbook of research on multicultural education* (pp. 699–715). San Francisco: Jossey-Bass.

Motha, S. (2014). *Race, empire, and English language teaching: Creating responsible and ethical anti-racist practice.* New York: Teachers College Press.

Ngai, M. (2004). *Impossible subjects: Illegal aliens and the making of modern America.* Princeton: Princeton University Press.

Ong, A. (1996). Cultural citizenship as subject making. *Current Anthropology, 37*(5), 737–751.

Pease, D. (2009). *The new American exceptionalism.* Minneapolis: University of Minnesota Press.

Reyes, A. 2007. *Language, identity and stereotype among Southeast Asian American youth: The other Asian.* Mahwah: Lawrence Erlbaum Associates.

Rios-Rojos, A. 2014. Managing and disciplining diversity: The politics of conditional belonging in a Catalonian Institute. *Anthropology and Education Quarterly, 45*(1), 2–22.

Rosaldo, R. (1994). Cultural citizenship and educational democracy. *Cultural Anthropology, 9*, 402–411.

Skilton-Sylvester, E. (1997). *Inside, outside and in-between: Identities, literacies and educational policies in the lives of Cambodian women and girls in Philadelphia* (Unpublished doctoral dissertation). University of Pennsylvania, Philadelphia, PA.

Skilton-Sylvester, E. (2009). 'Who cares?': Relationships, recognition & rights in the democratic education of Cambodians in the United States. *Inter-American Journal of Education for Democracy, 2*(2), 274–294.

Skilton-Sylvester, E., & Chea, K. (2010). The other Asians in the other Philadelphia: Understanding Cambodian experiences in neighborhoods, classrooms and workplaces. In M. Osirim & A. Takenaka (Eds.), *Global Philadelphia: Immigrant communities, old and new* (pp. 270–191). Philadelphia: Temple University Press.

Taylor, C. (1992). *Multiculturalism and the "politics of recognition."* Princeton: Princeton University Press.

Tuan, M. (1999). *Forever foreigners or honorary whites: The Asian ethnic experience today*. New Brunswick: Rutgers University Press.

UNHCR (2016). Global trends report 2015. Retrieved from http://www.unhcr.org/statistics/unhcrstats/576408cd7/unhcr-global-trends-2015.html

Revisioning curriculum in the age of transnational mobility: Towards a transnational and transcultural framework

Shibao Guo and Srabani Maitra

ABSTRACT

Under the new mobilities paradigm, migration is conceptualized as circulatory and transnational, moving us beyond the framework of methodological nationalism. Transnational mobility has called into question dominant notions of migrant acculturation or assimilation. Migrants no longer feel obligated to remain tied to or locatable in a "given", unitary culture. Rather, they are becoming embedded within a shifting field of increasingly transcultural identities. While migrants are becoming more transnational and adopting fluid, transcultural identities, there is a lack of focus and engagement with transnationalism as well as transculturalism in the official Canadian public school curricula. As scholars contend, Canadian school curricula are still based on Eurocentric, homogenizing, nationalistic discourses that tend to normalize values, norms, and behaviours that are perceived as "different" from the dominant norm. In response to the limitations of Canadian official curricula, as noted by various scholars who have examined curriculum documents, this essay proposes a revision of Canadian curricula in the context of transnational mobility with the aim of developing an approach that would integrate transnational and transcultural perspectives into the existing system. The article thus proposes a transnational and transcultural framework as an alternative to build a more ethical and inclusive school curriculum in Canada.

In recent years, scholars have claimed that a "new mobilities" paradigm, also known as a "mobility turn", is taking place within the social sciences to transcend disciplinary boundaries (Hannam, Sheller, & Urry, 2006, pp. 1–2; Sheller & Urry, 2006). A powerful discourse in its own right, one that creates its own effects and contexts, the emerging mobility paradigm challenges the "a-mobility" of much research in the social sciences. It problematizes both "sedentarist" approaches in the social sciences that "treat place, stability and dwelling as a natural steady-state", and "deterritorialized" approaches that "posit a new 'grand narrative' of mobility, fluidity or liquidity as a pervasive condition of postmodernity or globalization" (Hannam et al., 2006, p. 5). Deploying a critical eye to develop the paradigm further, Cresswell (2010) argues that mobility is best understood in terms of "constellations of mobility" that is, "historically, and geographically specific formations of movements, narratives about mobility and mobile practices" (p. 17). Thinking about mobility in this way implies a focus on "the fact of movement", the "shared meanings" that flow from representations of movement and the "experienced and embodied practice of movement" (p. 19). Doing so allows Cresswell to emphasize how human mobilities and the unequal power relations that produce and distribute mobility are inextricably bound. It underscores the importance of interrogating the politics of mobility, treating mobility as a political concept that is implicated in the production of power and hierarchical relations of domination.

Under the new mobilities paradigm, migration is now conceptualized as circulatory, processual, and transnational, thereby moving beyond the framework of methodological nationalism (Faist, 2010; Lie, 1995). As Lie notes, the idea of transnationalism "challenges the rigid, territorial nationalism that defines the modern nation-state; the dividing line is replaced by the borderlands of shifting and contested boundaries" (p. 304). In this view, migrants are best understood as "transmigrants" who engage in transnational mobility, involving "multiple, circular and return migrations, rather than a singular great journey from one sedentary space to another, occur[ing] across transnational spaces" (Lie, 1995, p. 304). Transnational mobility has called into question dominant notions of migrant acculturation or assimilation. Scholars suggest that transnationalism is making cultural boundaries and identities porous, hybrid, and dialogic. Migrants are no longer perceived to be obligated to remain tied to or locatable in a "given", unitary culture (Grosu, 2012). Rather, they are seen as embedded within a shifting field of increasingly transcultural identities (Kraidy, 2005). These new paradigms of migration have led to the emergence of new research protocols put together to explore the impact of transnational mobility on the identity, culture, and integration of migrant populations spanning several nations simultaneously (Guo, 2016).

A relatively understudied area in this context is the intersections between transnational mobility and education, particularly in relation to school curriculum. A handful of scholars have attempted to weave together the new mobilities paradigm and curriculum studies, pointing out that a growing number of students in contemporary classrooms "read, write, act, think, know [in ways] that are critically informed by a transnational standpoint" (Skerrett, 2015, p. xii). We need to ask whether the school curricula are able to engage productively with such transnationalism. Relatedly, Coloma (2012, p. 56) points out that a transnational framework is particularly germane for Canadian curriculum studies, "whose prevailing interpretive parameters remain bounded within the nation-state". This is so despite the fact that under existing conditions of global migrations, whether brought about by choice or forced by circumstances such as war, the existing boundaries of nation states have become porous in unprecedented ways. To talk about school curriculum without taking into account the effects of transnationalism and transculturalism is to shy away from the world-historical changes currently under way. This is especially true in the classrooms of Canada, which house a wealth of diverse experiences brought on by the processes of transnationalism and transculturalism (Ali, 2009). Yet, the official public school curricula of Canada continue to largely ignore the experiential knowledge of both teachers and students (Bickmore, 2014). At best, the curricula seek a tokenistic assimilation of cultural plurality while in practice insisting on a Eurocentric, singular, authentic, national culture that is generous enough to include its subordinated "Other" (Ali, 2009; Bickmore, 2005, 2014; Lightman, 2015, 2016).

By curriculum, we are specifically referring to the "curriculum-as-plan" (Aoki, 1993), a conception that signifies officially designed and sanctioned "set of learning objectives, instructional materials and approaches" as well as "learning activities and assessments" (Skerrett, 2015, p. 40) that Canadian students are expected to engage with in K-12 classrooms. Clearly there is no reason to assume that the officially designed curriculum is precisely and consistently implemented and taught in all classrooms (Bickmore, 2014). Still, it is important to pay attention to the ideology and politics behind curriculum planning, for people in positions of power, provincial governments, school authorities, and other stakeholders are often primary agents when decisions are made on the content of the curriculum, as well as instructional materials and texts chosen, thereby legitimating and enforcing what students should learn and teachers ought to teach (Bickmore, 2005; Skerrett, 2015).

Against this backdrop, it is therefore the purpose of the essay to examine the limitations of official Canadian public school curricula, as noted by various scholars who have examined curriculum documents, with the aim of developing an approach that would integrate transnational and transcultural perspectives into the existing system. The essay begins with a theoretical discussion of transnationalism and transculturalism which provides the conceptual lens for the examination, followed by a summary of secondary literature on official public school curricula in Canada. It ends with a discussion of a transnational and transcultural framework (TTF) as an alternative approach to building a more ethical and inclusive curriculum in Canada.

Theorizing Transnationalism and Transculturalism

Transnationalism is not a new concept per se. According to Kivisto (2001), the earliest articulation of transnationalism was by cultural anthropologists (Schiller, Basch, & Szanton Blanc, 1995). In the early 1990s, the concept offered a novel analytical approach to understanding contemporary migration. Sociologist Alejandro Portes is most responsible for popularizing and expanding the use of transnationalism (Portes, 1999; Portes, Guarnizo, & Landolt, 1999). When analyzing transnationalism, individuals and their support networks are regarded as the proper units of analysis. According to Portes et al., a study that begins with the history and activities of individuals is "the most efficient way of learning about the institutional underpinnings of transnationalism and its structural effects" (p. 220). Unlike early transnationalism, which was often limited to elites, contemporary grassroots transnational activities are examined as a reaction to government policies – and to the condition of dependent capitalism foisted on weaker countries – to circumvent the permanent subordination of immigrants and their families. At the grassroots level, Portes (1999) points out elsewhere, transnationalism offers an economic alternative to immigrant's low-wage dead-end employment situation, gives them political voice, and allows them to reaffirm their own self-worth.

Transnational activities can be organized into three types: economic, political, and socio-cultural (Portes et al., 1999). The main goals of each type are different. To illustrate with specific examples, transnational economic entrepreneurs are interested in mobilizing their contacts across borders in search of suppliers, capital and markets; transnational political activities aim to foster political power and influence in sending or receiving countries; and socio-cultural transnationalism is oriented toward the reinforcement of a national identity abroad or the collective enjoyment of cultural events and goods. In response to the fear that transnational activities will slow down the process of assimilation in immigrant host nations, Portes (1999) maintains that transnational activities can actually facilitate successful adaptation by providing "an alternative path of socioeconomic and political adaptation to the host society not envisioned by traditional models of assimilation" (p. 887).

The integration of a "transnational optic" into the understanding of migrant mobility is said to have re-configured the notions of race, class, ethnicity, and nation-state as bounded concepts in both social science and popular thinking (Schiller, Basch, & Blanz-Szanton, 1992). For example, conventional social science theories have conceived nation-states as territories with borders, characterized by linguistic, cultural, and ethnic homogeneity (Vertovec, 2004). Moreover, social scientists working within the paradigm of structural functionalism have repeatedly conceptualized immigrant population, ethnic groups or cultures as discrete, "bounded units" who live in one place and bear a "unique and readily identifiable culture" (Schiller et al., 1992, p. 6). Culture has thus been considered as unitary, static, and territorialized, "reproducing the image of the social world divided into bounded, culturally specific units, typical of nationalist thinking" (Wimmer & Schiller, 2002, p. 305). These forms of imagining national cultures as bounded categories have in turn reified certain dominant power relations and hierarchies of race or ethnicity as *natural* corollaries of national cultures rather than as historical effects of inequality and often violence (Maitra, 2015).

The concept of transnationalism offers an alternative to the bounded imaginaries of nationhood, providing a framework that posits a significant shift in the understanding of borders and national identities, thereby raising contentious questions about the cohesiveness of host societies, "identitive solidarity" (Heisler, 2001, p. 237), and orthodox assimilation theories (Vertovec, 2004). Such a framework posits migrant population as fluid, with multiple identities simultaneously grounded in their societies of origin as well as settlement. Moreover, identity itself in this framework gets refracted as a constant negotiation between divergent power relations and social hierarchies. The corollary that emerges from this critical transnational perspective is that transmigrants do not remain tied to the common sense hegemonic practices, habits, racial, and ethnic categories that pervade any particular nation-state. On the contrary, because of their navigation through various class backgrounds and racial and ethnic positionings, transmigrants selectively assimilate, incorporate, and develop their own notions of categories of identity by creating new cultures and social spaces (Schiller et al., 1992). Thus, transnational identity formation implies a process in which "identity is not singular but plural and always evolving" (Wong & Satzewich, 2006, p. 12). Clearly, this understanding of migration poses serious challenges to state policies and any attempt to institutionalize migrant citizenship within readily identifiable and static paradigms of cultural identities.

The study of transnational migrants and their fluid and mobile identity can be further nuanced through the framework of transculturalism. As with transnationalism, the prefix *trans* before culturalism also suggests movement across spaces and borders, conveying a synthetic and dynamic understanding of the interstices and relationships between cultures (Kraidy, 2005). The notion of transculturalism was developed by Ortiz (1940), who conceptualized transculturalism based on José Marti's idea of intercultural peoples (*mestizaje*) published in his article "Nuestra America" in 1891. For Ortiz, transculturalism did not just signify transition from one culture to another or simple acquisition of a new culture.

Rather, it meant a simultaneous synthesis of deculturalization of the past and a *mestizaje* with the present. The concept of mestizaje has been subsequently critiqued by many Latin American and Afrocentric scholars for being a colonialist and racialized discourse, that has erased the African Black heritage in Latin America and ignored the resistance that many indigenous communities have demonstrated to the idea that they need to become *mestizos* (Hale, 2002; Kraidy, 2005). In other words, the celebration of hybridity as necessarily desirable becomes untenable when viewed through the historical lenses of power and social domination. The unequal distribution of power therefore becomes a central concern of transculturalism that aims to be truly emancipatory and inclusive.

The concept of transculturalism has gained popularity since the 1990s, paralleling the emergence of transnationalism, and suggests a process through which "individuals and societies chang[e] themselves by integrating diverse cultural life-ways into dynamic new ones" (Hoerder, Hébert, & Schmitt, 2006, p. 13). This process of transculturation sees cultures as fluid, and places them in constant interaction with other cultures (Zhang & Guo, 2015). New cultures form; others dissolve. Transculturation is, moreover, implicated within various structural constraints, notably those of race, class, gender, sexuality, and ethnicity, which makes it a highly charged political process. Transculturalism then is different from cross- or multiculturalism as these concepts tend to "study contacts between individuals from different cultures that are assumed to be discrete entities" (Kraidy, 2005, p. 14). Proponents of transculturalism, by contrast, believe "all cultures to be inherently mixed" (Kraidy, 2005, p. 14), relational, and mutually transforming. Additionally, Berry and Epstein (1999) maintain that transculturalism enables a reflexive identity, where individuals can distance themselves from their own cultural moorings and can participate in "self-criticism of one's own cultural identities and assumptions" (p. 307).

Transculturalism has also been seen by many scholars as a more viable framework for understanding identity and mobility than multiculturalism (Cuccioletta, 2001/2002). They have highlighted that multiculturalism, despite being adopted as a policy in countries such as Canada, has in reality impeded rather than facilitated the integration of immigrants into Canadian society. It has reinforced borders and boundaries based on cultural categories, and failed to foster the recognition of the "Other" (Cuccioletta, 2001/2002). Cuccioletta (2001/2002), therefore, advocates for a transcultural framework that breaks down boundaries, opposes singular traditional cultures, recognizes cosmopolitan citizenship and develops the understanding that one's culture is multiple and fluid.

In the following sections, we present a summary of scholarly research that examines Canadian public school curricula, especially such courses as Social Studies, History, and Civics vis-à-vis transnationalism and transculturalism. Our interest in exploring the intersections between school curriculum and transnationalism and transculturalism stems from our own position as transnational scholars, who have moved extensively between one national context and another (for education and research), have experienced living between cultures in transnational contexts and have felt deeply the impact of having familial, cultural, and linguistic ties across geographical borders.

We hope that our discussion of the Canadian public school curriculum will have significance for other countries where classrooms are becoming increasingly diverse in the wake of increasing migration and, in particular, the current global refugee crisis (Santoro & Forghani-Arani, 2014). Given the global scope of migration, the children and youth of today's mobile populations are by definition culturally and linguistically diverse and are growing up in highly transnational contexts. Unavoidably, they are developing complex, multi-layered, socio-cultural relationships across geographical borders (Bickmore, 2005). Yet, standardized, official school curricula, in many countries (e.g. US, Britain, Sweden) fail to productively engage with such transnationalism and the "multiliterate, multilingual, and transcultural repertoire" that transnational children and their families develop (Skerrett, 2015, p. 7). Therefore, through a critique of official, Canadian, public school curricula, we want to provoke educationists and curriculum developers to develop curricula in relation to the national, cultural, or linguistic pluralisms that transnational and transcultural children bring to classrooms. Such innovative curriculum will enable all students to recognize the value of diversity and prepare them to be civic participants in a globalized world (Ali, 2009).

Researching School Curriculum in Canada

In Canada, with its four-decade history of official multiculturalism, a greater emphasis has been placed on "encouraging immigrants to engage in transnational social practices and to develop transnational social identities" (Wong & Satzewich, 2006, p. 1). Yet, official curriculum in Canadian public schools has been slow to respond to the transnational realities (Lightman, 2015). Kelly (2015), for instance, notes that despite the fact that fifty to sixty percent of children in some Toronto schools are transnational Filipino-Canadians, there is a striking lack of Filipino content and culturally responsive pedagogy in schools. The problem of a lack of transnational and transcultural perspective in Canadian school curricula is compounded by the fact that there is considerable variation between official, provincially mandated public school curricula.

In this paper, we concentrate on the work of scholars who critically examine official public school curricula across different provinces from a transnational and transcultural perspective, taking into consideration issues such as citizenship, nationalism, cross-cultural awareness, and global politics. Most of these studies have examined the Social Studies curriculum because it is a core curriculum course in all provinces and includes citizenship education, global citizenship, and nationalism, all topics relevant to our discussion of transnationalism and transculturalism (e.g. Ali, 2009; Bickmore, 2005, 2014; Lightman, 2015, 2016). Where relevant, we also draw on critiques of related courses such as History or Civics. Based on a survey of this scholarly research, we arrived at three themes these courses continue to uphold. We recognize that this is in no way an exhaustive discussion of official Canadian school curricula. What we have attempted instead is to focus on broad commonalities emerging from transregional contexts in Canada.

Eurocentrism

Critical educators argue that Canadian curriculum needs to be analyzed in light of the role played by colonialism and European settler domination (Neeganagwedgin, 2011). For the early colonizers, schooling was one of the main media through which they embarked on a process of cultural and psychological subordination of the colonized "Other", who was perceived as "inferior", "traditional", and "backward" (Kanu, 2003). Accordingly, school curriculum was developed with an explicit agenda of assimilation and neutralization of difference. A trenchant critique of the assimilationist moorings of education has come from the Indigenous scholars who have highlighted how school curriculum has been a tool of the colonizer's civilizing mission and reinforcement of European superiority (racial and cultural) in the settler nation (Battiste & Henderson, 2009; Neeganagwedgin, 2011; Weenie, 2008).

Concurrent arguments about the scant or distorted representations of contributions by various ethnic groups (e.g. Asians and Blacks) towards Canadian nation building have emerged in the wake of the critical analyses of Indigenous scholars (Broom, 2012; Finlayson, 2015). For instance, Ali (2009) points out that the history curriculum in Ontario, while glorifying the contribution of white men, largely ignores the role of Chinese workers in building the railways and other national infrastructural developments in Canada. Such Euro-dominated school curriculum seriously undermines the identity and knowledge of those who do not belong to the dominant racial, cultural, and ethnic groups of Canadian society. Additionally, histories of other nations are largely absent in the Social Studies curriculum in provinces like British Columbia, although such global perspectives are vital to understanding transnational mobility in the age of globalization (Broom, 2012). Thus, the school curriculum, while claiming to be part of a multicultural value system, both re-creates and subtends hierarchies of race and national belonging.

Homogenizing National Identity

The "curricular imagination" in Canada is also said to be mediated by a nationalistic discourse that propagates what Stuart Hall (1992) calls the "myth of cultural homogeneity" (p. 297) through its emphasis on common language, history, and culture. This nationalistic discourse functions as a vehicle for "ideological assimilation and homogenization" (Kanu, 2003, p. 71). Its role is to neutralize values, norms, and behaviour that are perceived as "different" from the dominant norm of the nation and to make individuals "fit into a single set of imaginaries about national citizenship" (Kanu, 2003, p. 71).

In particular, Canadian national history is conceptualized in school curriculum as homogenized and assimilationist. For instance, Ali (2009), exploring the curriculum to which a growing population of transnational youth in Canada is exposed, argues that current Ontario Social Studies school curriculum focuses on teaching a homogenous ideal of nationalism and Canada's role in world affairs. As corrective measures, she advocates for the inclusion of areas like international political–economic relations or international laws that might not only "validate the students' Canadian identity and affiliation, but will also open up generative possibilities for their multi-lingual, multi-cultural and multi-national identities and affiliations" (p. 239). Bickmore (2014), analyzing nationalistic discourses in relation to citizenship education imparted as part of Social Science, History, Civics or Language Arts, maintains that the curriculum of citizenship education in some provinces may formally advocate for multiple and diverse sources and viewpoints in light of the growing diversity and transnationality of Canadian population. However, the curriculum-in-practice fails to inspire critical awareness of social injustices experienced by different groups or to provide for a nuanced reading of hierarchical power relations.

Furthermore, there is a contradiction in Canadian schools between the variegated demands of national and global citizenship education that seek to address globalization and international mobility. Richardson and Abbott (2009) reveal this contradiction by showing how Canadian school curriculum reinforces a nationalist and European perspective even as it attempts to address transnational mobility. As Bickmore (2014) aptly concludes, even though "transnational issues and perspectives are included more than in previous years, some Canadian school curricula may reinforce ignorance and stereotypes about other nations and peoples and about the causes and effects of global problems such as war" (pp. 266–267).

Celebratory Multiculturalism

The adoption of multiculturalism as a state policy in 1971 and the Canadian Multicultural-ism Act in 1988 have made multicultural education an integral part of Canadian school curricula. The focus of such multicultural education, however, has been critiqued for being primarily based on tokenistic celebration of specific events, ethnic songs, dance and rit-uals and the assumption that exposure to such cultural practices will by themselves lead to sensitivity and understanding of cultural diversity, without actually disrupting a norma-tive sense of Canadianness (Ali, 2009; Richardson & Abbott, 2009). What is also problem-atic about such celebratory orientations to multicultural education is that it is primarily geared towards accommodating ethnocultural groups as subordinates without actually complicating or seriously undermining the power relations that exist between different racial, ethnic, and cultural groups. Moreover, under the rubric of such multicultural curricu-lum, categories of race, ethnicity, and culture are unproblematically depicted as biological, stable, eternal, and predetermined categories (Montgomery, 2005). A case in point is the secondary Social Studies curriculum for Ontario and Manitoba which hardly have any criti-cal content to address Canadian youth's complex transcultural identities and multiple attachments (Hebert, Wilkinson, & Ali, 2008). Even when historical racism or discrimination is discussed in the curriculum, the overarching message is still one of national cohesions implying that social hierarchies or inequalities are issues of the past that have been unequivocally resolved in the present (Bickmore, 2014; Montgomery, 2005). The success of official multiculturalism is therefore often alluded to in the school curriculum as being capable of controlling, limiting, and managing differences and saving the Canadian nation from ethno-cultural and racial divisiveness (Montgomery, 2005).

Conclusion: Towards a Transnational and Transcultural Curriculum

In this paper, we emphasize, first, how mobility and migration should be re-thought in an era of globalization as a multi-directional process in which diverse identities, forms of attachment and belonging inscribe the experiences of people as they move across geo-graphical, cultural, national and linguistic boundaries. Second, we argue that school edu-cation as a primary site of identity formation must recognize the transnational and transcultural movements of individuals whose identities are already inscribed by inequal-ities of power and structural violence. Such recognition is especially significant in the post-9/11 global order of cultural xenophobia and intolerance of difference, when there has been a hardening of mono-cultural and assimilationist ideals of citizenship, identity, and belonging. Consequently, diversity and plurality have become empty rhetoric that nations often pay homage to but do not embrace in reality. The hardening of singular cul-tural identities has also seeped into the school system and official curricula, where the overriding message is one of "social cohesion and integration" into Eurocentric main-stream society, thereby marginalizing other experiences and viewpoints (Bickmore, 2014). School curricula, therefore, must be brought into conversation with the wider ramifications of globalized migration and the distinctive webs of knowledge formation necessitated by transnationalism and transculturalism; otherwise, school curricula, especially in western countries, will continue to reinforce the limited perspectives of national and territorial fixities and bounded cultural domains.

As an alternative to the dominant, Eurocentric and assimilationist orientation of the official Canadian school curricula, we therefore propose transnational and transcultural curricula that will reject traditional, Eurocentric foundations of knowledge currently being circulated through the school curricula. Such a framework would broaden the knowledge base of students and inspire greater transcultural interactions in the classroom. As well, it will provide them with opportunities to engage with alternative narratives of history, science, language or literature by validating and incorporating multiple perspectives based on historical, cultural, and geographical diversity. The goal would be to enable their understanding of the connection between knowledge and power as well as stimulate empathy for people, issues, and worldviews across cultural and geographical borders. The students would then "experience the school space as more relevant and meaningful[ly] located within the continuum of their life spaces" (Kim & Slapac, 2015, p. 23).

Beyond this, a transnational and transcultural framework would align curricula with the shifting ideas of culture, language, and identity. By going beyond the "border-centered" conceptualization of culture, language, and identity, such a framework would move the curriculum from a "mere celebration of differences" toward an understanding of how, within transnational and transcultural social spaces and, despite their mobile identities, migrants remain implicated within unequal power relations of gender, race, ethnicity, class and occupy a range of dominating and dominated positions (Lightman, 2016). In the Canadian curriculum context, such understanding of mobile identities would create among students "an openness to others… so as to be able to imagine oneself as another, to take up new belongings, and to move across cultural, linguistic, religious, ethnic, racial spaces of interaction and boundaries" (Hébert et al., 2008, p. 51). Moreover, going beyond apolitical and normalized notions of race, culture, or ethnicity in the curriculum, a transnational and transcultural framework would foster democratic spaces for students to reflect on discrimination, stereotyping, and social injustice. It will nurture students toward becoming well-informed, engaged, cosmopolitan citizens dedicated to the cause of building a just and equitable world order.

Acknowledgments

The authors wish to thank the three anonymous reviewers for their insightful comments and suggestions.

Disclosure statement

No potential conflict of interest was reported by the authors.

References

Ali, M. A. (2009). Preparing citizens for a globalized world: The role of the social studies curriculum. *InterAmerican Journal of Education for Democracy, 2*(2), 238–256.

Aoki, T. T. (1993). Legitimating lived curriculum: Towards a curricular landscape of multiplicity. *Journal of Curriculum and Supervision, 8*(3), 255–268.

Battiste, M., & Henderson, J. S. Y. (2009). Naturalizing Indigenous knowledge in Eurocentric education. *Canadian Journal of Native Education, 32*(1), 5–18, 129–130.

Berry, E. E., & Epstein, M. E. (1999). Transcultural experiments: Russian and American models of creative communication. New York: St. Martin's Press.

Bickmore, K. (2005). Foundations for peacebuilding and discursive peacekeeping: Infusion and exclusion of conflict in Canadian public school curricula. *Journal of Peace Education, 2*(2), 161–181.

Bickmore, K. (2014). Citizenship education in Canada: 'Democratic' engagement with differences, conflicts and equity issues? *Citizenship Teaching & Learning, 9*(3), 257–278.

Broom, C. (2012). Citizenship, nationalism, "nation-building" stories, and the "good citizen": Associating citizenship education and public schooling. In C. Broom, & D. Reid (Eds.), *Citizenship Education Research Network (CERN) Collection* (pp. 7–17). Comparative and International Education Society of Canada.

Coloma, R. S. (2012). Theorizing Asian Canada, reframing differences. In N. Ng-A-Fook & J. Rottmann (Eds.), *Reconsidering Canadian curriculum studies: Provoking historical, present and future perspectives* (pp. 119–136). New York: Palgrave Macmillan.

Cresswell, T. (2010). Towards a politics of mobility. *Environment and Planning D: Society and Space, 28* (1), 17–31.

Cuccioletta, D. (2001/2002). Multiculturalism or transculturalism: Towards a cosmopolitan citizenship. *London Journal of Canadian Studies, 17*, 1–11.

Faist, T. (2010). Towards transnational studies: World theories, transnationalisation and changing institutions. *Journal of Ethnic and Migration Studies, 36*(10), 1665–1687.

Finlayson, M. (2015). Cultural sustainability of African Canadian heritage: Engaging students in learning, the past, the present and the future. *Improving Schools, 18*(2), 142–156.

Grosu, L. M. (2012). Multiculturalism or transculturalism? Views on cultural diversity. *SYNERGY, 8*(2), 102–111.

Guo, S. (2016). From international migration to transnational diaspora: Theorizing "double diaspora" from the experience of Chinese Canadians in Beijing. *Journal of International Migration and Integration, 17*(1), 153–171. doi:10.1007/s12134-014-0383-z

Hale, C. (2002). Does multicultural governance menace? Governance, cultural rights and the politics of identity in Guatemala. *Journal of Latin American Studies, 34*, 485–524.

Hall, S. (1992). The question of cultural identity. In S. Hall, D. Held, & T. McGrew (Eds.), *Modernity and its futures* (pp. 292–297). Cambridge: Polity.

Hannam, K., Sheller, M., & Urry, J. (2006). Mobilities, immobilities, and moorings. *Mobilities, 1*(1), 1–22.

Hébert, Y., Wilkinson, L., & Ali, M. (2008). Second generation youth in Canada, their mobilities and identifications: Relevance to citizenship education. *Brock Education, 17*, 50–70.

Heisler, M. O. (2001). 'Now and then, here and there': Migration and the transformation of identities, borders, and orders. In M. Albert, D. Jacobson, & Y. Lapid (Eds.), *Identities, borders, orders* (pp. 225–247). Minneapolis: University of Minnesota Press.

Hoerder, D., Hébert, Y. M., & Schmitt, I. (2006). *Negotiating transcultural lives: Belongings and social capital among youth in comparative perspective.* Toronto: University of Toronto Press.

Kanu, Y. (2003). Curriculum as cultural practice: Postcolonial imagination. *Journal of the Canadian Association for Curriculum Studies, 1*(1), 67–81.

Kelly, P. F. (2015). Transnationalism, emotion and second generation social mobility in the Filipino-Canadian diaspora. *Singapore Journal of Tropical Geography, 36,* 280–299.

Kim, S., & Slapac, A. (2015). Culturally responsive, transformative pedagogy in the transnational era: Critical perspectives. *Educational Studies, 51*(1), 17–27.

Kivisto, P. (2001). Theorizing transnational immigration: A critical review of current efforts. *Ethnic and Racial Studies, 24*(4), 549–577.

Kraidy, M. M. (2005). *Hybridity, or the cultural logic of globalization.* Philadelphia: Temple University Press.

Lie, J. (1995). From international migration to transnational diaspora. *Contemporary Sociology, 24*(4), 303–306.

Lightman, N. (2015). Caught in a transnational nexus: Teacher practices and experiences in a context of divergent ties to the homeland. *Citizenship Education Research Journal, 4*(1), 29–40.

Lightman, N. (2016). Situating secondary schooling in the transnational social field: Contestation and conflict in Greater Toronto Area classrooms. *Critical Studies in Education,* 1–18. doi:10.1080/17508487.2016.1186709

Maitra, S. (2015). The making of the 'precarious': Examining Indian immigrant IT workers in Canada and their transnational networks with body-shops in India. *Globalisation, Societies and Education, 13*(2), 194–209.

Montgomery, K. (2005). Banal race thinking: Ties of blood, Canadian history textbooks and ethnic nationalism. *Paedagogica Historica, 41*(3), 313–336.

Neeganagwedgin, E. (2011). A critical review of Aboriginal education in Canada: Eurocentric dominance impact and everyday denial. *International Journal of Inclusive Education,17*(1), 15–31. doi:10.1080/13603116.2011.580461

Ortiz, F. (1940). Del fenómeno de la transculturación y su importancia en Cuba. *Revista Bimestre Cubana, 27,* 273–278.

Portes, A. (1999). Conclusion: Towards a new world – the origin and effects of transnational activities. *Ethnic and Racial Studies, 22*(2), 463–477.

Portes, A., Guarnizo, L. E., & Landolt, P. (1999). The study of transnationalism: Pitfalls and promise of an emergent research field. *Ethnic and Racial Studies, 22*(2), 217–237.

Richardson, G. H., & Abbott, L. (2009). Between the national and the global: Exploring tensions in Canadian citizenship education. *Studies in Ethnicity and Nationalism, 9*(3), 377–394.

Santoro, N., & Forghani-Arani, N. (2014). Interrogating practice in culturally diverse classrooms: What can an analysis of student resistance and teacher response reveal? *European Educational Research Association, 38*(1), 58–70.

Schiller, N. G., Basch, L., & Blanc-Szanton, C. (1992). Transnationalism: A new analytic framework for understanding migration. *Annals of the New York Academy of Sciences, 645,* 1–24.

Schiller, G., Basch, N., & Szanton Blanc, L. C. (1995). From immigrant to transmigrant: Theorizing transnational migration. *Anthropological Quarterly, 68*(1), 48–63.

Sheller, M., & Urry, J. (2006). The new mobilities paradigm. *Environment and Planning A, 38,* 207–226.

Skerrett, A. (2015). *Teaching transnational youth: Literacy and education in a changing world.* New York: Teachers College Press.

Vertovec, S. (2004). Transnationalism and modes of transformation. *The International Migration Review, 38*(3), 970–1001.

Weenie, A. (2008). Curricular theorizing from the periphery. *Curriculum Inquiry, 38*(5), 545–557.

Wimmer, A., & Schiller, N. G. (2002). Methodological nationalism and beyond: Nation-state building, migration and the social sciences. *Global Networks, 2*(4), 301–334.

Wong, L., & Satzewich, V. (2006). Introduction: The meaning and significance of transnationalism. In V. Satzewich & L. Wong (Eds.), *Transnational identities and practices in Canada* (pp. 1–17). Vancouver: University of British Columbia Press.

Zhang, Y., & Guo, Y. (2015). Becoming transnational: Exploring multiple identities of students in a Mandarin–English bilingual programme in Canada. *Globalisation, Societies and Education, 13*(2), 210–229.

"We are here because you were there": On curriculum, empire, and global migration

Roland Sintos Coloma

ABSTRACT

If knowledge production is indelibly central to curriculum inquiry, then a critical investigation into the conditions of racialized minority and diasporic subjects in general and of Filipina/os in particular can shed light on the intersection of curriculum, empire, and global migration, a topic which has received relatively little attention in curriculum studies. Racialized and diasporic subjects resist efforts to erase their marginalization, and declare their undeniable presence, contributions, and interventions in metropolitan and colonial body politic by claiming that "we are here because you were there." Employing my ongoing research as examples, I will foreground US imperialism and the historical construction of colonized others as well as Canadian neoliberal globalization and the contemporary migration of labouring bodies. I will also showcase the intellectual and pedagogical efforts by Filipina/o American and Filipina/o Canadian studies scholars in resisting curriculum epistemicide. As an insurrection of subjugated knowledges, what is needed is a paradigmatic shift that challenges received ideas and interpretations and that struggles for radical impossibilities.

In *Welcome to the Jungle*, cultural critic Kobena Mercer (1994) argues that racialized minority and diasporic subjects become embodied "reminder and remainder" of imperialist pasts and their legacies in metropolitan centres and settler colonial states (p. 7). Forging crucial intellectual and political connections in the discursive, structural, and affective nexus of race, empire, and global migration, he contends that these subjects are paradoxically visible and invisible in metropolitan and settler spaces. On the one hand, they are made visible in spaces of whiteness through phenotypical and cultural differences that mark them as simultaneously exotic, to be commodified and consumed, as well as deviant, to be repelled or reformed. On the other hand, they are invisible through the state's silencing of their experiences of racism and colonialism and its failure to provide them with equal protection and citizenship rights under the law. According to Mercer, racialized minority and diasporic subjects resist efforts to erase their marginalization, and declare their undeniable presence, contributions, and interventions in metropolitan and colonial body politic by claiming that "we are here because you were there" (p. 7).

In this article, I will focus on the Philippines and the Filipina/o diaspora in the United States and Canada to address what historical anthropologist Ann Laura Stoler (2001) calls the "tense and tender ties" of curriculum, empire, and global migration. Following Stoler, I am particularly interested in bringing together "two distinctive historiographies" – postcolonial studies and North American history – to explore the linkages "in the making of racial categories and in the management of imperial rule" (p. 829). By tracking transnational movements across the Pacific between Asia and North America, I want to rethink conventional understandings of the "relationship of core and periphery" as unidirectional, and instead "treat metropole and colony as one analytic field" for "new ways of imagining and documenting how knowledge was produced along paths that went from metropole to colony and the other way around" (pp. 847–848).

The Philippines and the Filipina/o diaspora are important cases to consider as nodes at the intersection of curriculum, empire, and global migration, especially in relation to the United States and Canada. The Philippines came under United States colonial rule at the end of the Spanish–American War in 1898 until the onset of the Second World War. Although the Philippines gained political independence in 1946, scholars contend that the US continues to maintain neocolonial control over the archipelago (Manalansan & Espiritu, 2016; Miller, 1982; Schirmer & Shalom, 1987). Moreover, while the United States dominates as an empire, Canada manoeuvres globally as a subempire, "a lower-level empire that depends on the larger structure of imperialism" (Chen, 2000, p. 15). Since Canada's political, economic, and cultural structure is subordinated to the United States, Canada as a subempire focuses on "weaker countries, rather than more robust capitalist areas" as "its targets of expansion" (p. 15).

Even though Canada has never occupied or governed the Philippines as a colony, its economic relations began in 1895 with the establishment of Sun Life of Canada in the Philippines, the country's first life insurance company. Within the past four decades, Canadian mining companies, including Peter Munk's Barrick Gold, the world's largest gold-mining corporation, have become major players in the control and extraction of billions of dollars' worth of gold, silver, copper, nickel, and zinc. These companies have assumed such control in the Philippines that their combined power and infrastructure have formed what has been referred to as "Imperial Canada Inc." (Deneault & Sacher, 2012).

Moreover, the Philippines has become one of the largest sources of migrants to the United States and Canada. According to the US Census, the Philippines was the fourth top-sending country to the United States in 2011, with Mexico, China, and India representing the top three (Stoney & Batalova, 2013). That year alone, there were over 1.8 million Filipina/o immigrants residing in the United States, constituting 4.5% of the total foreign-born population. In Canada, the Philippines was the leading country of birth among people who immigrated to Canada between 2006 and 2011, followed by China and India (Statistics Canada, 2011). In 2011, it was estimated that there were 662,600 Filipina/os living in Canada, constituting about 2% of the country's total population (Statistics Canada, 2011).

Various push and pull factors have contributed to the migration of Filipina/os to both countries. Push factors, such as political corruption and instability, overpopulation, lack of sustained economic development, limited employment, and low wages, have led to abject poverty and uncertain futures, thereby compelling Filipina/os to leave their home country (Parreñas, 2001; Rodriguez, 2010). These factors are largely conditioned and rein-forced by structural adjustment programmes imposed on developing countries since the 1950s by the International Monetary Fund and the World Bank, financial institutions that are controlled by major donor countries like the United States and Canada (Mohan, Brown, Milward, & Zack-Williams, 2000). Pull factors, such as targeted immigration and labour pro-grammes for professional, skilled, and temporary workers, prospects for career and educa-tional advancement, promise of better life through hard work and perseverance, living abroad and sponsoring family members, as well as possibilities of adventure and freedom from certain cultural norms, have enticed many Filipina/os to seek opportunities else-where. In turn, the United States and Canada have developed and promoted these factors to garner more skilled and educated workers for their own economic interests and national prosperity.

Remember: *we are here because you were there.*[1] The presence of Filipina/os in the United States and Canada is primarily conditioned by US and Canadian involvement in the Philippines for over 100 years and by transnational push–pull factors that drew Filipina/os to these countries. Yet, what do we know of the Philippines and of diasporic Filipina/os from the vantage point of these imperial and subimperial centres? And why does such knowledge matter? If knowledge production is indelibly central to curriculum inquiry, then a critical investigation of racialized minority and diasporic subjects in general and of Filipina/os in particular can shed light on the intersection of curriculum, empire, and global migration, a topic which has received relatively little attention in curriculum studies. Hence, in this article, I will explore this intersection by addressing US imperialism and the historical imagining of the other as well as Canadian neoliberal globalization and the contemporary migration of precarious labour. Utilizing my ongoing research as exam-ples, I will make schematic distinctions between the United States and Canada and between past and present in order to clarify assertions and facilitate explanations, while recognizing substantial overlaps in these spatial and temporal contexts. I will end the arti-cle by showcasing intellectual and pedagogical efforts by Filipina/o American and Filipina/o Canadian studies scholars in resisting curriculum epistemicide.

Imagining Others

Elsewhere I have argued for the use and relevance of empire as an important analytical category for educational research (Coloma, 2013a). Understanding empire "heuristically as a geopolitical entity and as an enactment of power" (p. 641), its formation begins by acquiring surrounding areas and/or expanding control over other parts of the world through imperialism and colonialism. While imperialism exerts dominating power from the metropolitan centre and establishes unequal relations with subordinated states and subjects, colonialism operates territorially by occupying and claiming sovereignty over lands and controlling people and resources through military rule and biopolitical govern-mentality. Even though the United States was founded in its struggle for independence against the British empire, it asserted its own imperial and colonial force, initially, through the pillage and genocide of indigenous lands and peoples within what has become the contiguous geopolitical boundaries of the nascent nation-state. Then the United States emerged as a global empire at the turn of the twentieth century with its illegal overthrow of the Hawaiian monarchy in 1893 and its military defeat of Spain in 1898, whereby the

United States acquired colonies in the Pacific and the Caribbean. Consequently, empire is inextricably part and parcel of US national formation, its history, and ongoing development.

When the United States acquired and gained control of the Philippines, the end of the Spanish–American War indexed an important historical moment that symbolized the rise of the United States as a global colonial power. By the early 1900s, the US government and general public had very little knowledge about their first colony in Asia, and relied heavily on visual images circulated by the US media and the reports and letters mailed by US colonial personnel stationed in the islands (Coloma, in press). In constructing Filipina/os as colonized others, the discursive grammar of race was mobilized: individually and collectively, Filipina/os were repeatedly represented as dark-skinned savages who were primitive in their appearance and behaviour. They were also seen as developmentally child-like based on Western metrics of maturity and civilization. Although the empire's imaginary about colonized subjects travelled and disseminated transnationally, it was grounded domestically in US colonial officials and educators' views and experiences with racialized minority and indigenous peoples within their national borders. In other words, the empire's imagined knowledge of colonized others *over there* was fashioned in relation to metropolitan and settler conceptualization of minority and indigenous subjects *over here*.

Imperial knowledge in the form of discursive portrayals of colonized others as culturally backward and developmentally immature, therefore, functions as a powerful technique not only in imagining racialized populations elsewhere, but also in designing political, economic, social, and educational policies and programmes for them. Indeed, how those in power construe colonized and racialized others shape how they are treated. Moreover, these representations gain discursive currency during their circulation period and hold lasting effects and legacies in our current times. In *Imperial Curriculum*, historian James Anthony Mangan (1993) suggests that metropolitan and settler education is complicit in "the promulgation of racial stereotypes, the creation of ethnocentric attitudes, and the 'labeling' of colonial peoples," which subsequently result in the development of "attitudes of dominance and deference within an imperial context" (pp. 1–2). "The power of past images," he further contends, "should not be underestimated. They remain impressed on a culture as a palimpsest, shaping and coloring all the images that evolve at later dates" (p. 1).

Moreover, the discursive grammar of race operated within a comparative and transnational framework. It employed optical associations that conveyed similarities and differences across various groups under US imperialist rule and control. In an article previously published in *Curriculum Inquiry*, I provide an illustrative example of a political cartoon from a popular US magazine that demonstrates the visual lexicon of race intersecting with empire and curriculum (Coloma, 2009). In 1899, the *Puck* magazine published a cartoon entitled "School Begins," which features:

> a bewildered Filipino dressed in the Western style of long-sleeved shirt and pants and seated in the front row with three other students representing Hawaii, Puerto Rico, and Cuba. All four students are looking up at the towering, bespectacled Uncle Sam who is leaning over his desk with a stick in hand. Underneath the image are the words of Uncle Sam's stern lecture to these newly arrived students: "Now, children, you've got to learn these lessons whether you want to or not! But just take a look at the class ahead of you, and remember that in a little while, you will be glad to be here as they are!" (Coloma, 2009, p. 501)

My analysis of this cartoon suggests that Filipina/os had four options in the US project of race, empire, and curriculum. The first option was to be assimilated into the US norms of whiteness, represented by White teens reading silently behind the front row. The books held by these students, who seem to be maturing under Uncle Sam's tutelage, denote California, Texas, New Mexico, Arizona, and Alaska, the territories that the expanding United States had previously acquired by war or purchase. The second option was for Filipina/os to follow the Native American who is reading an upside-down book and sitting alone by the front door. The Native American image signifies the boarding school policy, considered an "education for extinction" (Adams, 1995), which removed and isolated indigenous students from both mainstream White America as well as their own indigenous communities. The third option was to be barred entry, like the Chinese, standing outside of the school door, due to the Chinese Exclusion Act of 1882. The final option was for Filipina/os to become like the African American who, due to manual–industrial training, is perched on a ladder and is washing the classroom window. Since the options of whiteness, extinction, or exclusion were not completely tenable for Filipina/os in the Philippines, the US-controlled public education system employed the policy and curriculum for African Americans in the US South as its educational template for Filipina/os across the Pacific (Coloma, 2009).

Hence, in the production of colonial knowledge about Filipina/os at the turn of the twentieth century, domestic minority and indigenous subjects served as the main reference points for transnational imaginaries of the colonized elsewhere. In this historical case, populations who were othered *over here* were necessary in empire's imagining of others *over there*. Hence, during the US occupation of the Philippines, the logic of Black schooling, especially for industrial–manual training, dominated the thinking and practice of colonial officials and educators. It was applied to Filipina/o children and youth in the public school system with the aim of turning them into useful, productive, and docile subjects whose extracted labour and products end up benefitting metropolitan centres and settler colonial states (Choy, 2003; Rodriguez, 2010).

Becoming Servants of Globalization

From 1981 to 2011, more than 1.8 million Filipina/os migrated to other countries – an average of 60,000 departures each year (Scalabrini Migration Center, 2013). The majority (60%) of Filipina/o migrants are women, and 3 out of 10 have college or university degrees. Approximately half of the total migrants are single and between the productive working ages of 25 and 59 years old. Based on this data, the typical profile of a Filipina/o migrant is a single, educated woman of working age. In *Migrants for Export*, sociologist Robyn Magalit Rodriguez (2010) indicates that the top occupations of recent Filipina/o migrants are in the following areas: household service workers, waiters, cleaners, nurses, caregivers/caretakers, and labourers/helpers. Deployed in over 200 countries and territories, Filipina/o workers have become so "ubiquitous around the globe" that their "worldwide distribution" is "perhaps unmatched by any other labor-sending country" (p. xii).

Among the top destination countries of Filipina/o migrants from 1981 to 2011, the United States and Canada ranked first and second, respectively (Scalabrini Migration Center, 2013). During that time period, over 1.2 million Filipina/os migrated to the United

States (or 64.84% of the total Filipina/o migrants) and over 310,000 Filipina/os to Canada (16.75%). From 2000 to 2012, the remittances sent by Filipina/os abroad to their families in the Philippines constituted a substantial portion of the country's gross domestic product, ranging from 7.5% to 10.4% annually. Not surprisingly, the United States and Canada also topped the list of origin countries of remittances. Due to their hard work and sacrifices to support their families as well as the economic benefits proffered to their home country, Filipina/os working overseas have been deemed by the Philippine state as its *bagong bayani* or new heroes. While the state may view them in such an elevated status, critical scholars and labour advocates take quite a different position: they consider Filipina/o migrant workers as "global servants of late capitalism" (Parreñas, 2001, p. 243).

While Filipina/os as colonized subjects in the Philippines were represented by the imperial United States as primitive, child-like savages in the early 1900s, in Canada they are seen and construed as domestic workers in the current age of neoliberal globalization and labour migration (Coloma, McElhinny, Tungohan, Catungal, & Davidson, 2012). Such perceptions of Filipina/os dramatically differ from the initial wave of mostly professional migrants who came as nurses, doctors, medical technicians, and office workers in the 1950s and 1960s. By the late 1970s, the age, gender, and occupational profile of the Filipina/o community in Canada started to shift. Instead of professionals, more clerical, manufacturing, and service workers were recruited by the Canadian state and companies. Through the immigration policy of family reunification, the initial wave of migrants also began sponsoring family members, including their spouses, children, parents, and siblings.

Subsequently, many Filipina/os entered Canada as domestic workers through the Foreign Domestic Movement in the 1980s, which was replaced by the live-in caregiver programme (LCP) in 1992 (Pratt, 2004; Stasiulis & Bakan, 2005). Between 1980 and 2001, almost 60% of Filipina/o migrants to Canada were women, and close to 12% arrived under the LCP category. Most of the women recruited through the LCP are college educated and often professionals who worked as nurses, midwives, educators, and office staff in the Philippines. They become desirable workers in middle- and upper-income households with children, elderly, and/or disabled family members. As a result of their labour, Canadian families are cared for and supported, and with more Canadian professionals in the workforce, the national economy prospers. Yet in return, Filipina/o domestic workers find themselves in precarious labour and living conditions. They must live in their employers' home, which constrain their privacy, prolong their work hours, and put them at risk for various forms of abuse. As temporary workers, they do not come to Canada as immigrants, thereby limiting their legal, health, and workers' rights. They must wait for two to three years of ongoing employment before they become eligible to file for permanent residency. By the time they become legal immigrants and save enough money to sponsor and bring their family to Canada, they have often been away from their loved ones for at least 8 to 10 years.

Filipina/o and labour advocates have long considered the LCP as keeping migrant workers in "indentured servitude and in some cases in situations of human trafficking for labor" (Migrante BC, 2014). The impact of the LCP on Filipina/o families and communities in Canada has been devastatingly negative. In our study on Filipina/o elderlies in Toronto, Canada's most populous and diverse city, we find that the overwhelming majority (7 out of 10) of Filipina/o seniors live in poverty, a rate that is six times more than the figure for all elderlies in Canada (Coloma & Pino, 2016). Those who migrated as live-in caregivers or were sponsored by children who were/are employed as caregivers struggle economically. Those in the LCP do not earn enough to accrue substantial savings, personal assets, or private pension plans. Hence, when they become seniors or when they sponsor elderly family members, Filipina/o elderlies rely primarily on government financial assistance for living expenses. In his study on Filipina/o youth in Canada, Philip Kelly (2014) finds that Filipina/o youth generally have lower educational and employment attainments in comparison to their parents and their peers in other racialized groups, a trend that differs from the overall pattern of upward social mobility among children of immigrants. He identifies three factors affecting the downward trajectory of Filipina/o youth: limited family resources of money and time, closed networks and information flows for educational and labour market, and skewed representation and racialized identity.

For many Filipina/o workers, elderlies, and youth in Canada, the deprofessionalization or deskilling of Filipina/os has led to economic marginalization, downward social mobility, and family tension and separation:

> Even though many immigrants from the Philippines fulfill Canada's point-system requirements for English language proficiency, educational attainment, and work experience, they confront an abysmal mismatch between their previous employment in the Philippines and what is made available to them in Canada. Their educational degrees and work experiences in the Philippines are usually not recognized as legitimately on par with normative standards by employers and accrediting associations in Canada. Even with higher educational attainments compared to the general population, many Filipina/os take survival jobs with downgraded pay and little to no fringe benefits to make ends meet. (Coloma & Pino, 2016)

Nurses become live-in caregivers, engineers become machine operators, dentists become dental hygienists, and university professors become supply school teachers. As Filipina/os continue to be recruited as servants of globalization, what do we know of their lives, of their historical and contemporary conditions, and of what can be done *over here* and *over there* for equity and justice?

Working Against Curriculum Epistemicide

My research on US and Canadian curriculum and on history textbooks in particular reveals that curricular content on the Philippines and the Filipina/o diaspora hardly exists in metropolitan and settler colonial societies (Coloma, 2012, 2013b). Filipina/os are virtually invisible in US history textbooks, appearing in merely 0.18% to 0.65% of published pages, in spite (or perhaps because) of its history of colonial occupation and ongoing neocolonial involvement. In Canadian history textbooks, the terms "Filipino" and the "Philippines" appear only as brief references in statistical figures of immigrants and late arrivals to Canada. Even though Filipina/os are one of the largest immigrant and racialized minority communities in the United States and Canada, and both countries have over 100 years of international relations with the Philippines, the official curriculum barely registers their historical and contemporary contributions and linkages. The virtual absence of Filipina/os in US and Canadian trans/national narratives, ultimately, enables those in the empire and subempire to forget that *we are here because you were there.*

To redress such curriculum absence or neglect, critical education scholar Joao Paraskeva (2016) suggests that we need "to move beyond questions, such as 'what/whose knowledge is of most worth,' despite not having figured out a correct answer" (p. 43). Instead, he urges researchers and practitioners "to fight for (an)other knowledge outside the Western epistemological harbor" and "to engage in the struggle against curriculum epistemicide" (p. 43). Like Paraskeva, I am inspired by the intellectual and political work of Boaventura de Sousa Santos who, in his book *Epistemologies of the South: Justice Against Epistemicide* (2014), "proposes a *teoria povera*, a rearguard theory based on the experiences of large, marginalized minorities and majorities that struggle against unjustly imposed marginality and inferiority, with the purpose of strengthening their resistance" (p. ix). He urges "imagining the new" which renders "creativity and interruption possible under hostile conditions that promote reproduction and repetition" (p. 5). Santos suggests "a possible way of living the impossibility of communicating the unsayable in a productive way, thereby creating new possibilities" (p. 7). In order to do so, we need to live and work through "the impossibility of radicalism" that is grounded in the belief that "capitalism, colonialism, patriarchy, and all other satellite-oppressions be can overcome" (p. 11).

In the spirit and praxis of working against epistemicide, scholars in Filipina/o American studies and Filipina/o Canadian studies continue to generate new ways of theorizing and mobilizing to contest hegemonic ideas and interpretations. For instance, in the latest academic collection on Filipina/o studies, editors Martin Manalansan and Augusto Espiritu (2016) view the academic field as a scholarly, political, and pedagogical project:

> to engage and assess the legacies of imperial power and its ideas, and redirect the trajectories of American empire by creating a set of critical optics to frame ongoing intellectual engagements with the exigencies of colonialism and postcolonialism, as well as the contemporary challenges of transnationalism, globalization, and diaspora. (p. 2)

The book sections focus on the field's intellectual genealogy and directions; questions of empire, colonialism, and nationalism; and the relevance of body and culture. In addition, in the first anthology on Filipina/o Canadian studies, my co-editors and I "ask how the contours of Canadian political, academic, and social institutions, both historical and contemporary, shape the politics of Filipina/o invisibility" (McElhinny, Davidson, Catungal, Tungohan, & Coloma, 2012, p. 5). Toward this end, we organized the book sections to address difference and recognition; gender, migration, and labour; as well as representation and youth in order to document and scrutinize pressing issues facing Filipina/o diasporic communities in Canada.

Working against curriculum epistemicide is not solely about learning and accumulating knowledges about racialized minority, diasporic, and colonized populations, although such an approach is a helpful starting point. It is not about incorporating such knowledges within existing liberal, multicultural, or even conservative frameworks that propagate "us" versus "them" or centre versus margin perspectives that maintain whiteness as universal in explicit and implicit ways. Such frameworks distinguish and reinforce other peoples, cultures, spaces, and ways of being and knowing as marginal to often-unmarked norms of dominance along separate and intersectional lines of race, gender, class, sexuality, ability, religion, language, and citizenship. Moreover, learning about others, even under the rubric of culturally relevant, responsive, or competent pedagogy, can end up essentializing and calcifying certain ideas, customs, and behaviours that may be selective, tolerable, or perpetuating stereotypes and that may constrain the othered group's rich range of knowledges, performances, and possibilities.

For racialized minority, diasporic, and colonized subjects and for those in solidarity with them, to work against epistemicide is to generate and enact a paradigmatic shift in the curriculum of empire and global migration. It is fundamentally a critical project that calls into question received ideas, destabilizes interpretations, imagines other possibilities, and struggles for educational and societal transformation. To work against curriculum epistemicide is to bring forth what historian–philosopher Michel Foucault (1980) calls an "insurrection of subjugated knowledges" (p. 81). Subjugated knowledges are "historical contents that have been buried and disguised," including the historical and ongoing governmentalities and technologies of empires and subempires; as well as knowledges considered "naïve," "low-ranking," and "disqualified as inadequate," including the experiences of transnational migrants who have become servants of globalization (pp. 81-82). They constitute "historical knowledge of struggles" against dominant logics and practices that render other ways of knowing and doing illegible and illegitimate (p. 83). The will to resist epistemicide and to generate critical, transformative knowledges, therefore, needs to be at the core of curriculum inquiry.

Research into the intersections of race, empire, and global migration is crucial in the intellectual, political, and pedagogical advancement of curriculum studies as an academic field and a liberatory space of praxis. For instance, inquiries into how racialized minority, diasporic, and colonized subjects are represented in the official curriculum of metropolitan and settler colonial states are significant in the national development of a democratic and equity oriented society as well as the transnational relations between Western powers and subordinated peripheries.

In this article, I have demonstrated how the Philippines and the Filipina/o diaspora serve as important case studies to investigate both the history of colonial representations and the contemporary migration of precarious labour that primarily benefit the US empire and the Canadian subempire. Under these conditions, Filipina/os are relegated as primitive yet corrigible natives who could be fixed under benevolent tutelage and as docile servants of global capitalism who ought to be grateful for opportunities provided abroad. From the perspective of mainstream US and Canadian governments and populace, the imperial metropole saves the colonized others *over there*, and provides opportunities for a better life through migration *over here*. Therefore, the task of critical curriculum scholars working against epistemicide is to track and interrupt such hegemonic narratives and to imagine and enact anew the impossibility of radical thought and practice.

Note

1. Borrowing from Kobena Mercer (1994), in this article when invoking the phrase "we are here because you were there", I am employing the term "we" to refer to racialized minority and diasporic subjects, and "you" to refer to both US and Canadian government, military, and corporate interests as well as US and Canadian white subjects.

Disclosure statement

No potential conflict of interest was reported by the author.

References

Adams, D. W. (1995). *Education for extinction: American Indians and the boarding school experience, 1875–1928*. Lawrence: University Press of Kansas.

Chen, K.-H. (2000). The imperialist eye: The cultural imaginary of a subempire and a nation-state. *Positions, 8*(1), 9–76.

Choy, C. C. (2003). *Empire of care: Nursing and migration in Filipino American history*. Durham: Duke University Press.

Coloma, R. S. (2009). "Destiny has thrown the Negro and the Filipino under the tutelage of America": Race and curriculum in the age of empire. *Curriculum Inquiry, 39*(4), 495–519.

Coloma, R. S. (2012). Abject beings: Filipina/os in Canadian historical narrations. In R. S. Coloma, B. McElhinny, E. Tungohan, J. P. C. Catungal, & L. M. Davidson (Eds.), *Filipinos in Canada: Disturbing invisibility* (pp. 284–304). Toronto: University of Toronto Press.

Coloma, R. S. (2013a). Empire: An analytical category for educational research. *Educational Theory, 63* (6), 639–658.

Coloma, R. S. (2013b). Invisible subjects: Filipina/os in secondary history textbooks. In D. C. Maramba & R. Bonus (Eds.), *The "other" students: Filipino Americans, education, and power* (pp. 165–182). Charlotte: Information Age.

Coloma, R. S. (in press). Becoming a problem: Imperial fix and Filipinos under United States rule in the early 1900s. *Postcolonial Directions in Education*.

Coloma, R. S., McElhinny, B., Tungohan, E., Catungal, J. P. C., & Davidson, L. M. (Eds.). (2012). *Filipinos in Canada: Disturbing invisibility*. Toronto: University of Toronto Press.

Coloma, R. S., & Pino, F. L. (2016). "There's hardly anything left": Poverty and the economic insecurity of elderly Filipinos in Toronto. *Canadian Ethnic Studies, 48*(2), 71–97.

Deneault, A., & Sacher, W. (2012). *Imperial Canada Inc.: Legal haven of choice for the world's mining industries*. Vancouver: Talonbooks.

Foucault, M. (1980). *Power/knowledge: Selected interviews and other writings, 1972–1977*. New York: Pantheon.

Kelly, P. (2014). *Understanding intergenerational social mobility: Filipino youth in Canada* (No. 45). Montreal: IRPP.

Manalansan, M. F., IV & Espiritu, A. F. (2016). The field: Dialogues, visions, tensions, and aspirations. In M. F. Manalansan IV & A. F. Espiritu (Eds.), *Filipino studies: Palimpsests of nation and diaspora* (pp. 1–11). New York: New York University Press.

Mangan, J.A. (1993). Introduction. In J. A. Mangan (Ed.), *The imperial curriculum: Racial images and education in the British colonial experience* (pp. 1–5). New York: Routledge.

McElhinny, B., Davidson, L. M., Catungal, J. P. C., Tungohan, E., & Coloma, R. S. (2012). Spectres of (in) visibility: Filipina/o labour, culture, and youth in Canada. In R. S. Coloma, B. McElhinny, E. Tungohan, J. P. C. Catungal, & L. M. Davidson (Eds.), *Filipinos in Canada: Disturbing invisibility* (pp. 5–45). Toronto: University of Toronto Press.

Mercer, K. (1994). *Welcome to the jungle: New positions in Black cultural studies*. New York: Routledge.

Migrante, B.C. (2014). Live-in caregivers: Kenney's new scapegoats. Retrieved from http://www.migrantebc.com/2014/07/06/live-caregivers-kenneys-new-scapegoats-statement-migrante-bc/

Miller, S. C. (1982). *"Benevolent assimilation": The American conquest of the Philippines, 1899-1903*. New Haven: Yale University Press.

Mohan, G., Brown, E., Milward, B., & Zack-Williams, A. B. (2000). *Structural adjustment: Theory, practice and impacts*. New York: Routledge.

Paraskeva, J. M. (2016). *Curriculum epistemicide: Towards an itinerant curriculum theory*. New York: Routledge.

Parreñas, R. S. (2001). *Servants of globalization: Women, migration, and domestic work*. Stanford: Stanford University Press.

Pratt, G. (2004). *Working feminism*. Philadelphia: Temple University Press.

Rodriguez, R. M. (2010). *Migrants for export: How the Philippine state brokers labor to the world*. Minneapolis: University of Minnesota Press.

Santos, B. D. S. (2014). *Epistemologies of the south: Justice against epistemicide*. Boulder: Paradigm.

Scalabrini Migration Center. (2013). Country migration report: The Philippines 2013. Makati: International Organization for Migration.

Schirmer, D. B., & Shalom, S. R. (Eds.). (1987). *The Philippines reader: A history of colonialism, neocolonialism, dictatorship, and resistance*. Cambridge: South End.

Stasiulis, D. K., & Bakan, A. B. (2005). *Negotiating citizenship: Migrant women in Canada and the global system*. Toronto: University of Toronto Press.

Statistics Canada. (2011). Immigration and ethnocultural diversity in Canada: National household survey, 2011. Retrieved from http://www.cic.gc.ca/english/resources/statistics/facts2010/permanent/10.asp

Stoler, A. L. (2001). Tense and tender ties: The politics of comparison in North American history and (post) colonial studies. *Journal of American History, 88*(3), 829–865.

Stoney, S., & Batalova, J. (2013). Filipino immigrants in the United States. Retrieved from http://www.migrationpolicy.org/article/filipino-immigrants-united-states-0

Arab Spring, *Favelas*, borders, and the artistic transnational migration: toward a curriculum for a Global Hip-Hop Nation

Awad Ibrahim

ABSTRACT

Straddling between the purely political and the poetically artistic, I am arguing, is a Global Hip-Hop Nation (GHHN), which is yet to be charted and its cartography is yet to be demarcated. Taking two examples, the first a Hip-Hop song from within the Arab Spring and the second from the *favelas* in Brazil, my intent is to show what Hip-Hop can do socially, racially, and politically, on the one hand, and how, despite the fact that this GHHN is clearly global, it grounds itself deeply in the local, on the other. Through these examples, I call for an ill-literacy, one where creativity is taken as serious as grammar and where literacy becomes ill: intimate, lived and liberatory.

"In order for music to free itself," writes Deleuze (1993) "it will have to pass over to the other side." The other side "where territories tremble, where the structures collapse, where the ethoses get mixed up, where a powerful song of the earth is unleashed, the great ritornelles that transmutes all the airs it carries away and makes return" (p. 104). Nowhere are these boundaries collapsed, borders pushed to their limits, citizenship totally revamped and redefined, and the "powerful song of the earth unleashed" than in the Global Hip-Hop Nation (GHHN) (Alim, Ibrahim, & Pennycook, 2009; Ibrahim, 2012, 2016). This is a semiotic, boundary-less, and arts-based Nation that has its own "language" and ways of speaking, including the spoken word, the body, the dance, the gesture, the music, graffiti, and all forms of linguistic and extra-linguistic expressions. These complex semiological languages, as Barthes (1983) would have called them, allow the French *to speak* to the Americans, the Venezuelans to the Finnish, and the Japanese to the Brazilians in ways that we are yet to fully understand; hence this article. Taking two examples from across the globe – a Hip-Hop song from within the Arab Spring and another from the *favelas* in Brazil that show what Hip-Hop can do socially, racially and politically, I will show how, despite the fact that this GHHN is clearly global, it grounds itself deeply in the local.

All of us, it seems, are in flow, in motion, and on the move; be it nomads, immigrants, refugees, students, company executives, academics and farmers. This is true even if physically we stay put. For Bauman (1998), in a time where "immobility is not a realistic option in a world of permanent change" (p. 2), being totally local, which is virtually impossible, is a sign of social deprivation. Therefore, flow, immigration, emigration, movement, displacement and globalization, it seems, especially post-Internet, is the intractable fate of the world (Appiah, 2006). This intractable fate, however, on the one hand, seems to magnify the wealth of a few and worsen the world's majority (Nussbaum, 2011). With the power of the globalized meaning-making machines (media, Internet, popular culture, etc.) and time/space compression, on the other hand, this situation is as much a threat to the local as it is a space for future hope and possibilities for wide-awakeness (Greene, 1995; Rautins & Ibrahim, 2011). It is in this space of tension between threat and hope that I am locating this GHHN. These two examples are used as a backdrop to illustrate the power of Hip-Hop (pers); Hip-Hoppers' creativity in localizing the global; and Hip-Hoppers ongoing deterritorializaiton of the State, replacing it with a creative and radically hopeful GHHN.

The Hip-Hop That Ignited the Arab Spring Revolution

As we are watching Syria burning, one cannot help but think that the flames of protest that started on 15 March 2011[1] were sparked by three preceding events: first, Cairo's Tahrir Square Revolution (started on 25 January 2011),[2] second, the Tunisian Jasmine Revolution (as it was/is known in Tunisia and assumed to have started on 17 December 2010 with the act of self-immolation of Mohammed Bouazizzi, the 26-year old street vendor whose harassment and humiliation reached its peak when the police confiscated his only possession: his fruit and vegetable vending cart).[3] However, the third event, for which I have attempted to create a genealogy elsewhere (see Ibrahim, 2016), is what concerns me in this article. It is a Hip-Hop song, and thanks to it, as we shall see, we can say: The Revolution Will be Televised (contrary to Gil Scott-Heron's prophetic song).[4]

Asen (2011) titled his hiphopdiplomacy article on the same topic: *The Rap that Sparked a Revolution: El General (Tunisia)*. Asen uses "spark" and I use "ignite." For this article, I am using the two terms interchangeably and purposefully. Hip-Hop, as we know, is not a political party, it is an artistic, cultural and musical expression and movement. Born to a large extent within the African American history and tradition, however, this artistic and musical expression and movement is deeply marinated in the political history of oppression, marginalization and struggle (see especially Alim, 2011; Perry, 2004; Rose, 1994; Chang, 2005, for the impact of the Latino and Caribbean influence on Hip-Hop style and message). In this sense, Hip-Hop revolutionizes and makes people think and hence "ignite" and "spark" their desire for change. The Hip-Hopper in question, El Général, did exactly that. In early December 2010, just before Mohammed Bouazizzi's self-immolation act, then a relatively unknown Hip-Hopper whose songs were strictly underground, quietly released a track, *Rais Lebled* or *Mr. President*, along with a simple video on his Facebook site. No bling, no special production but a raw and angry track addressed directly to then President Zine al-Abidine Ben Ali. Within days, it had gone viral and was on the lips of people as they defiantly went on the streets in the face of death (Asen, 2011).

It was one man, one mic, and a revolutionary message: "Mr President ... people have become like animals ... We are living like dogs." A caveat and an explanation are in order here. As an event that is produced within a sociality, history, time and space, Hip-Hop does not just speak its name. Hip-Hop is a testimony, an account and a witness to the historical moment in which it is born. As such, El Général's "one mic" does not just belong to him. That is to say, this one man/one mic has to be read within a genealogy of sociality, history, time and space, where his voice and message belong as much to him as they do to other oppressed, marginalized and struggling communities (both in Tunisia and globally). "[T]oday," El Général raps, "I am speaking in the name of myself and all the people who are suffering in 2011."

Clearly, El Général understood this ethics of witnessing, of speaking up and of telling, hence the song and the video, which were bold products that landed him in jail and detention for days. He was not released until he was forced to sign a statement to no longer make any political songs. As with all dictators, they bring it on themselves. Before his release, the video was picked up by a number of human rights organization and the Global Hip-Hop community. It was then reposted all over the Internet.[5] In imprisoning El Général, not only did he become well known to all in Tunisia and internationally, but *Rais Lebled* became the anthem of the "Jasmine Revolution," as it is/was known in Tunisia (Wright, 2011). El Général was only 21 years old.

So, when Mohammed Bouazizzi set himself on fire on 17 December 2010, it was *Rais Leblad* that was on people's lips.

> Mr. President, today I am speaking in the name of myself and of all the people
> who are suffering in 2011, there are still people dying of hunger
> who want to work to survive, but their voice was not heard
> get off into the street and see, people have become like animals …
> You know these are words that make your eyes weep
> as a father does not want to hurt his children
> then this is a message from one of your children
> who is telling of his suffering
> we are living like dogs
> half of the people living in filth
> and drank from a cup of suffering[6]

The beauty is all over this text: first, in its locality (i.e. how it speaks to and in the process politicize local social issues); second, in its deeply rooted Hip-Hop aesthetic, especially in being a voice for the voiceless; third, *à la* Public Enemy and in a typical Hip-Hop style, in speaking truth to power (especially in its appellation and interpellation to "Mr. President"); fourth and finally, in its collective voice, where one becomes a witness to the suffering of others and hence feeling the need to speak up even if it means being thrown in jail or sentenced to death (Ibrahim & Alfonso, 2016).

When Bouazuzzi stood in front of the municipal building and set himself on fire, that act caught on, literally, and spread across the country and the region, into Algeria, Morocco, Egypt, Yemen, Bahrain, Libya, and now Syria. Interestingly, Asen (2011) explains, when Egypt's revolution erupted in Tahrir Square a month after Tunisia on January 25, 2011, what was heard was not the usual Koran recitation, national anthem, and "traditional" poetry, but El Général's *Rais Leblad*. It was now an infamous phrase: "People want the régime to fall." It was the image of Bouazizzi's self-immolation that was burned in people's imagination and it was El Général's Hip-Hop song *Rais Leblad* that was on people's tongues first in Egypt, then Yemen, then Bahrain, then Libya and now in Syria (Wright, 2011). Around the same time, Ghosh (2011)[7] of *Time Magazine* tells a very interesting story about how *Rais Leblad* was taken up in Bahrain:

At 6:30 p.m. on Feb. 15 [2011], as thousands of people gathered to protest against their ruler at a busy intersection in Manama, the capital of the small island nation of Bahrain, you could just about hear over the general hubbub the anthem of the young people who have shaken regimes from North Africa to the Arabian Gulf… A reedy female voice shouted out, several times, the first line of "Rais Lebled," a song written by the Tunisian rapper known as El Général. "Mr. President, your people are dying," the woman sang. Then others joined in. "Mr. President, your people are dying/ People are eating rubbish/ Look at what is happening/ Miseries every-where, Mr. President/ I talk with no fear/ Although I know I will get only trouble/ I see injustice everywhere (n.p.).

Interestingly, Ghosh explains,

Bahrain, as it happens, doesn't have a President; it's ruled by a King, Hamad bin Isa al-Khalifa. No matter. The protesters in Bahrain knew that "Rais Lebled" was the battle hymn of the Jas-mine Revolution that brought down Tunisia's dictator, Zine el Abidine Ben Ali, and that it was then adopted by the demonstrators in Cairo's Tahrir Square who toppled Hosni Mubarak. Now it had come to Bahrain, as rage against poverty and oppression swept the Arab world from west to east. It isn't just songs that are being copied.

Ghosh explains further,

in a nod to the Egyptians, organizers in several countries have dubbed their demonstrations Days of Rage, and the popular Tunisian chant, "The people want the regime to fall," has been taken up by protesters from Algeria to Yemen. (n.p.)

A Hip-Hop song, it seems, can spark and ignite a revolution and El Général's *Rais Leblad* is a case in point. A Hip-Hop song, it is also worth noting, can be a perfect illustration of how the global is creolized, where the local and the global can and do co-exist. In doing so, it does away with boundaries; the question of the nation and its boundaries in a time of hyper-media and hyper-communication is no longer relevant. Boundaries are certainly relevant for politicians; one only needs to listen to US politicians talking about "the wall" between the USA and Mexico. Yet not for Hip-Hoppers, whose poetic intervention is mak-ing Hip-Hop belong as much to the Tunisian Jasmine Revolution, Cairo's Tahrir Square, and the current Syrian struggle for human dignity as it does to African Americans, Aborigi-nals, Latino/as and other marginalized communities in North America and across the globe. Hip-Hop therefore moves the Nation into Global Nation, thus creating what Alim, Ibrahim and Pennycook (2009) and Ibrahim (2012) call GHHN. As we shall see next, this GHHN is constructed around four pillars: culture, social class, historical oppression, and youth rebellion.

Conversational Sampling and the Gueto in Brazil

Brazil offers another very interesting example of how this GHHN "speaks." Clearly, it speaks a language of its own, where African American Vernacular English (AAVE) is its default lan-guage (Ibrahim, 2012). Speaking AAVE does not require its mastery (it is built around cer-tain linguistic codes, such as: "whassup homeboy," "yo," the "N" word as term of endearment, etc.). Moreover, the category "language" includes a series of what Barthes (1983) calls *complex semiological languages*. These are signs that are open for signification and different readings because they cannot produce verbal utterances yet they are ready to speak, including dance, bodily gestures (e.g. swaging as one is talking or singing), DJing, graffiti, photographs, cloths, *maquillage* and hair styles, among others. Similar to

AAVE, to become a citizen of this GHHN one does not need to fully master all its aspects. One gets his/her passport stamped by gesturing to the Nation. One can only do Krumping,[8] a form of underground b-boying and b-girling breakdance, and this qualifies one to become a citizen of this Nation. Put simply, this is a borderless Nation that has its own linguistic code, ways of speaking and ethics of witnessing and, by and large, it is socially conscious and politically active.

In her sociolinguistic work in Brazil, Roth-Gordon (2009) provided strong explanations, on the one hand, for how Hip-Hop was localized and made Brazilian and, on the other, how in the process it has become the voice of the *favelas* (shantytowns in the outskirts of big cities). For Roth-Gordon, the first membership or entrance of Brazil into the GHHN began with the incredible success of the Sao Paulo based group Racionais MC's, especially their album *Sobrevivendo no Inferno* (Surviving in Hell) in the late 1990s. That was the *ignition* for the booming of Hip-Hop culture in the *favela*. For Roth-Gordon, the many facets of this culture included and continue to include: the large murals and graffiti depicting album covers and song lyrics; US sports teams and reference to New York especially, and fans taking on nicknames of popular rappers.

"Though most Brazilian rappers and rap fans have limited access to English," Roth-Gordon explains, "this infusion of Hip Hop culture relied heavily on ideas and images of the United States (i.e. familiarity with the "code" of the GHHN). Taking inspiration from groups such as Public Enemy and KRS-One, politically conscious Brazilian rap focuses on the daily realities of Brazil's social and geographic periphery, highlighting the transnational similarities between situations of social inequality, crime, drug use, police brutality, and racism. They perform," she continues, "the aggressive and confrontational style of conscious rap and attract attention in particular for embracing US ideas [i.e. ideas that are found or more pronounced in the US, of course among other places] of structural violence (including institutional racism) and a Black–White racial dichotomy, as these themes directly contradict Brazilian ideals of racial democracy" (pp. 63–64).

To understand the complexity of this GHHN, its localization in Brazil, its ways of speaking and what it decides to talk about, Roth-Gordon (2009) made use of Osumare's (2007) notion of "connective marginalities," one where Hip Hop becomes a GHHN by resonating with young people across the globe in four main fields: culture, social class, historical oppression, and youth rebellion. Rapping about these four issues and fields, Roth-Gordon concludes, youth thus actively and consciously create connections between Brazil and the United States, especially the African American experience of marginalization and social exclusion and that of the *fevala*. In doing so, the Brazilian Hip-Hoppers "traffic" (i.e. metaphorically, artistically and linguistically borrow or "talk about") nationally opposed racial ideologies, especially the Brazilization of the US Black–White dichotomy.

Race is not a comfortable issue to discuss in Brazil, Roth-Gordon explains; it is a taboo. The imaginary of the nation is a racial democracy: one where all races in Brazil intermingle and mix in ways that do away with racism. However, Hip-Hop groups like Racionais MC's brought the issue of existing racial disparity, discrimination, poverty and White supremacy to the forefront.[9] They did that by naming what they saw as the racial similarities between themselves and the United States. In this sense, for the Brazilian Hip-Hoppers, South Bronx becomes a racialized urban symbolic site of power and social, political and racial inspiration and identification. One may conclude thus: Brazilian Hip-Hoppers localized the global and in the process localized racial politics.

Toward a Curriculum for a Global Hip-Hop Nation

In his recent video #hiphopishiphop,[10] KRS-One – one of the founding figures of Hip-Hop and one of its most intellectual (he teaches courses at Yale and Cornell with Cornel West) – demonstrates perfectly well the formation of the GHHN, on the one hand, and how it speaks, on the other. Its speech is grammaticalized, i.e. it is a second nature and common knowledge for the citizens of this Global Nation. Put otherwise, it is a code known to/by all. On the video, we have 14 Hip-Hoppers from 14 countries speaking their own languages and using their own styles to speak about their own local realities. It is the "connective marginalities" that bind them together and it is their deciphering of the code of the GHHN that makes them part of its citizenship. All 14 Hip-Hoppers talk about: social class struggle and equitable distribution of wealth; local culture; historical oppression and fighting against colonialism and race, gender and other forms of social oppression; and youth rebellion against hopelessness.

Elsewhere, I demonstrated that Hip-Hoppers across the globe are increasingly becoming our new cultural (not to say curriculum) theorists and cultural critics (Ibrahim, 2015, 2016).[11] I drew examples from Japan, where Hip-Hop introduced the notion of rhyme to the Japanese language, which did not have rhyme before Hip-Hop, and Hong Kong, where Hip-Hop normalized the Cantonese language, which used to be looked down upon as a street and working class language, as mainstream language. Hip-Hoppers place themselves as witness to social oppression, marginalization and youth rebellion; and propose a vision for a better future. KRS-One opens his video with, "Let's Unite!"

To engage this new cartography of curriculum, we as cultural theorists and cultural workers need to pay closer attention to our young people, their identities and their speech. This is a relatively uncharted, deterritorialized and nomadic cartography where Hip-Hoppers continue to push creatively against the apparatus of the State. From Brazil to Japan and from Hong Kong to Tunisia, Hip-Hoppers dare to imagine a different world, a GHHN, which is also deeply local. This creative push against the apparatus of the State, it is worth noting, does three things. First, it reminds us that Hip-Hop is a social and historical product. As such, it cannot escape the beauty but also the ugly face of history. Hip-Hop, I have argued elsewhere (Ibrahim, 2014), can also act as a hegemonic space where the bad and the ugly can be produced, including homophobia, misogyny and extreme and vulgar capitalist consumption. Second, the push brings to the fore the complex and not so easily distinguishable dynamic between that which is facilely appropriated and that which is radically transnationally translated. To explain, I was challenged once to think about El Général as "just a rapper who is simply imitating and reciting globally circulating images." When analysed closely, however, one finds that El Général, as a citizen of the GHHN, is deploying, invoking, making use of and speaking the GHHN complex semiological languages, but the mic he is using and the message he is igniting and sparking are so radically local, fresh and politicized that any notion of naïve consumption and appropriation has to be dismissed offhand. Third and finally, from a curriculum perspective, this push moves literacy to "ill-literacy," where what is known in linguistic anthropology as "semantic inversion" is the standard. In semantic inversion, "ill" and "sick" are inverted from their negative sense to mean "amazing" and "brilliant." "That cat is ill" means "That poet in incredibly skilled or skillful" (Alim, 2011, p. 120). Samy Alim points out that, while the vast majority of public discourse, including some academics (especially those who see nothing else in education but testing), are quick to point to Hip-Hop culture's "illiteracy" (meaning lack of literacy), Hip-Hop youth are even quicker to point to Hip-Hop's ill-literacy. They are quick to point to its rich aesthetic, bold politics, incredible orality and creativity and prophetic linguistic production and poetry.

In schools, I have argued elsewhere (Ibrahim, 2016), the focus can oftentimes be almost exclusively on grammar as opposed to creative, artistic and semiotic production. Within GHHN curriculum, this has to be rethought. We need to remember that schools can no longer afford to blind themselves from this global and ever present phenomenon. As we saw with Racionais MC's and El Général, English is no longer the only medium of Hip-Hop. Hip-Hoppers are speaking their own languages and in the process, creolizing (i.e. mixing the local and the global) and politicizing their local issues.

Here *ill*-literacy – that is, the literacy ability that enables Hip-Hoppers to witness, decipher and speak about local realities – becomes a reference to three components of literacy as proposed by Alim (2011) and Ibrahim (2016): literacy must be *I*ntimate, *L*ived, and *L*iberatory. As such a GHHN curriculum seeks to move literacy from simply reading the world to naming the world. Only in naming the world are we able to say we are living, especially that we are living in the world. If we follow or live in the world as named by others, we are just that: followers. In following others' path, we become dispossessed (in all the sense of the word). Here, a GHHN curriculum should enable all of us, but especially our youth, to recognize ourselves in an educational context where what is taught becomes relevant; to name our world. When we do, we are no longer just followers or consumers of knowledge, but producers and possessors of knowledge. Only then can we as critical pedagogues hope to link people's world with their word; only then can the dispossessed own their own voice, their own lives, and themselves; and only then can the politics of recognition become possible.

Notes

1. http://www.bbc.com/news/world-middle-east-26116868.
2. http://www.aljazeera.com/news/middleeast/2011/01/201112515334871490.html.
3. Warning: this is a graphic video of the self-immolation: https://www.youtube.com/watch?v=jHw_auqod6Y.
4. https://www.youtube.com/watch?v=qGaoXAwl9kw.
5. See this as an example: https://www.youtube.com/watch?v=leGlJ7OouR0.
6. This is a hybrid English lyric translation drawn from different sources including Youtube, Time Magazine, Newanthem blog (Jones, 2011), and Kimball (2014) in Hiphopdiplomacy blog (see reference section; see also Ibrahim, 2016).
7. http://www.time.com/time/magazine/article/0,9171,2050022,00.html#ixzz2ZuRiI599.
8. https://www.youtube.com/watch?v=7oddy9YoqO4.
9. With Racionais MC's, we see similar patterns to the ones we see in El Général: one mic, one message, one turntable/DJ, raw issues and one MC. If one is to conduct a semiotic exercise, I highly recommend you turn off the volume in both videos and focus on visual representations and just watch. One will see exceptional similarities between how people dress, walk and move their heads, fingers and the rest of their bodies. This is how the GHHN "speaks." Similar to El Général, the message that Racionais MC's talk about include: police brutality, systemic and institutional racism and social class issues. They certainly "roc the mic right" (Alim, 2006): https://www.youtube.com/watch?v=-2Cie49l0WE;https://www.youtube.com/watch?v=RVvoeWak-WM2006): https://www.youtube.com/watch?v=-2Cie49l0WE;https://www.youtube.com/watch?v=RVvoeWak-WM.

10. https://www.youtube.com/watch?v=ppR7s19c1RY.
11. Listen to, respectively, Obasi Davis (a 16-year old from Oakland, California) giving his political diagnosis and curriculum and cultural theorizing of the ills of the US political system and Hiwot Adilow (a 15-year old from Philadelphia, Pennsylvania) talking about and theorizing what it means to be young, Black, immigrant and talented: Obasi Davis: https://www.youtube.com/watch?v=myhuAaVwzZ8; Hiwot Adilow: https://www.youtube.com/watch?v=pc6CJ_kUNYc.

Disclosure statement

No potential conflict of interest was reported by the author.

References

Alim, S. (2006). *Roc the mic right: The language of hip hop culture*. New York: Routledge.
Alim, S. (2011). Global ill-literacies Hip Hop cultures, youth identities, and the politics of literacy. *Review of Research in Education, 35*(11), 120–146.
Alim, S., Ibrahim, A., & Pennycook, A. (2009). *Global linguistic flows: Hip-Hop cultures, youth identities, and the politics of language*. London: Routledge.
Appiah, K. (2006). *Cosmopolitanism: Ethics in a world of strangers*. New York: W. W. Norton.
Asen, J. (2011). The rap that sparked a revolution: El General (Tunisia). Retrieved from: http://hiphop diplomacy.org/2011/01/31/the-rap-that-sparked-a-revolution-el-general-tunisia/.
Barthes, R. (1983). *Elements of semiology*. New York: Hill and Wang.
Bauman, Z. (1998). *Globalization*. New York: Columbia University Press.
Chang, J. (2005). *Can't stop, won't stop: A history of the hip-hop generation*. New York: St. Martin's Press.
Deleuz, G. (1993). *Essays critical and clinical*. London: Verso.
Ghosh, B. (2011). Rage, rap and revolution: Inside the Arab youth quake. Retrieved from: http://www.time.com/time/magazine/article/0,9171,2050022,00.html#ixzz2ZuRil599.
Greene, M. (1995). *Releasing the imagination: Essays on education, the arts, and social change*. San Francisco: Jossey-Bass.
Ibrahim, A. (2012). Global Hip-Hop nation language: A (semiotic) review of Languages of Global Hip Hop. *Journal of Sociolinguistics, 16*(4), 547–552.
Ibrahim, A. (2014). *The rhizome of Blackness: A critical ethnography of Hip-Hop culture, language, identity, and the politics of becoming*. New York: Peter Lang.
Ibrahim, A. (2015). Youth: Our new cultural theorists. *Jeunesse: Young People, Texts, Cultures, 7*, 5–9.
Ibrahim, A. (2016). Critical Hip-Hop ill-literacies: Re-mixing culture, language and the politics of boundaries in education. *Journal of the American Association for the Advancement of Curriculum Studies, 11*, 1–11.

Ibrahim, A., & Alfano, A. (2016). Macklemore: Strong poetry, Hip-Hop courage and the ethics of the appointment. In S. Steinberg, & A. Ibrahim (Eds.), *Critically researching youth* (pp. 102–115). New York: Peter Lang.

Jones, A. (2011). *Anthems for a new generation.* Retrieved from http://newanthems.blogspot.ca/2011/01/rayes-lebled-hamada-ben-amor-el-general.html

Kimball, S. (2014). Rapping the Arab Spring. Retrieved from: http://hiphopdiplomacy.org/2014/01/14/rapping-the-arab-spring/.

Nussbaum, M. (2011). *Creating capabilities: The human development approach.* Cambridge: Harvard University Press.

Osumare, H. (2007). *The Africanist aesthetic in global Hip-Hop: Power moves.* New York: Palgrave Macmillan.

Perry, I. (2004). *Prophets of the hood: Politics and poetic of Hip Hop.* Durham: Duke University Press.

Rautins, C., & Ibrahim, A. (2011). Wide-awakeness: Toward a critical pedagogy of imagination, humanism and becoming. *International Journal of Critical Pedagogy, 3*(2), 24–36.

Rose, T. (1994). *Black noise: Rap music and Black culture in contemporary America.* Middletown: Wesleyan University Press.

Roth-Gordon, J. (2009). Conversational sampling, race trafficking, and the invocation of the Gueto in Brazilian hip hop. In S. Alim, A. Ibrahim, & A. Pennycook (Eds.), *Global linguistic flows: Hip-Hop cultures, youth identities, and the politics of language* (pp. 41–55). London: Routledge.

Wright, R. (2011). *Rock the Casbah: Rage and rebellion across the Islamic world.* New York: Simon & Schuster.

Emotions in the curriculum of migrant and refugee students

Sardar M. Anwaruddin (iD)

ABSTRACT

Emotions are often used to categorize migrant and refugee populations, and to place them into particular subject positions. In much of the literature on the education of migrant and refugee students, emotions are viewed through a therapeutic lens. Against this backdrop, I argue that curriculum inquiries need to pay more sustained attention to how emotions are generated and circulated through complex discursive practices and to their potential implications for the curricular experiences of migrant and refugee students. I discuss some principles of Critical Emotion Studies, which constitute an analytical framework for future curriculum inquiries.

"no one leaves home unless

home is the mouth of a shark.

. . . .

you have to understand:

no one puts their children in a boat

unless the water is safer than the land."

(Shire, 2015)

Migration is an inherently emotional process. It is not only the migrant who is frightened, anxious or nostalgic, but people in the societies that receive migrants may also express fear, anger and suspicion towards the migrant. Emotions become particularly harmful when they are used to produce essentializing labels that categorize migrants as certain types of subjects. In this essay, I argue that the field of curriculum studies needs to take emotions into account when studying the educational experiences of migrant and refugee students. This approach is urgent in the current xenophobic climate, in which migrants and refugees in general, and their school-going children in particular, are being marginalized through various emotion-based discourses. For example, Harding (2009) shows how emotion-words are used to define refugees, and to simplify and universalize their experiences. Refugees have to demonstrate that they are "genuine refuges deserving of compassion and asylum, and as such, dejected and dependent." Then they have to "transform themselves into good refugees, by making a life [...] as economically independent productive subjects." In this process, the refugees are "expected to transform themselves in emotional terms and exercise a degree of emotional management" (Harding, 2009, p. 275).

When it comes to formal schooling, education gets into an emotional tangle. Here the tension is between creating a condition for care that is often incommensurate with the political agendas imposed by the state. Through case studies conducted with British teachers who worked closely with asylum-seeking and refugee students, Arnot, Pinson, and Candappa (2009) found that teachers "identified caring as the most important emotional response and often saw compassion in the sense of caring as part of their professional identity" (p. 254). These teachers were also "aware of the dangers of associating compassion with pity, and even with victimhood" (p. 254). Yet, in their professional work, teachers were caught up in a political relationship, which was based on the discrepancies between the interests of the children and the interests of the state. Arnot et al. (2009) concluded that the "central government's priorities to reduce immigration are seriously disruptive of educational agendas such as helping every child to achieve their potential, to achieve a sense of well being and security" (p. 251). The UK is not the only country whose policies violate the (educational) rights of migrant and refugee children. Australia's mandatory detention policy and its consequences for education are noteworthy. A study on children in detention described their condition as "a living nightmare" (quoted in Christie & Sidhu, 2006, p. 459).

In this essay, I propose an approach to curriculum inquiry that aims to account for how emotions are mobilized to describe and categorize migrant and refugee students and how such mobilization may affect their curricular experiences. First, I discuss migration as an emotional process. Then I make a case for why we need to focus on emotions in the curriculum of migrant and refugee students. In the third section, I provide examples to demonstrate how emotions are used as a categorizing label. I also delineate some principles drawn from Critical Emotion Studies (CES) and develop an analytical frame for curriculum inquiry. Inquiries, informed by CES, will move beyond providing recipes for supporting the emotional well-being of migrant and refugee students, who are recurrently portrayed as emotionally vulnerable "problems" in need of fixing. I will argue that this frame is important because emotions are being used to simplify and generalize complex experiences and identities of diverse migrant and refugee populations and to present them as a "homogenous" group. I conclude the essay with a proposal that critical studies of curriculum and emotion be conducted at schools that serve migrant and refugee students.

Migration and Emotion

Migration – whether by choice or by force – is a hallmark of the contemporary world. As Skrbiš (2008) puts it, "We are, of course, more likely than ever to live across borders and boundaries, thus eroding the possibility, and historically well-tested expectations, that places of birth, life and dying will be the same" (p. 232). Historically, economic rationality has been used as a dominant theoretical lens for understanding migration. This theory uses a variety of "push–pull" factors and views migrants "as 'rational actors' who weigh the costs and benefits for themselves, or for their households, when making the decision to immigrate" (Kimberlin, 2009, p. 763). However, a growing body of contemporary work shows that the migrant life is shaped by complex processes that are beyond the economically driven instrumental rationality (Skrbiš, 2008; Svašek, 2012). Shire's (2015) poem "Home," which opens this essay, demystifies this theory of rationality. It shows that the migrant life is filled with complex and ambivalent emotions. Experiences of mobility pose emotional challenges to both migrants and the people in the destination societies. While the former "deal with emotions of loss, trauma, suffering and physical hardship," the latter "may experience fear, anger, anxiety, resentment and hatred for migrants" (Zembylas, 2012, p. 169).

When it comes to the education and well-being of the children of migrant families, the stakes are very high. These children often suffer from prejudice, racism and discrimination. Their "experience of displacement results in nightmares and violent memories that haunt [them] as they struggle to live their life in strange schools and societies" (Chan, Phillion, & He, 2015, p. 253). Yet, too much focus on their emotional "damage" may promote a tendency to look at migrant and refugee students through what Pupavac (2002) described as "therapeutic spectacles" (p. 489). Therefore, curriculum inquiry must not turn away from the closely connected relationships between migration, emotion and education.

Emotion and the Curriculum of Migrant and Refugee Students

The contemporary global context of migration warrants an approach to curriculum studies that takes emotions seriously. In the last decade, scholars in the humanities and social sciences have taken remarkably diverse approaches to the study of emotions and their complex interrelationship with personal, social and political aspects of life.[1] Yet, focusing too much on the scholarly interest felt in the first decade of the twenty-first century is to undermine the important work done prior to this "affective turn." For instance, there was a long tradition of scholarly work that examined emotions beyond the mind–body relationship in individuals. In the 1960s, Raymond Williams introduced the concept of the "structure of feeling," which he described "as firm and definite as 'structure' suggests, yet it operates in the most delicate and least tangible parts of our activity" (1961/2009, p. 36). While "structure of feeling" remained a concept closely related to class, Williams also developed new ways of understanding emotions. He pointed not only to the intangibility of emotional episodes in our personal and social activities, but also to the difficulty in historical investigations to capture the "felt sense of the quality of life at a particular place and time" (1961/2009, p. 36).

Abu-Lughod and Lutz's (1990) anthropological work was another milestone in the critical study of emotions. Their inquiry focused primarily on language and the politics of emotions. They proposed a radical rupture from the orthodox view that "emotions are psychological processes that respond to cross-cultural environmental differences but retain a robust essence untouched by the social or cultural" (p. 2). Abu-Lughod and Lutz took emotion out of the biological human body and showed that sociocultural analyses of emotion were both important and feasible. In order to appreciate this long tradition of critical work on emotions, I refrain from using the term "affective turn" and instead, following Trainor (2006), refer to this field of inquiry as CES.

CES is an interdisciplinary approach to understanding "the relationship between emotion and whatever it is that a particular discipline studies, from brain chemistry to teacher education to election results" (Trainor, 2006, p. 645). Generally speaking, CES rejects the psychological model of emotion, which views emotion as an individual's internal property. It also rejects the dominant sociological view that considers emotions as "collective or atmospheric forces that operate external to the body" (Seyfert, 2012, p. 28). Instead, CES attempts to understand emotions as complex, unpredictable and ambivalent encounters between individuals, material entities and discourses. This third position has recently made noticeable advances and proves particularly useful.

Johansen (2015), for example, identifies a two-step development that goes beyond the individual mind–body to understand the emergence and cultivation of emotions. First, the de-privatization of the emotional aspects of our life may be understood by examining how emotions are "organized, cultivated and initiated through discursive practices, techniques of governance, education and upbringing" (p. 49). Here, de-privatization is used differently from its connotation in economics. It means losing the privacy of one's emotions. The de-privatization argument holds that emotions are not something only internal to be discovered in our heart and brain, but are, rather, to be seen as social practices organized and enacted by stories that we both tell and are told (Rosaldo, 1984).

The second step of development is not simply about the movement *from* the individual *to* the social, but rather about "a more radical dissolution of the distinction between subject and surroundings that opens up the possibility of analyzing affect as something that reaches across bodies, objects and spaces" (Johansen, 2015, p. 49). These developments in CES point to contingent and volatile unfolding of emotional arousals. Goldie (2000) argues that such unfolding has a narrative structure. In other words, if we want to make sense of one's emotional life, we have to "see it as part of a larger unfurling narrative, not merely as a series of discrete episodes taken out of, and considered in abstraction from, the narrative in which they are embedded" (p. 5). In this light, CES does not attempt to ontologize either the individual or the social. Instead, it aims to question and reveal "deeply held assumptions … about the relationship between embodied versus transpersonal modes of being" (Boellstorff & Lindquist, 2004, p. 438).

One notable scholar, Sara Ahmed, has made significant contributions in this line of analysis, showing how the relationships between the "situation" and emotional experiences are inherently ambivalent, complex and unpredictable. Ahmed (2012) departs from both the psychological and the sociological models of emotion. For her:

> "Emotions create the very effect of the surfaces and boundaries that allow us to distinguish an inside and an outside in the first place. So emotions are not simply something 'I' or 'we' have. Rather, it is through emotions, or how we respond to objects and others, that surfaces or boundaries are made: the 'I' and the 'we' are shaped by, and even take the shape of, contact with others." (p. 10)

This view of emotion and how emotions create varying effects are important to understand the educational experiences of students from migrant and refugee backgrounds.

This is not to say that the subject of emotion has not been taken up in the field of curriculum studies. Boler's (1999) work on emotion and education, with careful attention to race, class and gender, is noteworthy. Her work is a persistent attempt to liberate emotion from its gendered associations and to institute emotion as a legitimate scholarly topic. Boler shows how emotion plays a substantive role in our conceptualization of knowledge, processes of knowledge acquisition and other issues of educational and moral concerns. Similarly, a key argument in Zembylas's wide-ranging work on emotion and education is that "all pedagogies are essentially pedagogies of emotions" (Zembylas, 2014b, n.p.).

Britzman and Pitt's work on trauma, affect and education is also illuminating. In particular, their concept of "difficult knowledge" has played a notable role in the study of emotion and education (Britzman, 1998; Pitt & Britzman, 2003). The principal function of "difficult knowledge" is "to signify both representations of social traumas in curriculum and the individual's encounters with them in pedagogy" (Pitt & Britzman, 2003, p. 755). Difficult knowledge that stems from profound social and historical traumas invites us to construct emotional significance of individual and collective actions. For example, Tarc (2011) shows how emotional responses to encounters with the difficult knowledge of traumatic histories of mass human violence may contribute to the production of what she calls a "reparative curriculum." Analysing beginning teachers' engagement with the traumatic history of residential schools in Canada, as depicted in Robert Arthur Alexie's novel *Porcupines and China Dolls*, Tarc underscores the potential of a reparative curriculum to develop "the learner's capacity to feel for the unimaginable lives and worlds of others" (p. 350). Here, reparative learning demands emotional responses to difficult knowledge, and such responses ask us "to face what is most undesirable about feeling and being human in a world teeming with unspoken atrocity" (p. 369).

Like the broad field of curriculum studies, migration studies has also begun to pay increasing attention to emotions (e.g. Skrbiš, 2008; Svašek, 2012). However, curriculum inquiries that focus particularly on the educational experiences of migrant and refugee students are yet to utilize the insights from CES in theorizing and enacting curriculum. Contemporary public discourses on migrants and refugees appeal to a range of emotions, such as suspicion, fear, anger and pity. These emotions are used not only to categorize migrants and refugees as unwanted subjects, but also to normalize xenophobic and violent attitudes towards them. This way of using emotions in public discourses may have significant consequences for the curriculum of migrant and refugee students because the experience that these "students have in schools is very much determined by the way that refugees are thought about, and represented in the public culture and how these representations are taken up or contested in schools" (Hattam & Every, 2010, p. 409).

Emotion as a Categorizing Label

An appeal to emotions is a familiar rhetorical trope in public discourses on migrants, asylum-seekers and refugees. For instance, we have seen this trope, using both positive and negative emotions, in the Brexit campaign (Wagner & Vasilopoulou, 2016). In such rhetorical use, emotions are employed as categorizing labels to represent migrant and refugees as homogenous groups. For example, an appeal to pity may develop a public perception of migrants and refugees as a vulnerable group deserving of protection. Similarly, an appeal to fear and anxiety may be an effective discursive tool to identify them as a dangerous group that must be kept outside the national border. Analysing the media portrayals of migrants and refugees, Esses, Medianu, and Lawson (2013) have identified various depictions that portray migrants and refugees as "enemies at the gate" trying to invade western nations (p. 518). These depictions suggest that "immigrants spread infectious diseases, that refugee claimants are often bogus, and that terrorists may gain entry to western nations disguised as refugees" (p. 518).

Historically, emotions have been used as powerful categorizing labels, with a concomitant significant impact on the portrayal of certain groups as inferior to others. For example, in Great Britain, the concept of emotion – coupled with that of civility – was used to create an imperial global order. Pernau's (2014) critical analysis of the British encyclopaedias from the eighteenth and nineteenth centuries shows how emotions were used as a criterion of difference at the global level. Her lexicographic study finds that "it was the management of feelings that marked the difference between wild, barbaric societies and civilized peoples, and thus became the ideological basis of colonial rulership" (p. 233). For instance, when British colonialism was facing resistance in some parts of India, especially by Muslim rulers in Mysore and Hyderabad, British encyclopaedias published and updated several entries on India. Those entries contained emotion-words to depict Indian Muslim rulers in derogatory ways (Pernau, 2014).

The same tendency to use emotion as a categorizing label is at work to this day. One contemporary arena in which the politics of emotion is playing out is transnational migration. As the numbers of migrant and refugee populations grow, so does an anti-immigration sentiment. For example, Muslim immigrants in western countries are being subject to enhanced screening and profiling because they are viewed as a potential threat to security. In this context, emotion-based discourses are nurturing a socio-political psyche that looks for the categorical essence of diverse groups such as Muslims. When it comes to school experience, Muslim students face surveillance, suspicion and prejudice. For instance, a 14-year-old student in a Texas school was arrested because he brought a home-made clock to school. His teachers mistook the clock for a bomb.[2] After this incident, questions were raised about whether or not the police would have been called if the student had not been a Muslim.

While many teachers are trying to come up with better curricular strategies for inclusive education, right-wing politicians are resorting to emotionally laden discourses that breed hatred and suspicion toward migrants and refugees. Donald Trump's 2016 campaign for US president is an illustrative example. He repeatedly warns US audiences that Mexico pushes its "drug dealers, criminals, and rapists" into the United States (The Chicago Tribune, 2016), promoting the construction of a giant wall along the US–Mexico border. He also wants to temporarily ban Muslims from entering the USA, in a desperate emotional bid to "make America safe again." In his campaign speeches, Trump is often heard promoting racial hatred towards non-whites and non-Christians.[3] As a powerful rhetorical tactic, he appeals not only to negative emotions such as hatred and fear, but also to positive emotions such as love (Carpentier, 2016).

The extreme xenophobic and neo-nationalist views that Trump embodies need to be understood within a genealogy of the historical development of a radical right-wing political sentiment. One notable antecedent to this sentiment was the rise of radical right-wing populist parties (RRWPPs) in western Europe. These parties advocate a free marketplace and a significant reduction of the government. They are known for their "rejection of individual and social equality, in their opposition to the social integration of marginalized groups, and in their appeal to xenophobia" (Betz, 1993, p. 413). Although these parties experienced ebbs and flows of public acceptance in the last three decades of the twentieth century, in recent years many of them have gained increasing support from voters. After the turn of the new millennium, many of these parties, including the Danish People's Party and the French National Front, continued to gain popularity. The global financial crisis in the late 2000s strengthened these parties. Additionally, a number of new RRWPPs emerged in the political arena (Lazaridis & Konsta, 2015). In national elections, the average share of vote for the RRWPPs "has increased from 8.0 per cent in the 1990s to 12.5 per cent in recent years" (Akkerman, de Lange, & Rooduijn, 2016, p. 1).

Keeping in mind this genealogy of neo-nationalism and xenophobia, below I juxtapose two quotations to show how emotions are used, in differing circumstances, as categorizing labels. Such labelling attempts to describe those who come from outside national borders as fearsome bodies that "deserve" hatred.

In announcing his presidential candidacy, Donald Trump said:

"When Mexico sends its people, they're not sending their best. They're not sending you. They're not sending you. They're sending people that have lots of problems, and they're bringing those problems with us [sic]. They're bringing drugs. They're bringing crime. They're rapists. And some, I assume, are good people." (quoted in Hee Lee, 2015, para. 1)

The following quotation is from the website of Aryan Nations, a white supremacist Christian religious group:

"It is not hate that makes the White housewife throw down the daily newspaper in repulsion and anger, after reading of yet another child-molester or rapist sentenced by corrupt courts to a couple of short years in prison or parole. It is not hate that makes the White working class man curse about the latest boatload of aliens dumped on our shores to be given job preferences over the White citizen who built this land. It is not hate that brings rage into the heart of a White Christian farmer when he reads of billions loaned or given away as 'aid' to foreigners when he cannot get the smallest break from an unmerciful government to save his failing farm. Not, it's not hate. It is Love." (quoted in Ahmed, 2001, p. 345)

In these quotations, certain emotions are mobilized and directed to the imagined other who threatens the imagined self.

In the first example, the speaker warns his audience of the potential "dangers" of letting Mexicans, and all migrants by implication, into the United States. By labelling the migrants as "drug dealers" and "rapists," he aims to create fear and anxiety among his audience, who will then direct their emotionally charged responses to the migrants. However, their responses are not likely to be based solely on fear and anxiety. As the scholarship on CES suggests, emotions often appear as "a cluster of emotions," for example, love may involve jealousy and anger may accompany grief (Ben-Ze'ev, 2000, p. 4). Due to such complexity of emotions, our fear and anxiety drive us to seek assurance and hope for a better "fear-less" future. Therefore, one viable option for people with xenophobic fear is to turn to right-wing politicians who promise to securitize national borders and keep migrants out. Thus, right-wing populist politicians draw upon people's emotional responses to outsiders and present the latter as a feared category. For example, we have seen how the Australian government's policies and practices relating to migrants, refugees and asylum-seekers are governed "through fear and anxiety generated in relation to outsiders," and how "the state draws on, and indeed creates, dispositions and feelings, generating a distinct politics of affect" (Tazreiter, 2015, p. 99). A recent example of such politics is *Operation Sovereign Borders* (OSB), one of Australia's border security policies. By analysing discursive and non-discursive practices of this policy, Hodge (2015) shows that OSB criminalizes asylum-seeker bodies in the name of securing the lives of Australian citizens.

In the second example, the members of the white Christian group justify their anger towards migrants and refugees by using a rhetorical tactic of reversal. They hate the outsiders because they love their fellow people. Here, the logic is that they hate others in order to love and protect their loved ones. In this way, reversal of emotions, such as love/hatred, is used as speech-acts for the justification of xenophobia and race-based violence. Elsewhere, I have described this rhetorical tactic as *metonymic practices of affective language* (Anwaruddin, 2016). Such practices allow us to call an emotional concept by a name other than its own. This renaming helps justify an action, which would otherwise be unjustifiable. For example, when the former president of the United States, George Bush, tried to justify his invasion of Iraq, he used this metonymic practice as a political strategy. He repeatedly told the American people that he went to war because he wanted to protect his "loved" Americans. Thus, he attempted to conceal his motives to go to war, i.e. his hatred for Iraq's then President Saddam Hussein and a desire to control an oil-rich region.

This rhetorical tactic, using the reversal of emotion, has both illocutionary and perlocutionary effects. It is illocutionary in the sense that the speaker of emotion-words expresses anger and hatred for others. It is perlocutionary because it has both intended and unintended consequences for the listener. While it may frighten, upset or sadden some, it may also encourage others to develop particular worldviews about the migrant and refugee populations. These worldviews not only categorize diverse people with certain labels of "concretized psychophysical states" (Lutz, 1988, p. 9), but they may also inspire people to engineer a social architecture and envision a political utopianism that simultaneously lives on and breeds hatred towards the perceived Other. The alarming rise of neo-nationalist sentiments, as expressed by Donald Trump and his supporters' desire to build a giant wall against Mexico and by Britain's decision to leave the European Union, exemplifies such a socio-political architecture.

In the contemporary cultural politics of emotions, the presence of the Other "is imagined as a threat to the object of love. It is this perceived threat that makes the hate reasonable rather than prejudicial" (Ahmed, 2001, p. 346). The tactic of reversal also contributes to what Ahmed (2012) calls the ripple effect of emotions. An emotion such as hate "'slides' sideways across signifiers and between figures, as well as backwards and forwards, by re-opening past associations whereby some bodies are 'already read' as more hateful than others" (Ahmed, 2001, p. 347). Due to this ripple effect, students are vulnerable to harm when they are subjected to emotion as a categorizing label in the course of their curricular experience. For instance, the immigrant/refugee status of students may be used to identify them as a "knowable categorization" (Rodriguez, 2015, p. 114). When this happens, the students are characterized as "emotionally damaged" subjects who are identifiable to their teachers and other students before they have even entered the school setting.

Such knowable categorization not only portrays migrant and refugee students as emotionally vulnerable, but also promotes the idea that emotions are the property of the experiencing individuals. This psychological focus is clear in the bulk of the literature on the education of migrant and refugee students. The central logic in this body of work is that these students experience significant psychological distress; therefore, they need to receive supports from schools (Sullivan & Simonson, 2016). By contrast, the CES approach to studying emotions suggests that we go beyond the individual, because emotions are always distributed across bodies, both material and discursive. Therefore, the exploration of emotions in curriculum should move "closer to the language of circulations, distribution and unfolding" of emotional arousals and episodes (Johansen, 2015, p. 50). Such explorations would then focus on how emotions are located across multiple and entangled personal, social and political spaces.

Thus far, the essay has focused mainly on negative emotions such as hatred, anger and anxiety. However, it is important to note that positive emotions are also invoked in discourses on migrants and refugees. The case of Canada can be an illustrative example. Historically, most Canadian political leaders have described Canada as a caring and compassionate nation. However, government policies and practices that aim to control and securitize the Canadian border create and perpetuate hierarchies of emotions. Recently, the Canadian parliament debated legislation regarding the detention of asylum-seekers. Kronick and Rousseau's (2015) critical discourse analysis of the parliamentary debates shows that the Canadian parliamentarians frequently invoked emotions such as compassion and empathy in ways that place "the state rather than the refugee in need of protection" (p. 544). Appealing to positive emotions, the parliamentarians made strong arguments for protecting refugee children from their "criminal" parents and human smugglers, thus, justifying the detention of children as a protective and humane measure. Through such emotional appeal, the parliamentarians portrayed Canada as a caring and compassionate nation. The detention of parents, and sometimes of children, was presented as a means of protecting borders and protecting children. Thus, "the government's power to control bodies is renamed as its capacity to care for children" (Kronick & Rousseau, 2015, p. 563).

Therefore, the CES approach that I propose should aim to investigate how negative as well as positive emotions are mobilized in complex, and often metonymic, ways in order to create social and political effects. It should also explore how emotions are used to identify migrant and refugee populations as essentialized categories, for example, vulnerable therefore deserving of pity, or dangerous therefore fearsome. As we see in Shire's (2015) poem,

> and if you survive
> and you are greeted on the other side with
> go home blacks, refugees
> dirty immigrants, asylum seekers
> sucking our country dry of milk,
> dark, with their hands out
> smell strange, savage –
> look what they've done to their own countries,
> what will they do to ours?

Essentializing labels of emotional signification, such as the ones contained in the above verse, are likely to ignite a hateful public imagination in, to use Spinoza's (1891) words, "superstitious persons, who know better how to rail at vice than how to teach virtue" (p. 230). In order to understand how emotions figure in students' curricular experiences, I recommend that the CES approach to curriculum inquiry be taken up in schools that serve migrant and refugee students. For example, a growing number of international schools in the USA that serve recently arrived migrants and refugees provide fertile ground for studying students' curricular experiences through a CES lens. Bajaj and Bartlett (2017) focus on three such schools. By exploring the curricular approaches of these international schools, Bajaj and Bartlett propose a "critical transnational curriculum," which not only responds to the academic needs of migrant and refugee students, but also recognizes the transnational realities and trajectories of their lives. The CES approach to curriculum inquiry that I have proposed might shed a different kind of light on the educational experiences of migrants and refugees in these international as well as other similar schools.

Concluding Remarks

In order to identify and resist the uses of emotions as harmful categorizing labels, in this essay I have proposed that curriculum inquiries examine the emotional encounters of migrant and refugee students and how they are positioned in discursive and material spaces. For such inquiries, the CES approach should prove helpful. A central tenet of this approach is that "emotions are not 'in' either the individual or the social, but produce the very surfaces and boundaries that allow the individual and the social to be delineated as if they are objects" (Ahmed, 2012, p. 10). I view this tenet as a productive dialogue between the dominant psychological–philosophical approaches that attempt to locate emotions in the individual body and the anthropological–sociological approaches that focus on the outside of the individual. Researchers examining the social and cultural politics of emotions in the curricular experiences of migrant and refugee students will readily recognize the ambivalent, complex and contextual nature of emotions. Through such inquiries, we may better understand how students sort through the tangle of emotions in their new schools and societies, and how they can resist harmful mobilizations of emotions that marginalize them.

Notes

1. See Clough (2007), Gorton (2007) and Zembylas (2014a) for reviews of the so-called "affective turn." Many authors have debated the distinction, or a lack thereof, between emotion and affect. Some have described emotion "as consciously apprehended and codified by a rational individual manifesting personal beliefs and intentions," and affect as non-recognizable, non-signifying and pre-personal sensations (Rushing, 2015, p. 74). However, I do not assume a distinction between affect and emotion. I agree with Ahmed (2010) who maintains that "the distinction between affect/emotion can under-describe the work of emotions, which *involve* forms of intensity, bodily orientation, and direction that are not simply about 'subjective content' or qualification of intensity. Emotions are not 'after-thoughts' but shape how bodies are moved by the worlds they inhabit" (p. 230).
2. http://www.cbc.ca/news/trending/ahmed-mohamed-arrested-clock-bomb-1.3230261
3. For examples of his racist remarks, see O'Connor and Marans (2016).

Acknowledgments

I'd like to thank Lucy El-Sherif and the editors of Curriculum Inquiry for their comments on an earlier draft of this paper.

Disclosure statement

No potential conflict of interest was reported by the author.

ORCID

Sardar M. Anwaruddin ⓘ http://orcid.org/0000-0002-5883-3238

References

Abu-Lughod, L, & Lutz, C. A. (1990). Introduction: Emotion, discourse, and the politics of everyday life. In C. A. Lutz & L. Abu-Lughod (Eds.), *Language and the politics of emotion* (pp. 1–23). Cambridge: Cambridge University Press.

Ahmed, S. (2001). The organisation of hate. *Law and Critique, 12*, 345–365.

Ahmed, S. (2010). *The promise of happiness.* Durham: Duke University Press.

Ahmed, S. (2012). *The cultural politics of emotion* (2nd ed.). New York: Routledge.

Akkerman, T., de Lange, S. L., & Rooduijn, M. (2016). Inclusion and mainstreaming? Radical right-wing populist parties in the new millennium. In T. Akkerman, S. L. de Lange, & M. Rooduijn (Eds.), *Radical right-wing populist parties in western Europe: Into the mainstream?* (pp. 1–28). London: Routledge.

Anwaruddin, S. M. (2016). Why critical literacy should turn to "the affective turn": Making a case for critical affective literacy. *Discourse: Studies in the Cultural Politics of Education, 37*(3), 381–396. doi:10.1080/01596306.2015.1042429

Arnot, M., Pinson, H., & Candappa, M. (2009). Compassion, caring and justice: teachers' strategies to maintain moral integrity in the face of national hostility to the "non-citizen." *Educational Review, 61*(3), 249–264. doi:10.1080/00131910903045906

Bajaj, M., & Bartlett, L. (2017). Critical transnational curriculum for immigrant and refugee students. *Curriculum Inquiry, 47*(1).

Ben-Ze'ev, A. (2000). *The subtlety of emotions.* Cambridge: MIT Press.

Betz, H-G. (1993). The new politics of resentment: Radical right-wing populist parties in Western Europe. *Comparative Politics, 25*(4), 413–427. doi:10.2307/422034

Boellstorff, T., & Lindquist, J. (2004). Bodies of emotion: Rethinking culture and emotion through Southeast Asia. *Ethnos, 69*(4), 437–444. doi:10.1080/0014184042000302290

Boler, M. (1999). *Feeling power: Emotions and education.* New York: Routledge.

Britzman, D. P. (1998). *Lost subjects, contested objects: Toward a psychoanalytic inquiry of learning.* Albany: State University of New York Press.

Carpentier, M. (2016). *Analysis of Donald Trump's recent speeches reveals what he loves.* Retrieved from http://www.theguardian.com/us-news/2016/feb/28/what-donald-trump-loves-recent-speeches

Chan, E., Phillion, J., & He, M. F. (2015). Immigrant students' experience as curriculum. In M. F. He, B. D. Schultz, & W. H. Schubert (Eds.), *The SAGE guide to curriculum in education* (pp. 249–258). Los Angeles: Sage.

Christie, P., & Sidhu, R. (2006). Governmentality and "fearless speech": Framing the education of asylum seeker and refugee children in Australia. *Oxford Review of Education, 32*(4), 449–465. doi:10.1080/03054980600884177

Clough, P. (2007). Introduction. In P. Clough & J. Halley (Eds.), *The affective turn: Theorizing the social* (pp. 1–33). Durham: Duke University Press.

Editorial: The ugly roots of Donald Trump's immigration plan. (2016, January 19). *The Chicago Tribune*. Retrieved from http://www.chicagotribune.com/news/nationworld/ct-trump-immigration-operation-wetback-edit-0120-20160119-story.html

Esses, V. M., Medianu, S., & Lawson, A. S. (2013). Uncertainty, threat, and the role of the media in promoting the dehumanization of immigrants and refugees. *Journal of Social Issues, 69*(3), 518–536. doi:10.1111/josi.12027

Goldie, P. (2000). *The emotions: A philosophical exploration*. Oxford: Oxford University Press.

Gorton, K. (2007). Theorizing emotion and affect: Feminist engagements. *Feminist theory, 8*(3), 333–348. doi:10.1177/1464700107082369

Harding, J. (2009). Emotional subjects: Language and power in refugee narratives. In J. Harding & E. D. Pribram (Eds.), *Emotions: A cultural studies reader* (pp. 267–279). London: Routledge.

Hattam, R., & Every, D. (2010). Teaching in fractured classrooms: Refugee education, public culture, community and ethics. *Race, Ethnicity and Education, 13*(4), 409–424. doi:10.1080/13613324.2010.488918

Hee Lee, M. Y. (2015). *Donald Trump's false comments connecting Mexican immigrants and crime*. Retrieved from https://www.washingtonpost.com/news/fact-checker/wp/2015/07/08/donald-trumps-false-comments-connecting-mexican-immigrants-and-crime/

Hodge, P. (2015). A grievable life? The criminalisation and securing of asylum seeker bodies in the 'violent frames' of Australia's Operation Sovereign Borders. *Geoforum, 58*, 122–131. doi:http://dx.doi.org/10.1016/j.geoforum.2014.11.006

Johansen, B. S. (2015). Locating hatred: On the materiality of emotions. *Emotion, Space and Society, 16*, 48–55. doi:10.1016/j.emospa.2015.07.002

Kimberlin, S. E. (2009). Synthesizing social science theories of immigration. *Journal of Human Behavior in the Social Environment, 19*, 759–771. doi:10.1080/10911350902910922

Kronick, R., & Rousseau, C. (2015). Rights, compassion and invisible children: A critical discourse analysis of the parliamentary debates on the mandatory detention of migrant children in Canada. *Journal of Refugee Studies, 28*(4), 544–569. doi:10.1093/jrs/fev005

Lazaridis, G., & Konsta, A.-M. (2015). Identitarian populism: Securitisation of migration and the far right in times of economic crisis in Greece and the UK. In G. Lazaridis & K. Wadia (Eds.), *The securitisation of migration in the EU: Debates since 9/11* (pp. 184–206). New York: Palgrave Macmillan.

Lutz, C. A. (1988). *Unnatural emotions: Everyday sentiments on a Micronesian atoll and their challenge to western theory*. Chicago: University of Chicago Press.

O'Connor, L., & Marans, D. (2016). *Here are 9 examples of Donald Trump being racist*. Retrieved from http://www.huffingtonpost.com/entry/donald-trump-racist-examples_us_56d47177e4b03260bf777e83

Pernau, M. (2014). Civility and barbarism: Emotions as criteria of difference. In U. Frevert, M. Scheer, A. Schmidt, P. Eitler, B. Hitzer, N. Verheyen … M. Pernau, *Emotional lexicons: Continuity and change in the vocabulary of feeling 1700-2000* (pp. 230–259). Oxford: Oxford University Press.

Pitt, A., & Britzman, D. (2003). Speculations on qualities of difficult knowledge in teaching and learning: An experiment in psychoanalytic research. *International Journal of Qualitative Studies in Education, 16*(6), 755–776. doi:10.1080/0951839031000163213S

Pupavac, V. (2002). Pathologizing populations and colonizing minds: International psychosocial programs in Kosovo. *Alternatives: Global, Local, Political, 27*(4), 489–511. Retrieved from http://www.jstor.org/stable/40645060

Rodriguez, S. (2015). The dangers of compassion: The positioning of refugee students in policy and education research and implications for teacher education. *Knowledge Cultures, 3*(2), 112–126.

Rosaldo, M. Z. (1984). Toward an anthropology of self and feeling. In R. A. Sweder & R. A. LeVine (Eds.), *Culture theory: Essays on mind, self, and emotion* (pp. 137–157). Cambridge: Cambridge University Press.

Rushing, S. (2015). Butler's ethical appeal: Being, feeling and acting responsible. In M. Lloyd (Ed.), *Butler and ethics* (pp. 65–90). Edinburgh: Edinburgh University Press.

Seyfert, R. (2012). Beyond personal feelings and collective emotions: Toward a theory of social affect. *Theory, Culture & Society, 29*(6), 27–46. doi:10.1177/0263276412438591

Shire, W. (2015). *Home*. Retrieved from http://www.theglobeandmail.com/opinion/home/article27608299/

Skrbiš, Z. (2008). Transnational families: Theorising migration, emotions and belonging. *Journal of Intercultural Studies, 29*(3), 231–246. doi:10.1080/07256860802169188

Spinoza, B. (1891). *The chief works of Benedict de Spinoza.* (R. H. M. Elwes, Trans.). London: George Bell and Sons.

Sullivan, A. L., & Simonson, G. R. (2016). A systematic review of school-based social-emotional interventions for refugee and war-traumatized youth. *Review of Educational Research, 86*(2), 503–530. doi:10.3102/0034654315609419

Svašek, M. (2012). *Emotions and human mobility: Ethnographies of movement.* London: Routledge.

Tarc, A. M. (2011). Reparative curriculum. *Curriculum Inquiry, 41*(3), 350–372. doi:10.1111/j.1467-873X.2011.00554.x

Tazreiter, C. (2015). Lifeboat politics in the Pacific: Affect and the ripples and shimmers of a migrant saturated future. *Emotion, Space and Society, 16,* 99–107.

Trainor, J. S. (2006). From identity to emotion: Frameworks for understanding, and teaching against, anticritical sentiments in the classroom. *JAC, 26*(3/4), 643–655.

Wagner, M., & Vasilopoulou, S. (2016). Emotions and Brexit: How did they affect the result? Retrieved from https://emotionsblog.history.qmul.ac.uk/2016/07/emotions-and-brexit-how-did-they-affect-the-result/

Williams, R. (2009). On structure of feeling. In J. Harding & E. D. Pribram (Eds.), *Emotions: A cultural studies reader* (pp. 35–49) (Original work published 1961). London: Routledge.

Zembylas, M. (2012). Transnationalism, migration and emotions: Implications for education. *Globalisation, Societies and Education, 10*(2), 163–179. doi:10.1080/14767724.2012.647403

Zembylas, M. (2014a). Theorizing "difficult knowledge" in the aftermath of the "affective turn": Implications for curriculum and pedagogy in handling traumatic representations. *Curriculum Inquiry, 44*(3), 390–412. doi:10.1111/curi.12051

Zembylas, M. (2014b). Making sense of the complex entanglement between emotion and pedagogy: Contributions of the affective turn. *Cultural Studies of Science Education.* Advance online publication. doi:10.1007/s11422-014-9623-y

Global mobilities and the possibilities of a cosmopolitan curriculum

Fazal Rizvi and Jason Beech ⓘD

ABSTRACT
This paper is aimed at exploring the possibilities that the notion of everyday cosmopolitanism can open up for pedagogic practices and, at the same time, the opportunities that pedagogy can provide for the construction of a cosmopolitan global ethics. Our argument is that students (and teachers) are involved in everyday experiences of cosmopolitan encounters and that these can and should be used as a starting point for the development of a cosmopolitan curriculum aimed at steering the cosmopolitan outlook of students towards morally open but productive directions.

We live in a world in which global mobilities are increasingly transforming the social spaces in which we now live, work and learn. It is a world in which despite great distances and notwithstanding the continuing presence and significance of national borders, certain kinds of relationships across these borders have become intensified. The idea of transnationalism has widely been used to understand the nature and scope of such relationships, problematizing the traditional nation-centric notions of identity and citizenship (Thiel & Friedman, 2016; Vertovec, 2009), public spaces and public cultures and even migration (Nail, 2015; Shortell, 2016). Global mobilities, these authors suggest, have changed the sense people have of their locality. While these changes are particularly evident among migrant groups, they nonetheless affect entire communities, not least because they bring diverse cultural traditions and practices into contact with each other as never before, both within and across national borders. Such contact of course creates a range of new challenges for living together, giving rise to a new politics of difference that is often globally stretched.

At the core of this politics are contrasting views about how to interpret and respond to global mobilities. On the one hand, the idea of the global flows of people has been celebrated. It has been argued that a globally integrated knowledge economy needs flows not only of capital and ideas but also of people. Not surprisingly, therefore most advanced economies have developed programmes designed to recruit skilled migrants, enabling business to be conducted across borders more easily. Given the choice, a growing number of people desire mobility and the lives associated with it. Yet, there are also a growing number of people across the world who fear its various economic and cultural consequences. In response, various political movements have cropped up promising to put up barriers to the global mobility of people, even threatening to build walls. Regimes of border protection are, for example, emerging throughout the world to prevent refugees from entering sovereign spaces. Opposition to immigration has become common in many countries, often around the reassertion of fixed categories of national, cultural and religious identity. A politics of fear of others is once again raising its ugly head, often exploited by expedient politicians. Increasingly, they promise to restrict the terms of global mobility – of who is allowed to move and how.

What is clear then is that we live in a world in which discourses that celebrate and promote fluidity of movement sit uncomfortably alongside discourses of political fixity and closure. Appadurai (1996b) wrote about this contradictory phenomenon as disjunctures across various scapes. He noted, for example, that technoscapes, ideoscapes and ethnoscapes are "disjunctive" and "chaotic" in character and supersede traditional geographical thinking. In his subsequent monograph, *Fear of Small Numbers*, Appadurai (2006) argues that the capacity of people, images and objects to move rapidly across local and global geographical space has given rise to high levels of anxiety, creating a space in which xenophobic and nativist politics potentially thrive.

Educational settings are not unaffected by the empirical realities of global mobilities and the political debates that surround them. For educators, this raises the normative question of how the curriculum should address the challenges forged by a contradictory space in which mobilities of various kinds have become more possible to occur on a larger scale, and have become more desirable by many, but are also feared. In other words, how should schools approach the task of helping students to interpret the nature and scope of global mobilities and understand the complex politics to which they have given rise? How can schools help them develop a normative sensibility towards the kinds of cultural exchange that has become an inevitable outcome of the processes of globalization?

In addressing such challenges, we want to argue, the notion of cosmopolitanism retains contemporary relevance, but not in its traditional philosophical sense. It needs to be re-thought. We suggest that cosmopolitanism be viewed both as a social fact and a political value. In our view, education has a major role to play in connecting the *facts* of cosmopolitan encounters and the *values* that cosmopolitanism espouses. What is needed, we suggest, is "cosmopolitan learning," which denies the abstractionism of the traditional theories of cosmopolitanism but underlines the realities and challenges associated with global mobilities (Rizvi, 2009). Thus, the educational challenge we face is how to help students move from an understanding of *empirical* cosmopolitan encounters to a set of *normative* ideas about how to live with cultural difference in a world in which mobilities are both valued and also characterized by their uneven and unequal consequences.

If we think of education as the process through which young people develop the means of orientation (Elías, 1994) that will help them interpret and act upon the world, then global mobilities need to be considered as part of the demands of any contemporary curriculum. Yet, it also needs to be acknowledged that the ways in which different groups and individuals interpret and respond to the contradictions of global mobilities are locally specific. Thus, totalizing universal educational solutions to this challenge are neither desirable nor possible (Todd, 2009). On the contrary, we want to argue that in the most optimistic scenario what we might aspire to is a series of context-specific and particular pedagogic practices. In that sense, our aim in this essay is to discuss the possibility of a *curricular approach* that can provide an overarching framework to address the challenges posed by global mobilities to education, but that is open enough to allow for spatially contingent interpretations and enactments that take the plurality of human experience as a starting point.

Abstract Normative Cosmopolitanism

The idea of cosmopolitanism has traditionally been linked to notions of social solidarity, cohesion and a global sense of belonging (Nussbaum, 2002). What cosmopolitanism challenges is the spatial reference for social solidarity. So if communitarianism is based on the idea of solidarity across a given community (Etzioni, 2004), and nationalism implies developing a sense of belonging to a nation (Smith, 2010), cosmopolitanism appeals to solidarity and belonging along the whole cosmos or the universe. As morally appealing as this notion might appear, a number of scholars have pointed out that this association between cosmopolitanism and the universal has contributed to the development of a highly abstract understanding of cosmopolitanism that overlooks issues of historical difference (Fine, 2007; Malcomson, 1998; Robbins, 1998). The cosmos or the universe is moreover difficult to grasp in practical and experiential terms, and consequently it is quite challenging to develop and promote a sense of belonging to such an abstract formation. Many attempts, coming from different political and philosophical perspectives, have thus been made to construct a narrative of cosmopolitanism that promotes intercultural understanding at the global level but does not assume its abstractionism (Holton, 2009).

We agree that abstract normative approaches to cosmopolitanism have conceptual, political and practical limitations, especially when they are used as foundation for the development of pedagogic strategies. Conceptually, one of the problems of these approaches is the way in which they associate cosmopolitanism to the idea of the universal and the search for universal values. In these accounts "the universal" is rendered as equivalent to the global on the basis of a binary distinction between universal/particular and global/local. In this perspective, the global and the universal are linked to the ubiquitous, the abstract, the amorphous and porous. They have no borders or confinement. The local, on the other hand, is seen as the locus of our everyday experience, linked to attachment and a feeling of security (Larsen & Beech, 2014). This binary spatial conception contributes to the construction of cosmopolitanism as an ideal of detachment (Robbins, 1998).

There are also a number of moral and political limitations to the abstract normative approaches to cosmopolitanism. The association of cosmopolitanism with the cosmos and the universe tends to promote a singular view of cosmopolitanism (Robbins, 1998). But even if we accept that there might be only one world in physical terms, there clearly can be many ways of engaging with that world and, consequently, many types of cosmopolitanisms. Actually, at different times and in different places, there have been distinctive conceptions of cosmopolitanism. The notion of a singular cosmopolitanism can quite often fall into ethnocentrism and an imperialist logic. The search for universal values tends toward global homogeneity and uniformity. But as Appiah (2006) argues, it is possible to imagine a type of cosmopolitan ideal that operates on a pragmatic belief that different cultures and ways of living can exist side by side harmoniously, without assuming a set of moral universals. Rejection of universalism does not imply rejecting the possibility of negotiating values across differences in an ongoing manner.

Finally, abstract normative views of cosmopolitanism are also faced with important limitations in practical terms. If we accept that most people are involved in cosmopolitan encounters on a day-to-day basis, and that these encounters might require certain ethical decisions, it becomes evident that it is quite difficult that abstract allegedly universal norms could provide a clear and unequivocal guide to these decisions. In real life, moral principles conflict with each other, and it is in the arena of competing principles that ethical decisions have to be made, deciding to privilege certain principles over others. In this sense, idealized moral constructions become impractical, since it is impossible for an individual to always respect all of the moral principles that are included within the theoretical construction of the perfect cosmopolitan. Accordingly, abstract normative views of cosmopolitanism tend to favour top-down pedagogical practices in which students are considered passive receptors of a list of "good cosmopolitan behaviours" that tend to be disconnected from their everyday experiences, and do not necessarily help them in their day-to-day decision-making.

This analysis suggests the need to consider alternatives to abstract universal normative views, bringing cosmopolitanism down from the pedestal at which Kant (1991) and more recently Nussbaum (2002) and others have placed it. Malcomson (1998) refers to the "long history of arrogance" (p. 241) of cosmopolitanism and calls for a more humble cosmopolitan ethos. In other words, the challenge is to locate cosmopolitanism and understand it as being related to everyday practices; scaling down, pluralizing and particularizing cosmopolitanism (Malcomson, 1998; Robbins, 1998).

In what follows, we want to argue that it is possible to view cosmopolitanism as an everyday practice that is unstable, complex and open to very different interpretations and enactments. Once we interpret cosmopolitanism in terms of actually existing practices, it becomes possible to suggest a plurality of cosmopolitanisms. A cosmopolitan project, as we understand it, should not be aimed at flattening those differences in the search for some kind of universal ethic, but rather promote conversations across difference. The starting point for such a project is not an approach from above, but from understanding actually existing everyday cosmopolitan experiences, keeping unstable the relationship between and across them. Such a project suggests modalities that go beyond interculturalism, focusing on the ways in which the local and national encounters are shaped by global forces and connections.

Everyday Cosmopolitanism

The concept of "everyday cosmopolitanism" points to the realization that most people are engaged in cosmopolitan encounters in their everyday life and are already developing an incipient organic sense of cosmopolitanism with which to engage the world of cultural difference (Skrbis & Woodward, 2013). Skrbis and Woodward (2013) use the term everyday cosmopolitanism to refer to those practices of cosmopolitanism that are now routine, becoming part of an emerging global consciousness. This consciousness suggests a broad sense of openness towards other people, cultures and ways of life. To assert the need to take instances of everyday cosmopolitanism more seriously is to be alert to their profound consequences for the social constitution of our discourses, relations and institutions. In this sense, everyday cosmopolitanism underlines the importance of an empirical openness to the ways in which everyday cosmopolitan encounters produce social meaning and increasingly affect many of our dispositions, experiences and aspirations.

In the current condition of ubiquitous global mobilities, cosmopolitan encounters are nothing unusual, nothing extraordinary. Rather, they are often routine ways of engaging with the contemporary realities of everyday life: they produce meaning and have deep impact on human practices, dispositions and experiences. They shape us even when we do not know how. Although most people are unable to travel extensively, no community is entirely unaffected by global shifts produced by increasing levels of international travel, social imaginaries circulating across transnational social media (Appadurai, 1996a) and the globalizing nature of economic exchange and work.

The notion of everyday cosmopolitanism can be relevant as an analytic foundation for the development of a cosmopolitan pedagogic approach. Cosmopolitan learning should be situated within the lives of young people, highlighting how their lives are part of wider social, political and economic relations. If cosmopolitan learning is seen as a learning process that has to do with individuals in context (Biesta & Lawy, 2006), it can be more meaningful for students than the discussion of abstract normative principles. A pedagogic approach that starts from everyday experiences can open up the possibility for multiple engagements with cosmopolitanism, and to a cosmopolitan approach that is situated and specific to the different contexts in which different students live and learn. It is through interaction with specific experiences, desires and expectations that abstract normative principles can be contextualized and made meaningful and relevant to the lives of students.

The point of departure could be the family histories of students and teachers, or an event in the daily news, or even a simple experience of consumption. From a simple reconstruction of the flows of people, objects and cultural artefacts that affect that experience, it is possible to go deeper into analysing the wider cultural, social, political and economic context of these encounters and exchanges. How are family histories of mobility linked to colonialism and global inequalities? How do our consumption practices affect distant people and global justice? Embedding these kinds of issues in real concrete experiences can potentially make learning more meaningful for students and contribute to contextualized conversations on moral issues, dispositions and attitudes towards difference. Furthermore, in this way it becomes visible for students how our everyday practices potentially have cosmopolitan dimensions and are affected by and affect relations of power on a global scale.

In order to move from experiences to the ways in which they are interpreted, it is useful to make an analytic differentiation between cosmopolitanism as an empirical reality and the way in which that reality is interpreted. Based on a sociological approach to understanding cosmopolitanism, Fine (2007) distinguishes between a cosmopolitan condition and a cosmopolitan outlook. Similarly, Beck (2006) refers to a process of latent cosmopolitanization differentiating it from a cosmopolitan outlook.

The cosmopolitan condition (using Fine's vocabulary) refers to the intensification of mobility and encounters with difference in the current world of globalization, and to the awareness of this "forced mixing" (Beck, 2006). In addition, the increasing global nature of social issues such as equity, justice, security and sustainability imply a degree of global interdependence in which the dangers and challenges of civilization become deterritorialized, reinforcing the cosmopolitan condition as a ubiquitous reality. Thus, global mobilities and interdependences have created an empirical cosmopolitan reality in which human experiences and references have been spatially stretched.

One of the ethical issues that are debated in the literature is the link between cosmopolitanism and socio-economic inequalities. Calhoun (2002) associates actual existing cosmopolitanism with those in the higher ends of the social economic scale who have opportunities to travel, of engaging in exotic consumption and, therefore, for cosmopolitan encounters. However, for a large number of the world population, cosmopolitan encounters are not a choice, but rather a strategy of survival (Malcomson, 1998). Thus, the notion that cosmopolitan encounters mostly take place between the privileged is questionable in the current spatial context in which diversity, mobilities and connectivities have become ubiquitous. From this perspective, cosmopolitan encounters are not the result of conscious and voluntary choices of an elite, but rather part of the effects of processes of globalization.

The cosmopolitan condition as an empirical reality has been widely documented and discussed in the social sciences. It is much more difficult to empirically identify and analytically make sense of the cosmopolitan outlook. The cosmopolitan outlook is the way in which the cosmopolitan condition is interpreted. It is constituted by attitudes, dispositions, imaginaries and beliefs. There is no inherent virtue in the cosmopolitan outlook. It does not necessarily "herald the first rays of universal brotherly love among peoples, or the dawn of the world republic, or a free floating global outlook, or compulsory xenophilia" (Beck, 2006, p. 13). It implies analytically considering the need to re-think political and cultural borders and differentiations such as internal/external and national/international or global. Awareness of the empirical realities of the cosmopolitan condition can trigger reactionary and xenophobic reactions as much as it can spark openness to diversity and the presence of the other. In other words, the cosmopolitan outlook is a domain of contested politics (Robbins, 1998, p. 12).

What is of major importance for our argument is that the cosmopolitan condition is a reality that is part of the lives of most (if not all) young people, and that young people have to interpret this cosmopolitan reality to make sense of and act upon the world in which they live. Their cosmopolitan attitudes, dispositions, imaginaries and beliefs are rarely organized in a coherent explicit narrative. On the contrary, the bargain of people with the cosmopolitan condition is messy, complex, sometimes contradictory and not necessarily explicit and organized. Consequently, we suggest that the way in which young people interpret the increasing cosmopolitanization of reality should be made explicit, understood and be the object of reflexive pedagogic practices. In this way, by working pedagogically with the cosmopolitan outlook of students, it is possible to think of transformative pedagogic practices that can steer the interpretations of cosmopolitan reality towards morally productive cosmopolitan values. In turn, this transformation could have an impact on the cosmopolitan condition itself and contribute to the development of a more ethical global reality.

When we emphasize the need to steer the cosmopolitan outlook of students towards morally productive directions, we are not thinking of a predefined set of values that demarcate a closed position to which the students have to be forced. Neither are we promoting some kind of moral relativism. We rather suggest that the definition of a morally productive cosmopolitan outlook is a collective task, that it is dynamic and always in the process of becoming and that its greatest significance is not so much in the conclusions to which a group can arrive, but rather in the process of learning itself.

Towards a Cosmopolitan Curriculum

Our view of cosmopolitanism is in line with what Appiah (1997) calls "rooted cosmopolitanism." From this perspective, cosmopolitanism does not contradict patriotism or other allegiances; neither does it need to be equated with universalism. Instead of seeing cosmopolitanism as linked to a logic of detachment, we see it as a reality of multiple attachment (Robbins, 1998). We promote a kind of cosmopolitanism that is not positioned as being in superiority to particularisms and "provincialisms," but rather a cosmopolitanism that promotes bridges among particularisms, as a move away from ethnocentrism. Rethinking cosmopolitanism requires reconceptualizing space, borders and belongings, and overcoming the simple binary of universal and particular (Robbins, 1998). Embracing the notion of multiple and overlapping belongings involves a significant shift in the ways in which the social sciences have tended to conceptualize the construction of collective identities. The either/or logic in which the demarcation of symbolic borders is a precondition for identity formation is replaced by the both/and logic of "inclusive differentiation" (Beck, 2006). From this perspective, the strong opposition between cosmopolitanism (as detachment) and national identities (as attachment) has been overstated.

We see cosmopolitanism as performative. It is messy, complex and put into play in everyday decisions. It is not an outcome; it is not an individual attribute, but rather a practice, a disposition that is always in process of changing as people interact across different contexts. As such, "cosmopolitan" is not something you are or you are not, or as Skrbis and Woodward (2013) put it, there is no such thing as an "end point" in cosmopolitanism. It is an ongoing project, both at the social and the individual level.

For Appiah (2006), the cosmopolitan project is about developing the capacity to participate in open-ended conversations with others without necessarily reaching an agreement or defining universal maxims. He uses the notion of conversation, both in its habitual meaning, and also as "as a metaphor for engagement with the experience and the ideas of others" (p. 85). From this perspective, a reflexive cosmopolitanism is about developing awareness of the complexity of life decisions, the value of considering other points of view and the consequences of our everyday decisions and actions for those that are close, but also for those that are far away in space and time.

The analytic distinction offered by Beck and Fine, between a cosmopolitan condition and cosmopolitan outlooks is a useful way to start thinking about a cosmopolitan pedagogic agenda. Such an agenda should take the everyday cosmopolitan experiences of students as a starting point, and through processes of discussion and conversation influence their cosmopolitan outlooks. If we can access and affect the cosmopolitan outlook of students, this can potentially have an effect on their ongoing cosmopolitan encounters that can then inform further classroom conversations. Hopefully, this kind of pedagogical work can then have an influence on cosmopolitan conditions, contribute to a more ethical approach to globalization and in this way move toward the more ambitious expectations for cosmopolitanism from below.

While students are experiencing a cosmopolitan reality that is contradictory, messy, and in many ways, dominated by consumer cultures and market narratives, schools provide them with abstract and allegedly universal values as a way of promoting their moral engagement with cosmopolitan reality. The problem is that these two narratives seem to be located in parallel planes that have no contact with each other.

An alternative view is to take seriously the possibility of forging cosmopolitan values from below, based on distributive and transformational practices embedded in everyday experiences. The challenge is to steer everyday experiences towards a critical and reflexive cosmopolitanism, as part of a broader pedagogical project that works in between the messiness of the actual social, political and cultural life of students and cosmopolitan aspirations that institutions often profess. The focus should be on cosmopolitan learning (Rizvi, 2009).

We do not however regard cosmopolitan learning as the acquisition of a fixed set of values and dispositions. Experience is a transaction between the self and the environment or context (Biesta & Burbules, 2003). Thus, cosmopolitanism should not be understood as an attribute of the individual, but has to do with individuals in context. When thinking about cosmopolitan experiences, we need to move into a notion of context (and thus experience) that considers space as relational, since mobilities, connectivities and diversity are distinctive characteristics of the context that is in transaction with the individual. The emphasis on context-specific cosmopolitan experiences as a pedagogic point of departure reinforces the impossibility of providing in this essay a detailed recipe for pedagogic action. It is the specificity of the context, the experiences of students and teachers, the resources that are available and the particular positions from which they live the contradictions of global mobility that should inform the ways in which the empirical is combined with the normative (Wahlstrom, 2014).

This demands making everyday cosmopolitan experiences – including its banal, consumerist and elitist forms – visible, open to scrutiny and competing interpretations. Once cosmopolitan experiences are made visible, the next step is to promote a critical and reflexive practice, avoiding binary thinking associated with an ethical good/bad approach, and getting deep into the messiness and complexities of moral everyday decisions in which different values and the rights of different groups are in conflict and overlap, both within and across national borders. This exchange should take the form of an open-ended collective conversation that provides an opportunity to discuss cosmopolitanism in relation to lived experiences of the participants, reflecting on the complexities that are inherent to every decision, no matter how trivial or profound. Conversations, Todd (2013) argues, are not about making decisions or reaching agreements, but rather about confronting each other, and providing an opportunity for "facing the particularly human face of disruption, resistance, outsidedness, in all its messiness and mundaneness" (p. 2).

These types of conversations should be aimed at overcoming purely individualistic notions of global responsibility, in which global problems are "couched in individualistic, psychological and moralistic terms – the result of a lack of individual responsibility, rather than an outcome of more structural causes" (Biesta & Lawy, 2006, p. 69). On the contrary, global problems, inequalities, risks and challenges should be historicized and politicized.

We argue that by identifying everyday cosmopolitan experiences, it is possible to steer these experiences towards a morally productive cosmopolitanism, where such a moral is itself something that is negotiated rather than imposed from above as a moral technology. Instead of learning about cultures in an abstract manner, a critical approach must help students to explore the crisscrossing of transnational circuits of communication, the flows of global capital and the cross-cutting of local, transnational social practices and their differential consequences for different people and communities. We believe that a pedagogically productive cosmopolitan conversation should not necessarily be aimed at reaching consensus and unanimous agreement. On the contrary, the value of having a profound discussion and listening to different positions with respect and an open mind should be promoted as a virtue in itself. If students learn, through their formal education, to participate in debates with those that have different positions, priorities and values, without the need for agreement, but with the need to understand other people's perspectives, this could potentially contribute to develop the ability to master the kind of cosmopolitan conversations that we are advocating.

Disclosure statement

No potential conflict of interest was reported by the authors.

ORCID

Jason Beech (iD) http://orcid.org/0000-0002-4971-7665

References

Appadurai, A. (1996a). *Modernity at large: Cultural dynamics of globalization*. Minneapolis: University of Minnesota Press.
Appadurai, A. (1996b). *Future as cultural fact: Essays on the global condition*. New York: Routledge.
Appadurai, A. (2006). *Fear of small numbers*. Durham: Duke University Press.
Appiah, K. A. (1997). Cosmopolitan patriots. *Critical Inquiry, 23*(3), 617–639.
Appiah, K. A. (2006). *Cosmopolitanism: Ethics in a world of strangers*. New York: W.W. Norton.
Beck, U. (2006). *Cosmopolitan vision*. Cambridge: Polity.
Biesta, G., & Burbules, N. (2003). *Pragmatism and educational research*. Lanham: Rowman & Littlefield.

Biesta, G., & Lawy, R. (2006). From teaching citizenship to learning democracy: Overcoming individualism in research, policy and practice. *Cambridge Journal of Education, 36*(1), 63–79.

Calhoun, C. J. (2002). The class consciousness of frequent travellers: Toward a critique of actually existing cosmopolitanism. *South Atlantic Quarterly, 101*(4), 869–897.

Elías, N. (1994). *Conocimiento y poder* [Knowledge and Power]. Madrid: La Piqueta.

Etzioni, A. (2004). *The common good*. Cambridge: Polity.

Fine, R. (2007). *Cosmopolitanism*. London: Taylor and Francis.

Holton, R. J. (2009). *Cosmopolitanisms: New thinking and new directions*. London: Palgrave Macmillan.

Kant, I. (1991). Perpetual peace: A philosophical sketch. In H. Reiss (Ed.), *Kant: Political writings*. Cambridge: Cambridge University Press.

Larsen, M., & Beech, J. (2014). Spatial theorizing in comparative and international education research. *Comparative Education Review, 58*(2), 191–214.

Malcomson, S. L. (1998). The varieties of cosmopolitan experience. In B. Cheah & B. Robbins (Eds.), *Cosmopolitics: Thinking and feeling beyond the nation* (pp. 1–19). Minneapolis: University of Minnesota Press.

Nail, T. (2015). *The figure of the migrant*. Stanford: Stanford University Press.

Nussbaum, M. C. (2002). Patriotism and cosmopolitanism. In J. Cohen (Ed.), *For love of country?* (pp. 3–17). Boston: Beacon.

Rizvi, F. (2009). Towards cosmopolitan learning. *Discourse: Studies in the Cultural Politics of Education, 30*(3), 253–268.

Robbins, B. (1998). Actual existing cosmopolitanism. In B. Cheah & B. Robbins (Eds.), *Cosmopolitics: Thinking and feeling beyond the nation* (pp. 1–19). Minneapolis: University of Minnesota Press.

Shortell, T. (2016). *Everyday globalization: A spatial semiotics of immigrant neighborhoods in Brooklyn and Paris*. New York: Routledge.

Skrbis, Z., & Woodward, I. (2013). *Cosmopolitanism: Uses of the idea*. London: Sage.

Smith, A. D. (2010). *Nationalism: Theory, ideology, history*. Cambridge: Polity.

Thiel, M., & Friedman, R. (2016). *European identity and culture: Narratives of transnational belonging*. New York: Routledge.

Todd, S. (2009). *Toward an imperfect education: Facing humanity, rethinking cosmopolitanism*. Boulder: Paradigm.

Todd, S. (2013, April). *Difficult conversations, or the difficult task of facing humanity*. Paper presented at the Impossible Conversations Series, National College of Art and Design, Dublin. Retrieved from http://www.hughlane.ie/phocadownload/exhibitions/cummins_conversation%203%20fin-26.pdf

Vertovec, S. (2009). *Transnationalism*. London: Routledge.

Wahlstrom, N. (2014). Toward a conceptual framework for understanding cosmopolitanism on the ground. *Curriculum Inquiry, 44*(1), 113–132.

Afterword: provisional pedagogies toward imagining global mobilities otherwise

Sharon Stein ⓘ and Vanessa de Oliveira Andreotti

ABSTRACT

In this afterword we bring insights from the special issue into conversation with the ongoing educational challenges of imagining the world differently. To do so, we consider how global mobilities are conceptualized and materialized within three "pillars" of the architecture of modern existence: the nation-state, global capital, and Eurocentric humanism. We consider how each of these pillars stands dependent upon racial and colonial expropriation, exploitation, and subjugation, and in response we propose a provisional pedagogy that would: interrupt and make visible the role of violence in producing contemporary existence (including global mobilities); ask how we might enact transformative modes of redress for the harms produced by this architecture; and facilitate the imagining of and experimentation with alternative possibilities of existence.

Like many key concepts in global education, ideas about mobility consistently risk becoming locked into ahistorical and depoliticized tropes that presume flattened geographies, opportunities without borders, and autonomous, raceless/genderless mobile subjects. Refreshingly, the authors of this special issue of *Curriculum Inquiry* avoid celebratory and simplistic scripts and instead offer layered portraits, nuanced analyses, and instructive critiques of power. In the process, they gesture towards different dimensions of an emergent critical curriculum of global mobilities that could prepare teachers and students alike to collectively face the complex contemporary challenges that are not bound by national borders; indeed, many of these challenges are a direct result of the creation and policing of those borders. The authors' efforts can help inform the creation of such curricula without foreclosing new possibilities or overdetermining the direction of this necessarily collective and contested work. In this afterword, we situate these articles and our response to them in relation to other efforts to address the educational challenges of imagining the world differently (Andreotti, 2016a).

In order to meet these educational challenges, which we elaborate further below, we propose the need for a pedagogy that can help us trace how we arrived at the colonial present so that we might be taught by existing mistakes, interrupt recurrent relations of domination, and learn to be together in the world differently – or perhaps, learn to make different worlds together. From this perspective, coloniality is reproduced not so much by a lack of knowledge as by the onto-epistemic framework of global modernity, which naturalizes Euro-supremacy, seeks certainty and control, and disavows its own colonial conditions of possibility (Silva, 2007). Dismantling this framework will, therefore, require not only learning about colonial histories, but also unlearning and cracking the colonial architecture through which we currently imagine the world and ourselves in it. In this sense, our greatest challenge is that we cannot simply talk, think, or write our way out of this.

We contend that the current architecture of global modernity is held up by three interdependent pillars: the nation-state, global capitalism, and humanism. We use "pillars" as a metaphor to describe the material, symbolic and affective processes, and social relations that (re)produce dominant global social, political, and economic systems, institutions, and subjectivities. Collectively, these pillars make lofty promises of safety, certainty, security, affluence, and autonomy for all. However, these promises are not only unevenly distributed, their fulfilment is made possible through processes of expropriation, exploitation, destitution, and dispossession that are rationalized by the very racial/colonial hierarchies that the architecture itself institutes. Thus, when we frame expanded access to modernity's promises as the solution to problems of inequity, we forget that modernity itself is dependent on those inequities for its continuation. These dynamics also operate in the context of global mobilities, where it has often been the case that certain populations are either made to move or barred from movement so that others might move freely. Thus, while we tend to think of mobility as something that creates opportunities, these opportunities are often subsidized by harms displaced elsewhere.

We, therefore, propose an approach to a curriculum of, for, and about global mobilities that is not reducible to curricula of, for, and about "mobile people," but which rather persistently denaturalizes and disrupts our satisfactions with the shared colonial architecture within which we are all produced as differentially mobile subjects. However, because our institutions, imaginaries, desires, perceived entitlements, and frames of intelligibility tend to be organized by the very colonial relations of global modernity that we seek to identify and denaturalize, it can be difficult to trace the dynamics that normalize these relations. Tracing the dynamics of just one of the pillars can be challenging enough, and more contradictions arise when we try to address all three at once. For instance, we may rely on humanist norms to critique the nation-state when it institutes overtly racist immigration policies and practices, or position the nation-state as a positive alternative or counterbalance to capital in order to contest the privatization of public services. In order for these critiques to be effective in efforts to make a particular strategic intervention, we may have to bracket that in fact the pillars are all intertwined, such that they cannot be easily disarticulated, and the fact that each pillar comes with its own set of problems.

Paradoxes are also produced by the messy histories of overlapping departures, arrivals, displacements, and containments that make up what Byrd (2011) describes as "the transit of empire," which in turn produces "a cacophony of contradictorily hegemonic and horizontal struggles" for justice (p. 53). This is especially important in the context of nation-states founded through conquest, like the United States and Canada (King, 2016), where the forced removals and ongoing colonization of Indigenous peoples serve as the conditions of possibility for others' arrival, and where the afterlife of the forced migration and enslavement of Black peoples shapes the racialized and gendered regimes of personhood into which new im/migrants arrive (Nopper, 2011).[1]

Grappling with global mobility, therefore, requires that we address not only potential solidarities but also the tensions, complicities, complexities, contradictions, and incommensurabilities of what Walia (2014) describes as the "interlocking struggles for the freedom to stay, move and return" (http://rabble.ca/news/2014/10/no-safe-haven-canadas-managed-migration). With these concerns, caveats, and educational imperatives in mind, for the remainder of this afterword, we draw on and extend the insights of the contributors in this special issue to consider how a combined critique of the imaginaries and infrastructures of citizenship (within nation-states), social mobility (within global capitalism), and universal moral reason (within humanism) might raise different questions for a curriculum of/for/about global mobilities. We conclude by conceptualizing an education oriented by *hope beyond hope*, and propose a pedagogy that might take us to the edge of our existing frames and interrupt our satisfaction with the promises offered by global modernity, without assuming that it will be possible to transcend them or that we will understand what lies beyond them if we do.

The Modern Nation-State

The modern nation-state formation is organized around the presumption of mutually exclusive territorial sovereignty and rigid borders. Particularly in the West, the state is imagined to be the result of a "social contract" in which citizens give up certain freedoms for the promise that the state will protect their life, liberty, and private property (Mills, 2015). The social contract grants authority for states to use violence to fulfil these promises and ensure national self-preservation domestically (through the police), internationally (through the military), and at the interface between states (through border policing). The nation, in turn, presumes a homogeneous and bounded ethical entity and community. Modern nation-state formations had their origins in Europe and in the settler colonies of Europe that later became independent nation-states.

In both metropole and settler colonial contexts, colonized and enslaved populations were not party to the social contract, or the nation; instead, their subjugation was/is rationalized by that contract, as they are always already deemed to represent potential violence towards the nation-state (Silva, 2009). The nation-state formation was later appropriated by colonized populations seeking independence, although the sovereignty of these nations is persistently undermined by Western nation-states and capital. Many racialized populations within the West continue to seek fulfilment of the nation-state's promises, but success in this realm is conditional and only possible when deemed to be in the interest of continued white dominance and capitalist growth (Bell, 1979; Melamed, 2006). Indigenous peoples to this day continue to resist colonial rule by those nation-states that still claim sovereignty over their ancestral territories.

On the whole, conceptualizations of global mobility continue to be largely framed as movement between nation-states, and even critical scholarship tends to presume nation-states are, at base, benevolent entities whose continued existence is inevitable. This presumption of benevolence can help to reproduce a collective amnesia around a country's colonial past and present, as Abu El-Haj and Skilton illustrate in their contribution to this special issue. Theories of transnationalism usefully complicate the notion of bounded nation-states or nationalities by conceptualizing the movement of people and ideas beyond the borders of a single nation-state. As Warriner points out in her article, scholars of education have recently refined these theories and grappled with the nuance, complexity, and power relations that shape lived transnationalisms. Contributions from Bajaj and Bartlett, Dryden-Peterson, Guo and Maitra, and Ibrahim in this issue all further this work. For instance, as Dryden-Peterson points out, "The trajectories of refugees do not fit neatly into the established policy categories of return, local integration, and resettlement. Instead, they are non-linear and complex permutations of migration, exile, and consistently re-imagined futures" (see p. 21). These trajectories are indeed transnational, but not in any predictable or predetermined way.

However, even the most nuanced approach to transnationalism does not necessarily question the nation-state formation itself. Identifying this limit, Abu El-Haj and Skilton gesture towards a curriculum that decentres the nation-state, while Bajaj and Bartlett challenge the teleology of citizenship in their consideration of how schools for im/migrant youth "rethink the fundamental assumption of national schooling systems—the expectation that schools should socialize students as citizens" (p. 27).

What might we learn from educational efforts to denaturalize the nation-state as a primary or determinate mode of social organization? As Patel points out in her contribution, nation-states are not immutable but rather contingent entities through which access to citizenship rights is often adjudicated according to racialized and gendered regimes of property and personhood. This means that, particularly in settler colonial nation-states like the United States and Canada, the safety and security that are promised to white male citizens through the social contract are dependent upon the denial of safety and security to others through the ongoing colonization of Indigenous peoples; anti-Black ethical and legal norms; and the racialized, gendered exploitation and expropriation of labour and resources at home and abroad. All three of these dimensions are backed by the threat of violence.

As Walia (2013) argues, Western states are the "major arbiters in determining if and under what conditions people migrate" (p. 39), just as they are also major contributors to the displacements that drive people to migrate in the first place; this includes their role in armed conflict, military occupation, climate change, environmental destruction, and economic instability. If this is the case, many questions arise: how have we arrived at a point where people have to ask permission to im/migrate to the very nation-state that contributed to the war, instability, or insecurity that led to their displacement? What does it mean to request permission to im/migrate to and/or become a citizen of a nation-state that is not only constituted through the forced removal of Indigenous populations but also governed by racialized (and specifically, anti-Black) regimes of citizenship? Once we acknowledge that the very promises that continue to make certain nation-states desirable destinations (political stability, relative affluence, national security, liberal democracy) are subsidized by ongoing violence both "here" and "there" (Byrd, 2011), what is our responsibility as educators to denaturalize these promises?

Global Capital

Capitalism is premised on the perpetual accumulation of profit, which takes the form of private property (including both material possessions and financial assets). Although contemporary capitalism dovetails with meritocratic promises of access to the middle class for all who work for it, capitalism is by nature unequal, premised on the exploitation and expropriation of labour, lands, and resources. Capitalism originated in the dispossessions of the transatlantic slave trade and colonization of the Americas, which provided its foundational conditions of possibility (Silva, 2014). In this way, capital was both a global and racial formation from its beginnings, and it has perpetually sought to eradicate other modes of organizing social relations (unless those relations subsidize capitalism through unwaged forms of labour).

As a result of the rapacious search for natural resources and the toxic wastes that it produces, capital not only produces environmental destruction, it also destroys land-based relations (Coulthard, 2014; Walia, 2013). Although liberal political economic theory treats the modern state and capital as if they were distinct entities, in fact from their very beginnings the two have been intertwined, if irreducible. Nowhere is this clearer than in the fact that one of the primary purposes of the state is to protect (with violence, if deemed necessary) the wealth/property produced through capitalism (Chakravartty & Silva, 2012).

The state has also been instrumental to shifts in hegemony from industrial to financial capital (van der Zwan, 2014). Financialization, along with the privatization of formerly public services, has been the most recent means for capital to reinvigorate itself in the face of resistance from both labour and anti-colonial movements in the 1960s/1970s, and the accompanying crisis of accumulation. Broadly, financialization has entailed the expansion of credit (and its converse, debt), the flexibilization of labour, and the incorporation of more middle-class people into (often-risky) financial systems, e.g. by way of mortgages and participation in pension plans.

Some have argued that the neo-liberal formation of capitalism represents a unique threat to liberal democracy (Brown, 2015). However, as is evident from the disproportionate impact of the 2007/2008 financial crisis and associated subprime mortgage crisis on racialized communities, it is necessary to consider how novel capitalist formations are layered on top of, remain dependent on, and made legible through, the architectures produced through earlier *and ongoing* processes of specifically racialized and colonial modes of state-sanctioned dispossession (expropriation, extraction, and commodification of lands, bodies, labour, and resources) (Bhandar & Toscano, 2015; Chakravartty & Silva, 2012). As Chakravartty and Silva (2012) suggest, because racialized and Indigenous subjects are deemed to be "lacking the moral attributes (self-determination, self- transparency, and self-productivity)…that distinguish the proper economic subject" (p. 368), they are also perpetually targeted for novel forms of dispossession, even as they are blamed for their own economic precarity/vulnerability. In fact, financial instruments like credit, insurance, and securitization were first developed in the context of Black enslavement (Kish & Leroy, 2015; Moten, 2013).

If capital was always global, it is now more mobile than ever, as corporations constantly seek new sources of value, and populations willing to work for the lowest wages in the most flexible arrangements. Today, it is nearly impossible to simply "opt out" of capitalism, and even when it has forsaken certain populations or geographies, its effects are felt through its absence and the destruction left in its wake. This in turn contributes to global migration flows that often manifest as the "return of the colonized." For instance, in his contribution to this issue, Coloma attributes the contemporary migration of Filipina/o workers to the lack of local opportunities, but traces their specific choice to migrate to the United States and Canada to the historical and ongoing imperial presence of these countries in the Philippines, asserting what is by now a familiar phrase for many working towards im/migrant justice: "we are here because you were there."

One of the ways capital orders our lives is by naturalizing the pursuit of social mobility in the form of necessity. Within a capitalist system, the only way to escape material conditions of poverty is to adhere to what is expected of a "proper economic subject" (Chakravartty & Silva, 2012). However, this subject position is not only generally unavailable to racialized and Indigenous people, it also relies on an inherently violent system of value creation. This results in a double bind for marginalized subjects who do not wish to contribute to others' marginalization in their efforts to "get ahead." The result of contemporary, financialized formations of capitalism is such that expropriation and exploitation are both increasingly generalized conditions (including among those who had once been relatively buffered from its most harmful effects), *but* are nonetheless still highly concentrated within certain populations who are always already deemed dispossess-able, and to blame for their own dispossession. Moreover, the generalization of capitalism's negative impacts is matched by the persistent and/or increasing imbrication of our lives and livelihoods with capitalist accumulation.

How should educators address the paradox that capitalism is, at the same time, harmful to all of us; more harmful to some than others; and a system that most of us cannot live without? How might we address the material harms and suffering that capitalism itself produces in ways that do not further feed capitalist expansion itself? How can we interrupt the production of "cheap" goods that rely on hyper-exploited (and often mobile) labourers and environmental externalities, while recognizing that many people have come to rely on these cheap goods in order to meet their basic needs on low salaries? How can we approach material injustice in ways that both recognize that racial/colonial capitalism has produced unpayable debts (for harm done) that nonetheless must be redressed, and in ways that interrupt the reproduction of business as usual?

Humanism

When the promises of the nation-state and global capital are understood to offer false comfort and be premised on invisibilized harms, many prefer to conceptualize mobility through humanist values premised on a universal moral code that is free from exclusionary national particularities or the cold calculations of economic rationality. Humanism often appears alongside other concepts utilized in the study of mobility, including cosmopolitanism, global citizenship, and, of course, global human rights. If at first blush humanism appears to offer an alternative option for relating to others beyond the confines of national citizenship or market relations, in fact it is premised on a racialized grid of humanity, not in spite but rather because of its claims of universalism. Because humanism's promise of universality presumes a set of shared values and knowledge, anyone who deviates from them may be deemed *less than* human, meaning that humanism polices the acceptable bounds of human difference.

Many anti-colonial scholars point out that the birth of European humanism "was and continues to be predicated on slavery and colonial imposition" (Jackson, 2013, p. 682). These relations of violence instituted an enduring racial/colonial hierarchy of humanity whose "absent presence" positions an ideal "universal" human – i.e. white, male, property-owning, master of universal reason – as the head of humanity and the height of human progress. In turn, all others (with their various racial and gendered "particularities") are purported to trail behind this "universal" human, which thereby justified their subjugation (e.g. Byrd, 2011; Césaire, 1972; Jackson, 2013; King, 2016; Silva, 2007; Wynter, 2003). This "universal human" and his "others" are not separate or independent from the nation-state or global capital, but rather produced as political and economic subjects within their architecture. Finally, this figure of the human is not only Eurocentric and androcentric, but also egocentric and anthropocentric, as evidenced in the humanist presumption that the rational will of (certain) individuals can and should determine our entangled futures. Such an approach is not only premised on absolute domination over others' existence, but it also disavows the interdependencies and incalculable responsibilities that we have to all humans and to other-than-human beings.

If admittance into universal humanity was formally denied to racialized and Indigenous peoples until the mid-twentieth century, starting after World War II, they were officially but conditionally welcomed into humanity's ranks. Yet this welcome remains contingent upon adherence to "universal norms" still defined by Eurocentric ideals and world views. As Chakravartty and Silva (2012) note, by the end of the Cold War, the global human rights paradigm generalized this particular notion of the human further still, and even became a pretence for Western nations' imperial interference under the guise of humanitarian intervention – contributing to new displacements and subsequent migrations. However, not only do Western governments and citizenries generally disavow their own role in prompting such mobilities, they also deploy Eurocentric humanisms to adjudicate peoples' ability to stay or move; often only if people can recognize themselves in im/migrants do they accept them, and only if they adhere to Eurocentric norms is im/migrants humanity affirmed (norms that include obedience to law, contributions to national prosperity, and gratitude for the opportunity to be there).

One response from critics of the Eurocentric liberal humanist guise of neutrality has been to propose alternative formations of humanism that would not be premised on a particular disguised as a universal, but rather finally fulfil Césaire's (1972) call for "a humanism made to the measure of the world" (p. 56; see also Jackson, 2013; Wynter, 2003). Similarly, many have tried to transform concepts commonly associated with humanism rather than dismiss them altogether, as Beech and Rizvi do in their paper on cosmopolitanism in this issue. However, questions remain about the extent to which such terms can ever be fully resignified from their European/colonial origins, even as we must nonetheless try (Jazeel, 2011; Lee, 2014). As long as these terms continue to orient many conversations about global justice and global education, they can be useful starting points for re-signification. Thus, any pedagogy that engages the figure of "humanity" and related terms should be committed to an open-ended process of disruption, decentring, and reflexivity towards different and unexpected possible meanings *and* alternatives, without a guarantee that something different will be achieved.

In this issue, Anwaruddin argues that examining the cultural politics of emotion in the context of im/migration might enable researchers to "recognize the ambivalent, complex, and contextual nature of emotions" (p. 121). We agree, and suggest that more generally acknowledging human complexity and contradiction within a curriculum of/for/about global mobilities might make possible a disenchantment with the humanistic frameworks of justice that are premised on our own innocence, moral goodness, and "humanity." Such frameworks require that we see others this way in order for us to deem them considered deserving of empathy and basic resources. A curriculum that emphasizes disenchantment with these frameworks would invite us to acknowledge the complex, often contradictory reasons why mobile people choose to leave, and why they choose to go where they do. Acknowledging human complexity also opens up space to consider how one may be both structurally vulnerable *and* complicit in harm towards others (Gordon, 1997). However, many questions remain for how we might imagine justice in relation to global mobilities if we wish to neither rely on universal humanist frameworks, nor absolute relativism.

How might we learn to not merely tolerate but to work and live together with those embedded in different knowledge and value systems? What would collaboration, solidarity, and collective action look like without consensus? How can justice between two parties with different, incommensurable imaginaries of justice be arbitrated? How can we remain answerable to the communities from which we come, those into which we arrive, and those that we have not yet and may never encounter? Are there limits to the kinds of human difference we can live with? What if someone's idea of humanity is not only different from ours, but is premised on the denial of our existence?

Hope Beyond Hope: Toward Other Imaginaries of Mobility

There is no doubt that even as the three pillars discussed earlier have been subsidized through subjugation, they have also been skilfully repurposed as tools to resist and/or subvert that subjugation (Brown, 2015). Whether done strategically or in earnest, mobilization of the promises of modernity against itself can help mitigate violence and alleviate immediate harm, including in the context of global mobility. For these efforts to be effective, it is generally necessary to bracket the full complexity of a problem, or to contingently employ at least one of the pillars as a means to critique the other (so that there is at least one "leg" left to stand on, so to speak). As important as these efforts are, they do not necessarily change the terms of the game, and may even rely on the reproduction of harm in another context. Thus, we also need to ask what else is possible – or, perhaps, to ask why some things appear possible while others appear impossible or unintelligible.

Many young people have already identified the limits and contradictions inherent in the promises of citizenship, social mobility, and universal moral reason, and are searching for other frameworks and ways of making meaning. For instance, in their article, Nieto and Bickmore observe that students in a Canadian school reproduced celebratory narratives about Canadian multiculturalism while also noting that their own im/migrant relatives faced economic instability or racist treatment. Without a systemic analysis, the students believed their relatives' bad experiences were due to individuals' racial biases, rather than 'structural processes and inequities' (p. 41) within Canada and the larger world. Meanwhile, Abu El-Haj and Skilton note that for Palestinian and Cambodian im/migrants, "the demands to 'buy into the program' did not line up with the identifications and understandings they had developed through their migration experiences" (p. 71). These students "could see the contradictions between the colonial fantasies with which they were being asked to line up, and the local and global injustices they knew so well" (p. 72).

Once we begin to problematize the gap between what is promised and what actually happens, we may become disenchanted with the modes of mobility that are deemed possible, desirable, and intelligible within global modernity. However, the immediate response to this disenchantment may be to search for hope elsewhere as a means to regain the sense of security, futurity, entitlement, and innocence that was promised to us. Thus, it is important to ask, as Duggan does, whether hope is "consistently a good thing, or a necessary thing, in the ways we often assume" (in Duggan & Muñoz, 2009, p. 276). In recognition of how hope often functions as a form of (re)colonization and containment, Muñoz proposes "a distinction between a mode of hope that simply keeps one in place within an emotional situation predicated on control, and, instead, a certain practice of hope that helps escape from a script in which human existence is reduced" (p. 278).

Following Muñoz, we argue for the need to shift away from existing modes of hope that are circumscribed by colonial frames, and are often expressed as a desire to improve the current system (protecting our futurity within it). We consider instead the possibility of "hope beyond hope," which acknowledges that many of our existing hopes and desires are subsidized by violence. Recognizing the importance of loss, and the generative potential of feeling disillusioned with the available possibilities, hope beyond hope invests in our capacity to be taught by the past, to honour our un-payable debts and entanglements in the present, and to walk differently together into unforeseen futures, without guarantees.

With the notion of hope beyond hope, we propose a provisional and transitional pedagogy that would push us toward the edge of what is possible, or what appears to be possible from within our current frameworks. In this way, we might begin to understand that we don't and can't understand what lies beyond, that in our efforts to try something different we will likely fail, and that it is precisely the lessons from these failures that can point to something radically different. At this edge we might nonetheless be invited and inspired to encounter those who have already been doing the work of dismantling these pillars, even as we must be cautious about the risk of appropriating their efforts and projecting our existing desires and dreams in ways that create more of the same dressed up as something different. We stress that such a pedagogy should not be understood as laying a linear path toward shinier, happier, conflict-free futures. Rather, it points to provisional tools to aid in the difficult, dissensual process of walking together differently: facing up to our own complicity in violence, disinvesting from a harmful mode of existence, cleaning up the messes we have collectively made, and finding other sources of joy.

Gaztambide-Fernández argues that in the current conjuncture, "educators are called upon to play a central role in constructing the conditions for a different kind of encounter, an encounter that both opposes ongoing colonization and that seeks to heal the social, cultural, and spiritual ravages of colonial history" (2012, p. 42). How might we create these conditions in ways that do not reproduce colonial relations and entitlements precisely in the moment we think that we have transcended them? We propose that at least three layers of educational intervention are necessary.

In the first layer, there is a need to trace how the past produces the present, so as to interrupt and make visible the violent relations that made and continue to make possible our contemporary existence. This includes identifying the patterns of social relations and subjectification through which we reproduce harmful worlds, often even when we try to do otherwise. It is in this layer that we might face the ugly truth about our weaponized sense of entitlement, autonomy, and immunity, and account for our responsibilities to one another within the entangled "transits of empire" (Byrd, 2011), while also asking how we might re-imagine relationships not premised only on calculations of historical debt.

In the second layer, there is a need to consider what the past demands of us in the present, and to ask what kind of an education would affirm our collective responsibility to dismantle the imperial frameworks within which all of our "transits" occur(ed), while recognizing that we each have different positions and roles to play in these efforts. This layer is not about simply offering apologies or demanding that people heal or make peace with an unfortunate past. Rather, it would entail asking what should be done in the present to enact transformative modes of redress for the unevenly distributed pain of colonization, so that we might make the future together differently. This will require looking outside of existing imaginaries of justice as it is adjudicated within any of the three pillars of global modernity (through the promises of prosperity with global capitalism, civil rights and sovereignty within the nation-state, or universal human rights and consensus in humanism). Justice produced within these pillars will only generate more of the same harms, because it cannot account for how such promises are premised on colonial violence from the outset (Byrd, 2011; Mills, 2015; Silva, 2014).

Finally, there is a need to shift existing orientations to the future, moving away from the narrowness of modern scripts of existence, but without losing track of what lessons modernity might teach. Rather than applying more cement to a cracking colonial architecture, we need to prioritize questions that gesture towards possibilities that are currently unintelligible within normalized imaginaries. Educationally, this would mean a curriculum that interrupts our satisfaction with our modern ontological securities and that dislodges the arrogance of any search and struggle for privileged epistemic space. This kind of curriculum is counter-intuitive, as it prioritizes decentring over leadership, entanglement over separability, consent over consensus, disarmament over empowerment, and experimentation over prescription, recognizing that the process of "hospicing" global modernity is trans-generational, life-long and life-wide, and has no guaranteed outcome (Andreotti, Stein, Ahenakew, & Hunt, 2015). A provisional and transitional pedagogy might help us trace the desires that produce harmful knowledge, identities, imaginaries, and relationships, and face the paradoxes and contradictions of our complex collective existence (Andreotti, 2016b). This approach is not without risk, particularly for those who are already denied promises of security, sovereignty, and stability within modernity's architecture. Yet, perhaps this precarious pedagogy of mobility will help us to develop the stamina, generosity, humility, and compassion to walk together differently into an unknown future, welcoming indeterminacy, without the option of turning our backs to one another.

Note

1. We borrow the term "im/migrant" from Abu El-Haj and Skilton, who in turn borrow it from Arzubiaga, Nogeuron, and Sullivan, as a means to "denote the variety of people included in the category of immigrant (for example, immigrant, transnational migrant, and refugee)."

Acknowledgments

The authors would like to thank the editorial team of Curriculum Inquiry, in particular editorial assistant Gabrielle de Montmollin, for their assistance throughout the publication process.

Disclosure statement

No potential conflict of interest was reported by the authors.

ORCID

Sharon Stein (iD) http://orcid.org/0000-0001-6995-8274

References

Andreotti, V. (2016a). The educational challenges of imagining the world differently. *Canadian Journal of Development Studies/Revue Canadienne D'études du Développement, 37*(1), 101–112.

Andreotti, V. (2016b). Multi-layered selves: Colonialism, decolonization and counter-intuitive learning spaces. *Arts Everywhere – Musagetes*. Retrieved from http://artseverywhere.ca/2016/10/12/multi-layered-selves

Andreotti, V., Stein, S., Ahenakew, C., & Hunt, D. (2015). Mapping interpretations of decolonization in the context of higher education. *Decolonization: Indigeneity, Education & Society, 4*(1), 21–40.

Bell, D.A. (1979). Brown v. Board of Education and the interest-convergence dilemma. *Harvard Law Review, 93*, 518–533.

Bhandar, B., & Toscano, A. (2015). Race, real estate and real abstraction. *Radical Philosophy, 194*. Retrieved from https://www.radicalphilosophy.com/article/race-real-estate-and-real-abstraction

Brown, W. (2015). *Undoing the demos: Neoliberalism's stealth revolution*. Cambridge: MIT Press.

Byrd, J.A. (2011). *The transit of empire: Indigenous critiques of colonialism*. Minneapolis: University of Minnesota Press.

Césaire, A. (1972). *Discourse on colonialism*. (J. Pinkham, Transl.). New York: Monthly Review Press.

Chakravartty, P., & da Silva, D.F. (2012). Accumulation, dispossession, and debt: the racial logic of global capitalism—an introduction. *American Quarterly, 64*(3), 361–385.

Coulthard, G.S. (2014). *Red skin, white masks: Rejecting the colonial politics of recognition*. Minneapolis: University of Minnesota Press.

Duggan, L., & Muñoz, J.E. (2009). Hope and hopelessness: A dialogue. *Women & Performance: A Journal of Feminist Theory, 19*(2), 275–283.

Gaztambide-Fernández, R.A. (2012). Decolonization and the pedagogy of solidarity. *Decolonization: Indigeneity, Education & Society, 1*(1), 41–67.

Gordon, A. (1997). *Ghostly matters: Haunting and the sociological imagination*. Minneapolis: University of Minnesota Press.

Jackson, Z.I. (2013). Animal: New directions in the theorization of race and posthumanism. *Feminist Studies, 39*(3), 669–685.

Jazeel, T. (2011). Spatializing difference beyond cosmopolitanism: Rethinking planetary futures. *Theory, Culture & Society, 28*(5), 75–97.

King, T.L. (2016). New world grammars: The "unthought" Black discourses of conquest. *Theory & Event, 19*(4). Retrieved from https://muse.jhu.edu/article/633275

Kish, Z., & Leroy, J. (2015). Bonded life: Technologies of racial finance from slave insurance to philanthrocapital. *Cultural Studies, 29*(5–6), 630–651.

Lee, C.T. (2014). Decolonizing global citizenship. In E.F. Isin & P. Nyers (Eds.), *Routledge handbook of global citizenship studies*. Milton Park: Routledge.

Melamed, J. (2006). The spirit of neoliberalism from racial liberalism to neoliberal multiculturalism. *Social Text, 24*(489), 1–24.

Mills, C.W. (2015). Decolonizing Western political philosophy. *New Political Science, 37*(1), 1–24.

Moten, F. (2013). The subprime and the beautiful. *African Identities, 11*(2), 237–245.

Nopper, T. (2011). The wages of non-Blackness: Contemporary immigrant rights and discourses of character, productivity, and value. *Tensions Journal*, (5), 1–25. Retrieved from http://www.yorku.ca/intent/issue5/articles/pdfs/tamaraknopperarticle.pdf

Silva, D.F.D. (2007). *Toward a global idea of race*. Minneapolis: University of Minnesota Press.

Silva, D.F.D. (2009). No-bodies: Law, raciality and violence. *Griffith Law Review, 18*(2), 212–236.

Silva, D.F.D. (2014). Toward a Black feminist poethics: The quest (ion) of Blackness toward the end of the world. *The Black Scholar, 44*(2), 81–97.

van der Zwan, N. (2014). Making sense of financialization. *Socio-Economic Review, 12*(1), 99–129.

Walia, H. (2013). *Undoing border imperialism*. Oakland: AK Press.

Walia, H. (2014). No safe haven: Canada's 'managed migration'. *Rabble.ca*. Retrieved from http://rabble.ca/news/2014/10/no-safe-haven-canadas-managed-migration

Wynter, S. (2003). Unsettling the coloniality of being/power/truth/freedom: Towards the human, after man, its overrepresentation – an argument. *CR: The New Centennial Review, 3*(3), 257–337.

Index

Note: Page numbers followed by 'n' refer to end notes